NAPOLEON

and His Collaborators

ALSO BY ISSER WOLOCH

Revolution and the Meanings of Freedom in
the Nineteenth Century, *Editor*

The New Regime: Transformations of the French Civic Order, 1789–1820s

Eighteenth-Century Europe: Tradition and Progress, 1715–1789

The French Veteran from the Revolution to the Restoration

The Peasantry in the Old Regime: Conditions and Protests, *Editor*

Jacobin Legacy: The Democratic Movement Under the Directory

NAPOLEON

and His Collaborators

THE MAKING OF

A DICTATORSHIP

ISSER WOLOCH

W · W · NORTON & COMPANY

NEW YORK LONDON

For information about permission to reproduce selections from this book,
write to Permissions, W. W. Norton & Company, Inc., 500 Fifth Avenue,
New York, NY 10110

The text of this book is composed in 11/14 Adobe Garamond with the display set in
Adobe Garamond and Shelley Andante, with Rococo Ornaments One
Composition by AW Bennett Inc.
Manufacturing by The Courier Companies, Inc.
Book design by Margaret M. Wagner

Library of Congress Cataloging-in-Publication Data

Woloch, Isser, 1937–

  Napoleon and his collaborators : the making of a dictatorship / Isser Woloch.
          p.   cm.
  Includes bibliographical references and index.
  ISBN 0-393-05009-2
  1. Napoleon I, Emperor of the French 1769–1821—Associates. 2. France—
Officials and employees—Biography. 3. France—Politics and government—
1789–1815. 4. Dictatorship—France.

DC203.9 .W785 2001
944.05'092—dc21
[B]   00-062230

W. W. Norton & Company, Inc.,
500 Fifth Avenue, New York, N.Y. 10110
www.wwnorton.com

W. W. Norton & Company Ltd.,
10 Coptic Street, London WC1A 1PU

1 2 3 4 5 6 7 8 9 0

To R. R. Palmer

Contents

Preface

I HOPE that this volume might be the second book taken up by a reader wishing to consider the era of Napoleon Bonaparte. The first would naturally be a full-scale biography, of which scores exist in various registers.[1] Whatever the perspective of such biographers, the trajectory of Napoleon's life remains at once familiar and elusive. The master narrative has changed little since the days of its first chroniclers in the 1820s, but this standard outline has never precluded a wide variety of opinions "for and against."[2] Any sound interpretation of Napoleon's career must in the end assess the balance between creativity and tyranny. All are bound to ponder the boundless ambition and hubris that ultimately led this remarkable individual to squander his talent, energy, and appeal.

Yet even if viewed from the top down, Napoleon's saga is not simply the story of a single man. Along the way, before the coup d'état of 18 Brumaire made him the head of the French state, his destiny lay only partly in his own confident hands. The young officer naturally depended on a succession of patrons and, in due course, on talented military subordinates. But at the critical juncture of Brumaire, his position even more manifestly intersected with the will of others.

In reality, the epochmaking Brumaire coup was a joint venture between a group of insecure republican politicians who had lost faith in their own Directory regime, and a general who had served the Directory outstandingly but had also come to see it as dysfunctional. Eventually, of course, this joint venture gave way to a dictatorship where one partner effectively swallowed the other. But even after Napoleon placed the imperial crown on his own head in 1804, his regime remained linked to his erstwhile partners of Brumaire as well as to others coopted soon after.

This book explores that joint venture and its aftermath, the relationship between Napoleon and his leading civilian collaborators. Stalwarts of the French Revolution, for the most part, who reached out to General Bonaparte preparatory to seizing power in Brumaire, and on whom Bonaparte then relied, their fate remained intimately bound with his. But apart from Talleyrand and Fouché—whose respective skills in diplomacy and police work have become legendary—Napoleon's prominent collaborators remain almost faceless men. Known only in narrow political circles, they generally lacked any national name recognition then or since. With proven talent in legislation, jurisprudence, science, or administration, most nurtured no ambition other than high state service with its material and psychological rewards: status and financial security, no doubt, but also self-fulfillment and a sense of honor. Most worked hard, although the more elderly or less apt were usually rewarded with sinecures.

Focusing on these men might seem at first glance a game of "Rosencrantz and Guildenstern" to Napoleon's Hamlet. In fact, it addresses an essential element of Napoleon's success: the precocious solidity and efficacy of the regime, which depended on the commitment and skills of his leading supporters. It should be noted, however, that this book deals only with Napoleon's civilian collaborators in France. Similar histories might well be written about Napoleon's relations with two comparable groups: his military commanders and his non-French collaborators in the annexed territories and satellite states of the Empire. But those generals and foreigners would not speak directly to a central question: the symbiosis of prominent former revolutionaries with Napoleon Bonaparte during his unforeseen passage from general of the republic and first consul to dictator and conqueror of Europe.

FROM THE OUTSET in 1789 the revolutionaries had repeatedly faced hard choices: whether to go along with some distasteful initiative for the sake of unity (the execution of the king, for example, or the annihilation of the Girondins, with worse to come under the Terror) or to stand on liberal principle and resist, at the risk of undermining the Revolution while endangering oneself. All moderates and many radical Jacobins were relieved when the end of the Terror seemed to free them from such pressures, even if it left behind scars to their revolutionary faith or their integrity. But Thermidor and the fall of Robespierre quickly brought new dilemmas about how far to go in the other direction. How far should punitive anti-Jacobinism be carried; or conversely, how strenuously must "reaction," the potential outrider of a royalist restoration, be resisted? Could a stable political equilibrium ever emerge from the resultant clashes?

Brumaire, as we shall see, promised an exit from this impasse, yet in its own way Bonaparte's ascendancy posed yet another dilemma for those in his camp who had once taken political and civil liberty seriously. After Brumaire the question of political choice took on a stark clarity: would one be serving the interests of France, along with one's self-interest, by serving Napoleon Bonaparte, no matter the direction in which he veered? Or putting it another way: could one really serve the best interests of a regenerated France by disavowing Napoleon at some point in his trajectory, after so much had come to depend on him personally? While the range of public argument and the possibilities of acceptable dissent eventually contracted almost to the vanishing point, prominent individuals in the regime still retained the option of what Albert Hirschman has called "voice" or "exit"[3]: they could remain true to themselves by firing off a volley of principled criticism, even if it might be their last public act; or they could fold their tents and, without any real risk, signal their personal alienation from the regime.

We do not entirely lack instances of principled liberal criticism of Napoleon. The rare displays of independence by men such as Pierre Daunou, Benjamin Constant, or Lazare Carnot are indeed indispensable in establishing perspective on this matter. As for quietly opting out, this depended on personal circumstances such as age, wealth, and vocation. Established intellectuals, for example, could be more self-reliant, at least if their income was assured. Disillusioned supporters of Brumaire such as Senators Volney, Cabanis, or Destutt de Tracy could turn from politics to their real work, their contributions (respectively) to scholarship, science, or philosophy, although it must be said that none resigned from their lucrative sinecures. But active men whose expertise and experience lay primarily in government and administration had much less latitude.

Reconciling self-interest and the public interest; deciding whether service to the nation meant serving the regime currently in power; deciding whether the alternatives were worse even if the current regime offended—these have been persistent questions in the public life of modern France, a nation where coups clothed in pseudo-legality have repeatedly changed the rules of the game, as recently as 1940. The dark circumstances of the Vichy period have in fact impressed on the term "collaborator" a nasty connotation that it did not necessarily possess before. As of 1800 the choices were less portentous than in 1940 but could still pose a serious conundrum. For how could one contribute to the consolidation of revolutionary gains and to the well-being of France after 1800 without offering the unconditional loyalty that Napoleon Bonaparte seemed to demand?

Threaded through this account, then, are a number of questions about key individuals and small groups pivotal to the civil side of the Napoleonic experience. What kinds of contributions did they make to the Napoleonic regime and what did they receive in return? What "gains of the Revolution" did they believe themselves to be defending and how effectively did they do so? How did they sustain their commitment as Napoleon's personal ambitions expanded beyond reason and as public liberty eroded? How, in the final analysis, do we go about assessing their behavior in light of the regime's equivocal if promising start, striking achievements, deplorable derogations, and ultimate disasters?

IN THE PAGES that follow I will introduce these men in narratives of certain key events and in various thematic discussions. A first set of chapters deals with the seizure of power in the joint venture of Brumaire; the organization of power in its wake, where patronage and depoliticization are the two principal motifs; the first transgressive assertions of raw willfulness by the first consul; and the responses pro and con to Napoleon's drive for untrammeled monarchical power. Then, in a different vein, come chapters on Napoleon's most intimate collaborator; Napoleon's relations with his leading subordinates in the routines of governance; the problem posed for his liberal servitors by the regime's reliance on such practices as preventive detention and censorship; and finally the impact on his minions of the Empire's collapse, the Bourbon Restoration of 1814, and Napoleon's return from Elba in 1815.

To aid the reader, I wish to identify at the outset a handful of men who emerged, without any preconceptions on my part, as figures of particular interest in this drama populated with ostensibly minor characters. Keep your eye out above all for Boulay de la Meurthe and Théophile Berlier. Ardent republicans and deputies in the legislature of 1799, they initially found themselves on opposite sides during the Brumaire crisis. In the thick of the plot, Boulay immediately became one of Napoleon's most loyal and able collaborators, from Brumaire to Waterloo. Berlier had nothing to do with Brumaire but was quickly coopted into the Consulate as a kind of house Jacobin, and like Boulay served the Napoleonic regime effectively until its last day. These erstwhile republican liberals, who transformed themselves into fully committed servitors of Napoleon, never entirely surrendered their sense of perspective and subsequently tried to chronicle and explain their public lives. Each stated that his memoirs were intended for his descendants rather than the general public, and ironically this intention seems to have prevailed since few if any historians have plumbed these rare and suggestive volumes.

The case of Antoine Thibaudeau is quite different. Somewhat similar in political profile to Boulay and Berlier, although far more mercurial, Thibaudeau came into his prime only after 1815 and precisely as the author of a series of memoirs that have since been used by most serious writers on Napoleon. Still, these remarkably detailed volumes proved fresh and revealing to me because I approached them for a different purpose. In the process, Thibaudeau perforce became one focus of my attention. So too did Regnaud de St. Jean d'Angély. A patriot deputy in the National Assembly of 1789, Regnaud was not much enamored of the republic after 1792. His relationship with General Bonaparte dated from the Italian campaign of 1797 (when he served as a military hospital administrator in Italy), and along with Boulay he quickly became one of Napoleon's preferred and most reliable collaborators after Brumaire—one of his three "iron men," as I will suggest. Regnaud produced no memoirs of any kind nor did he leave behind personal papers that I know of. Yet in the archives of the Napoleonic government and in the memoirs of others one cannot escape his low-keyed but persistent presence. Finally, there is Jean-Jacques-Régis Cambacérès, who must have been surprised but immensely pleased to find himself the right-hand man, so to speak, of First Consul Bonaparte and Emperor Napoleon. In a class by himself, Cambacérès merits a chapter of his own.

$\mathcal{N}$APOLEON

and His Collaborators

I

Seizing Power: The Joint Venture of Brumaire

*O*N AT LEAST two occasions the citizens of France had plausibly expected to see their revolution come to an end. The promulgation of the nation's first constitution in September 1791 marked the first such moment. Four extremely long years later—with Louis XVI and Robespierre in the grave, over a hundred thousand émigrés in exile, the Jacobin dictatorship dismantled, and the reign of terror at an end—the moderate thermidorians produced a new constitution and a new expectation of closure. The Directory, so named for its five-man executive, pledged that the republic would finally shed its revolutionary birth pangs for a kind of normalcy. But by 1799 that hope had waned. The Directory failed to create a national consensus or a normal politics just as it failed to allay the accumulated recriminations from the Revolution's fratricidal conflicts.

To be sure, the French Revolution had begun auspiciously when the Third Estate transformed itself into a National Assembly in June 1789 and proclaimed as its basic principles the sovereignty of the people and representative government. The Assembly instituted a reverent commitment to elections at all levels of government, and even demonstrated an admirable willingness to surrender power to new men once the constitution was in place. In 1791 the deputies adopted a "self-denying ordinance" rendering themselves ineligible for election to the forthcoming Legislative Assembly.

But the practice of a normal democratic politics eluded the new regime. As bitter contention exploded over relations with the clergy, the power of the king, the treatment of counterrevolutionaries, the prosecution of the war that began in April 1792, and the response to populist militancy, it became clear that the constitution had not provided an accepted, consensual basis for the nation's civic life. In this fast-changing and bewildering climate, new political imperatives eventually swamped commitments to legality and political compromise. In the name of revolutionary unity and public safety, Parisian militants overthrew the monarchy and with it the constitution of 1791. But the insurrection of August 1792 settled little, as citizens all across France chose deputies to a National Convention to fill the vacuum. The Convention, on which everything now hinged, found itself torn apart by factional conflict—a stalemate resolved only when the Montagnard-Jacobin alliance purged its Girondin rivals and thus achieved "unity by partition."[1] The reign of terror and the ascendancy of the Jacobins in turn came to an abrupt end after 9 Thermidor (27 July 1794) with the execution of the leading Robespierrists and subsequent purges of Jacobin stalwarts.

Even as it completed a new constitution in 1795 as the basis for political normalcy, however, the thermidorian Convention did not trust the electorate's wisdom or loyalty at this juncture, fearing that it was too inclined toward royalist reaction. The Convention not only declined to enact a new self-denying ordinance, but refused to call an open election for the two-house legislature that its new constitution created. Instead, in the name of preserving the republic, it adopted the controversial "two-thirds decree," which provided that only one-third of the new legislators would be chosen in the upcoming election, with the remaining two-thirds of the seats to be filled by sitting *conventionnels*, the justification being that in the future only one-third of the legislature would be up for election annually. For the moment, perpetuation in office served the same function as enforcing unity through purges. But would that suffice to assure stability?

REPUBLICANISM AND ITS DISCONTENTS

The official oath of loyalty in the directorial republic required a declaration of hatred for royalism and anarchy (the current epithet for Jacobinism). By most calculations the moderate political elite should have embraced the constitution of 1795 as a safe passage between those extremes—the practical alternative to the abortive Jacobin commonwealth of 1793 or to a royalist restoration. But the constitution of 1795 did not produce the anticipated equilibrium. Liberal enough to permit openings for oppositional movements, it did not preclude the government from taking repressive acts against royalists or Jacobins whenever it felt threatened.

Centrist supporters of the Directory stigmatized political parties as illegitimate, no better than cabals. They thereby impeded the development of normal politics, since among constitutional royalists and former Jacobins, at least, an impulse toward organized opposition or nascent party formation came naturally. But the directorials denounced such tendencies as potential conspiracies to overthrow the government. The Directory regime improbably combined a system of annual elections with a readiness to nullify the results of those elections if they seemed outside the pale. When the right or left showed any strength in the political arena, the Directory suspended the liberties pledged in its own constitution and adopted coercive measures.

With its allies in the legislature, the Directory thus organized two purges to undo the results of successive elections in 1797 and 1798. The coup of Fructidor Year V (1797) closed down the royalist press and ousted over two hundred deputies on the right who had tilted the balance in the legislature after that spring's elections. Following the next year's voting, the coup of Floréal Year VI (1798) struck at the left. The Directory orchestrated a purge of 127 deputies-elect, mostly Neo-Jacobins, having previously closed down their clubs and newspapers.

These purges provoked appreciative responses at the time from various constituencies, but cumulatively this succession of unconstitutional actions sapped the legitimacy of the republic itself. Yet as self-declared liberals and anti-terrorists who abhorred the guillotine, the directorials could not decisively quash opposition from the left or right. In the end, then, nothing could be taken for granted, least of all the integrity of the constitution itself. The electoral wars of the Directory years fractured, unsettled, and ultimately disillusioned the moderate political elites. As the last year of the century drew to a close, many who shared the original thermidorian consensus were ready to scrap their constitution altogether and start over. In search of a surer, more controlled political framework, they became "revisionists."[2]

Paradoxically, from 1798 onward it was the Neo-Jacobins who defended the constitution of 1795 most adamantly. They correctly feared that any attempt to shed or alter that framework would produce a more authoritarian or oligarchic regime—an even less democratic constitution, which would surely bar their own path to local or national power once and for all. Before the Brumaire plot even existed, the Neo-Jacobins could predict its outcome as far as they were concerned. Polemics in their surviving newspapers and resuscitated clubs, and remarks by deputies who had slipped through the purge, communicated a passionate commitment to defend the very constitution originally designed to erase their legacy. In response, moderates might have found even more reason to question their own devotion to that charter.[3]

The more so since the Directory had managed to bungle other areas of its stewardship. The treasury was empty and financial stringency inhibited the government at every turn, most visibly in its ability to supply the army. This was especially scandalous since the Directory's diplomacy had provoked the formation of a new anti-French coalition abroad, the outbreak of a war on three fronts, and an early string of victories by its enemies—Britain, Austria, and Russia. Within France, the government's seeming inability to suppress a tide of rural brigandage and highway robbery—some political in coloration and some simply criminal—further weakened the Directory's standing, although it was actually in the process of mounting a serious offensive against this terrifying disorder.[4]

Meanwhile, the secularists or Voltairians in the government (often moderate on other issues) had incited a different kind of backlash. "Republican institutions" in their lexicon translated into a *Kulturkampf* with Catholic values and the Catholic clergy. The republican calendar, its ten-day weeks a remnant of more radical times, became the entering wedge for the government's counterproductive ideological campaign. By insisting on the observance of the *décadi* instead of Sunday as the day of rest and even of worship, the Directory antagonized ordinary Frenchmen and women. A campaign of harassment against Catholic primary school teachers further alienated many parents from the republic. As one aggrieved priest argued shortly before Brumaire, the constitution of 1795 did not truly guarantee the precious freedom of religion at all, and the Directory seemed to feel "that to be a republican one must still cease being a catholic."[5]

IN THEIR RATIONALIZATIONS for Brumaire during and after the coup, its adherents indicted the recurrent electoral turmoil of the Directory regime for promoting factionalism at the expense of the public interest. Poorly designed organs of government compounded the damage, in this view, neither functioning effectively nor meshing harmoniously with each other.

The thermidorian architects of the constitution of 1795 had abandoned the universal male suffrage promised in the Jacobins' abortive constitution of 1793 by returning to a propertied franchise and indirect elections. (Local "primary assemblies" of all eligible voters chose electors who in turn convened in departmental "electoral assemblies" to choose deputies, judges, and local administrators.) While Jacobins deplored this abridgment of the franchise, the right to vote at the primary level still remained extensive; indeed, according to the brumairians, it permitted "the disastrous and irresistible influence of the multitude in the primary assemblies." As a result, "the fundamental base of the representative system is thrown upon a shifting and volcanic terrain."[6] Considering that voter turnout was notoriously low in the annual primary assemblies, perhaps averaging only 15 percent of eligible voters, this was a preposterous claim. Yet it did explain away for moderates the volatility of the electoral process: the often unsatisfactory choices of electors and deputies as well as the commotion that sometimes swirled around primary and electoral assemblies.[7] Another element of the indictment, in any case, was assuredly true: "The frequency and universal simultaneity of elections" compounded that volatility. Elections to renew a portion of the legislature and of local administrations took place each and every year, never giving political conflicts and historic animosities a chance to subside. As one apologist concluded with notable illogic, the Brumaire coup held out the promise "that the vivifying influence of elections will make itself felt without producing trouble or disorder anywhere"![8]

The character of the Directory's bicameral legislature magnified the appearance of instability created by the electoral process. Too large to begin with (one house of five hundred deputies, the other of two hundred fifty), it met day in and day out in the manner of the Convention, which had effectively ruled the country between 1792 and 1795. "Oppositionists are constantly in confrontation, opinions collide against each other, differences of opinion are exalted, the conflicts of yesterday are rekindled, to be engaged in again tomorrow. . . . [The legislature] can attain neither consistency nor poise."[9] Again, this judgment was entirely one-sided, but the revisionists could have justly complained that on numerous issues crying out for resolution the parliament was not making decisions. Either the Council of 500 (which initiated laws) could not come to agreement within its own ranks, or a bill finally hammered out in that chamber could not win approval in the Council of Elders.

Such frequent stalemates exacerbated the more obvious problem of occasional deadlock between the legislature and the executive for which no constitutional mechanism of resolution existed. Moreover, the five-man Directory itself could be frustrated by internal discord. The thermidorians had fashioned a collective executive precisely to avoid the danger of an excessively strong hand or dictatorship, but the Directory sometimes failed to maintain a collegial harmony. Internal conflict exploded twice, once in Fructidor (1797), and again on the eve of the Brumaire coup itself. Before three of the directors could nullify the royalist-tinged elections of 1797 by a purge, they had first to neutralize (i.e., oust and arrest) their two colleagues who vehemently opposed the plan. The three justified this manifest violation of the constitution by condemning their colleagues Barthélemy and Carnot for collusion with royalists who threatened the survival of the republic. The separation of powers was all well and good but did not offer much protection for constitutionalism in the absence of an underlying consensus.

IN SUM, the revisionists concluded after four years of experience that the defects of their own constitution promoted the very factionalism it was supposed to restrain. They were ready to jettison the open electoral arena with its annual confrontations; the clashing opinions endlessly ventilated in the legislature; the conflicts among the directors and between Directory and legislature; the liberal provisions that permitted public manifestations of Neo-Jacobinism and anti-republicanism—or anarchy and royalism, in the current formula.

This sour perspective was of course far from universal. Apart from the Neo-Jacobins who now defended the constitution of 1795, some centrist republicans held a more optimistic view; for example, Théophile Berlier, a veteran legislator from Dijon respected by Jacobins and thermidorians alike for his integrity and legislative skills. Berlier discerned a broad republican consensus behind the exaggerated partisan rhetoric of the annual electoral battles. He viewed the campaign of the Year VI (1798), which ended with the Directory's anti-Jacobin purge, as "for the most part simply a war of nuances among patriots of different degrees." (Berlier himself had been chosen by both factions of the schismatic Paris electoral assembly, and when the government validated the slate of the anti-Jacobin rump, he escaped the Floréal purge.) In the legislature, he believed, there were no veritable parties; "notwithstanding its nuances, the whole body was republican."[10] With this tolerant confidence in the republic's political culture, Berlier did not see the need for another coup, would not have supported it at the time, and would have been dismayed by its success. Berlier's equanimity was not widely shared, however, even if his ardent republicanism and liberal values still commanded the respect of his colleagues—some of whom would come to power in Brumaire and invite their ex-colleague to join them.

A PLOT TAKES SHAPE

Emmanuel-Joseph Sieyès, author of *What Is the Third Estate?* and founding father of the French Revolution, had at least two things in common with Napoleon Bonaparte in the fateful year of 1799. Each had been out of the country for a time and therefore had the aura of a fresh face. With the latitude of a comparative outsider, each seemed to stand above the partisan recriminations of the moment. Moreover, although they were securely imbricated with the new regime, each nursed an aversion for the politics and institutions of the directorial republic. Upon their respective returns to France (some five months apart), Sieyès and Bonaparte sensed the malaise that gripped the political elite, and each concluded that the regime must be toppled.

After his bold, decisive role in the founding acts of 1789–90, Sieyès's reputation endured but his influence receded. While he returned as a deputy to the National Convention (where he voted for the execution of the king) and continued on in the directorial legislature, Sieyès kept a low profile during the Revolution's subsequent phases. As he once famously remarked, his role during the reign of the terror was simply to have survived. Though thoroughly anti-Jacobin or thermidorian in spirit, Sieyès disapproved of the Directory from its inception. Fiercely proud of his conceptual powers in political theory, Sieyès found his ideas ignored in the constitution of 1795. Above all, that charter failed to incorporate his cherished proposal for a "constitutional jury," a third force standing between executive and legislature that could resolve constitutional deadlocks or annul transgressions of the constitution by either branch.[11]

Dejected by this snub, the sage of 1789 refused to accept a position as one of the five directors, which was his for the asking. Instead, he dropped into a kind of willed obscurity, resurfacing only briefly in late 1797 with an outburst against the ex-nobles whom he wished to bar completely from citizenship rights—an uncharacteristically radical position for this proponent of a moderate bourgeois republic, yet one consistent with his obsessional view of the former Second Estate, which he had attacked so memorably on the eve of the Revolution.[12]

Subsequently, just as Talleyrand helped launch General Bonaparte on his expedition to Egypt, the foreign minister placed Sieyès as the republic's ambassador to Berlin. This post he filled with a degree of satisfaction, dignity, and success, although his rapport with the Duke of Brunswick fueled speculation back home that Sieyès looked favorably upon some new form of monarchy for France. As diplomatic relations with the European powers deteriorated, France's vulnerability on its far-flung military lines became evident. A personal sense of danger shook the republic's diplomats after the assassination of French delegates to a negotiating conference in Rastadt, Germany. Sieyès decided to pack his bags and seek security back in Paris, where he was about to be offered a seat on the Directory again. This time he accepted.

Sieyès filled the annual vacancy on the five-man Directory for the Year VII. But shortly after he assumed his post, and before he began to assert himself, a coalition of frustrated moderates and angry Neo-Jacobins in the legislature executed a power play of their own, known as the coup of 30 Prairial (18 June 1799). Accusing three remaining directors of malfeasance, poor leadership, and tyrannical actions, the deputies forced their resignations, in effect ousting them. Subsequently the Council of 500 debated whether to prosecute these ex-directors, and came only three votes short of doing so. Inexplicably, however, the most notoriously corrupt and self-seeking of the veteran directors, Barras, was left in place, while the selection of three new directors seemed calculated to produce new conflicts. Two of the men elected by the Council of Elders—Gohier and Moulin—identified with the resurgent Neo-Jacobins, while Roger Ducos became a faithful follower of the implacably anti-Jacobin Sieyès.[13]

The legislature's performance in those months heightened the anxiety of the revisionists. Panic over military defeat in Italy and the Low Countries emboldened the Neo-Jacobins to activate their arsenal of draconian measures. As an anti-Jacobin backbencher later recalled, the war crisis "justified the clamors of the Jacobins up to a point and caused a number of others to pass into their ranks."[14] Not only did they come within a whisker of indicting the three ex-directors, but they won majorities for two muscular laws of exception: a forced loan—a kind of emergency tax with steeply progressive modalities to replenish the empty treasury—and the law of hostages, which authorized the interning of émigré relatives as a deterrent to the assassination of local republicans. Many moderates considered this no less than a revival of Jacobin spoliation and terrorism. The forced loan and the law of hostages later became part of the revisionists' litany in justifying their coup against the "destructive measures" and "convulsive movements" that ought by now to have been banished forever from French public life, regardless of circumstances.

Of course things looked different to those who advocated such laws. Deputies from the western departments beset by *chouannerie* (anti-republican violence) communicated the sense of peril and helplessness in the region's isolated rural communes. They urged their colleagues to respond by threatening prominent sympathizers of the *chouans*, such as émigré relatives, with incarceration and seizure of property should any republican official in a community be attacked. Théophile Berlier sat on the committee appointed to deal with this problem. His liberal republican convictions at first ranged him against such a "repugnant" law of exception. But the firsthand reports relayed from the West by its deputies won him over to the proposal. In the end, although he was not the bill's *rapporteur*, he made the most impassioned floor speech in favor of the law of hostages, and came to be regarded as its architect.[15]

Berlier was the *rapporteur* for a proposed law to establish the boundaries of press freedom. His long-pending draft addressed the perpetual conundrum of how to preserve liberty and curb license, how to assure the right of free expression to journalists while protecting the republic from subversion. Most immediately, Berlier's bill would have limited the government's power to shut down or otherwise censor dissenting newspapers—a power the Directory had used with abandon since the Fructidor coup in 1797. The Council of 500 was also debating how political clubs might be regulated in order to assure freedom of association yet prevent the abuse of that freedom. Unlike many of his friends in the Council of 500, Berlier did not belong to the Neo-Jacobin club that had recently started meeting at a public building known as the Manège. But he keenly wished to halt the closures of local Neo-Jacobin clubs that the Directory had repeatedly ordered. Berlier therefore submitted a detailed and balanced proposal "to normalize these assemblies [and to specify] the limitations required for public order," which would have provided a more secure basis for their existence.

Berlier's painstaking projects on press freedom and political associations never came to a vote. With opinion sharply divided, the Council of 500 could not reach consensus on either issue. Dissenting newspapers and clubs therefore remained vulnerable to government repression. Were my proposals on protecting and regulating newspapers and clubs "a vain utopia"? Berlier asked himself decades later. "Today I am strongly inclined to think so."[16] That may have well been true, for these issues bedeviled French governments until the 1880s. But the failure of the legislature in 1799 to codify a liberal framework for a free press and political association would make it much easier for Bonaparte to erase both kinds of liberty in the wake of Brumaire.

It also meant that the Neo-Jacobins would be fettered on the eve of Brumaire, since Sieyès was able to instigate the closure of the Neo-Jacobin's rallying point, the club of the Manège, three months before the coup. Not that his move was gratuitous. For the Neo-Jacobins detected in Sieyès a powerful enemy and had started attacking him personally. The preemptive strike against the Manège Club by Sieyès and his new police minister, Joseph Fouché, was effectively the preliminary skirmish of the Brumaire plot.

SUBJECT to fits of depression, Sieyès often fled to the sidelines and sulked, but he could also display fierce determination at crucial junctures and did so now with two clear objectives. First, to break the momentum of the Neo-Jacobins by deploying whatever powers the Directory had amassed over the years; then to lay the groundwork for a revision of the constitution. Given the inordinately protracted requirements for legal amendment, this meant some sort of coup, to be clothed as much as possible in the garb of legality. To this end, Sieyès recruited allies among moderates of all stripes in and outside the legislature, with particular focus on the Council of Elders. In the more fractious Council of 500, his most effective collaborator proved to be Boulay de la Meurthe, who would go on to become the quintessential revolutionary servitor of Napoleon from Brumaire to Waterloo.

Born in 1761 to a prosperous cultivator who died when his son was three, Boulay received an excellent education in a provincial *collège*. Under the tutelage of a clerical uncle he first considered a career in the church but opted instead for the bar. As a young man he practiced law in Nancy and then sought his fortune in Paris, where he observed the early events of the Revolution, sometimes from the spectators' gallery of the National Assembly. Back home in 1792, he enrolled in the volunteer battalion of the Meurthe department as a common soldier and saw combat at the historic battle of Valmy. After mustering out of the army, Boulay was elected a judge on the civil tribunal of the district, but was later purged as a moderate. Rejoining the army, he rose to the rank of captain but ill-health forced him out. Back home again, a threat of arrest for his past politics drove Boulay into hiding for several months during the Terror, but the fall of Robespierre released him from that miserable existence. For a second time his fellow citizens in the Meurthe chose him as a judge and then as the department's public prosecutor.

One of the very few republicans to be elected deputy in the royalist tide of 1797, Boulay embodied for his constituents their wish for moderation and reconciliation. But in the confrontational atmosphere that engulfed the legislature after the "new third" took its seats, he joined the directorials in their battle with the conservative and royalist opposition or Clichyites, as they were known, after the name of their club. Boulay backed the coup of 18 Fructidor, and along with Sieyès and Chazal, he was named to the committee that led the Council of 500 through the purge. Indeed, he became the committee's *rapporteur*, for as a young man Boulay had trained himself in oratory like Demosthenes, and his colleagues valued that talent.[17]

All supporters of the Fructidor purge agreed that no scaffolds should be erected for the vanquished side. But the Directory insisted on the penal deportation of the most notorious Clichyite deputies and journalists, and this extra measure of repression Boulay vainly opposed. Similarly, he deplored the tight rein of press censorship that the Directory imposed after the coup. Nor did Boulay share the anti-clerical, secularizing bias of the post-Fructidor Directory. In fact he led the parliamentary resistance to the Directory's anti-Catholic *Kulturkampf* in 1798–99, and successfully defended the prerogatives of private Catholic school teachers against proposals to regulate what went on in their classrooms. While he joined in engineering the ouster of three directors in Prairial for malfeasance and unconstitutional actions, he drew the line at putting them on trial.

Boulay de la Meurthe possessed a finely calibrated political sensibility that combined liberal values with a hard edge of realism. Like Berlier, he was respected by his colleagues and often found himself named to important ad hoc committees in the Council of 500. On three occasions the Council elected him as its president, most recently in September 1799. During his one-month term, General Jourdan, victor of Fleurus in 1794 and one of the most prominent Neo-Jacobins in the Council of 500, introduced a motion to declare the fatherland in danger (*la patrie en danger*). Was this a plausible response to dire military news from the front or a license to plunge France back into revolutionary dictatorship? Neither interpretation could be excluded, and this evocative, open-ended motion therefore provoked an impassioned debate.

Boulay worked strenuously to defeat the motion. As presiding officer he prevented a precipitous, emotional vote by stretching out the debate to a second day. Then he successfully lobbied for a rare *appel nominal* or roll call vote. These two tactics likely helped produce the desired outcome, for Jourdan's motion failed, 171 to 215 against.[18]

The timing was fortuitous. Within ten days, French armies under Generals Brune and Masséna finally halted the anti-French offensive with decisive victories in Holland and Zurich. The war crisis had been defused by ordinary means, for the most part, without plunging the country back into a revolutionary dictatorship. Sieyès could now begin to lay his plans in earnest.

BONAPARTE'S RETURN

A parliamentary coup at its core, the plot nonetheless depended on an overwhelming show of military force, organized by a popular general. Not that anyone expected a need to unsheathe the bayonets. Rather, the plotters intended the visible support of the army to dishearten their opponents and preclude any protests in the streets. Locking up support for the plot among army commanders in the Paris region would also deny potential resistors any recourse to a military countermove. Hence the famous comment by Sieyès, "Je cherche une épée"—I'm looking for a sword.

At the outset five generals had sufficient prestige to fill that role. But the favored Joubert had recently been killed in battle, and Jourdan, firmly aligned with the Neo-Jacobins, would have opposed the plot. Moreau, whom Sieyès esteemed, sympathized but wished to minimize his involvement in politics, while the opportunistic Bernadotte—recently removed as war minister by Sieyès—was immobilized by his conflicting instincts and ambitions. That left Bonaparte, who had slipped through a British naval blockade to reenter France in October 1799, just as the plot ripened.[19]

Technically, the general had committed a grave offense by leaving his army behind in Egypt without orders to do so. But who would dare or even wish to confront him? On the contrary, he received a hero's welcome everywhere he turned. His string of victories in Italy two years before had barely been tarnished by his questionable military exertions in the Near East. And even the Egyptian campaign received good press coverage because of its exoticism and veneer of scientific exploration.

Because the Revolution's political culture had not favored inordinate per-

sonal ambition or cults of personality, the position of national hero was problematic in revolutionary France, but also a vacuum waiting to be filled. Most
political figures had negligible name recognition (those who had it were dead),
and scarcely any generals had enjoyed consistent or dramatic success. Yet the
Revolution's ideological bias against dominant personalities and naked ambition could not suppress the natural inclination to identify with individual
achievement rather than abstractions. Ordinary French citizens, not to mention members of the new political elite, must have craved on some level to
celebrate an individual who embodied their highest values and personified
their republic's achievements.

Having assiduously cultivated his image back in France while on campaign in Italy and Egypt, General Bonaparte now savored the adulation that
burst around him, the greater for his having been out of the limelight for a
year. Splendid military and diplomatic achievement in 1797, embellished by
skillful news management, had elevated him above the dreary ranks of bick-
ering civilian politicians and almost all of his military peers. Apart from the
more reserved and enigmatic Moreau, Bonaparte seemed to be the only veritable hero of the republic, civilian or military. Moreover, he cultivated a
warm relationship with the leading scholarly, literary, and scientific lights of
the republic, now ensconced in the National Institute that had replaced the
old royal academies. Bonaparte himself held a membership in the Institute's
mechanics and applied science section, and went out of his way to express
admiration for the Institute's members and their work. To the various political figures seeking to enlist him in their corner upon his return, he first
responded noncommittally, keeping his options open like a good commander until he had studied the treacherous terrain.

It did not take long, however, for Bonaparte to indicate his distaste for the
Neo-Jacobins. This would not have surprised anyone familiar with *La France
Vue de l'Armée d'Italie*, a newspaper published by his command in 1797 and
edited by the devoted Regnaud de St. Jean de Angély, director of French military hospitals in Italy. Its masthead credo pledged to defend the republic
against the partisans of royalism or terror, to oppose factionalism, the greatest threat to the republic's well-being, and to promote national unity. In
broad outline, the sentiments of Bonaparte and Regnaud in 1797 could have
formed the epigraph for Brumaire: "Tired of discord, troubles and dissension, citizens seem by unanimous accord to approve exhortations to concord." At that juncture, the imminent threat to concord seemed to come
from the Clichyites, and General Bonaparte signaled his readiness to back the

Directory in any confrontation. Still, he repeatedly made it clear that his republic had no room for terrorists or *hommes de sang*.[20]

Already in 1797, while ostensibly defending the republic against subversion by the Clichyites, Bonaparte's tone was less than reverent for its charter. The constitution had many flaws, his journal conceded, including the absence of a mechanism like Sieyès's constitutional jury. "Thus it can be criticized, censured, assaulted—YES; but overthrown—NO." Unfortunately, the duly elected Clichyite legislature of 1797 was enacting laws "subversive of the social order, obviously contrary to the spirit and letter of the constitution." Accordingly, the Directory must be supported when it refuses to implement such laws and, presumably, when it finally acts to disencumber the republic from them by any means necessary.[21] With a change of emphasis, this becomes the formula for Brumaire: replace the term "constitution" with "underlying principles of the Revolution," and the rationale for the coup is already there in embryo.

Bonaparte's anti-Jacobinism sat well with Sieyès. It was the general's impatience and ambition that worried him. The inordinate public adulation for Bonaparte suggested to Sieyès that even if the revisionists succeeded, they might not emerge as masters of the situation. Instead of heading toward a safe harbor at last, Sieyès from the first sniffed a new tempest on the horizon. But at this juncture he was too committed to desist. "Now we all have to group ourselves around your brother," he morosely acknowledged to Lucien Bonaparte.[22]

For his part, General Bonaparte had reservations about Sieyès. At the outset, a question of protocol as to who should approach the other nettled the touchy pride of both men. The first occasions when the two found themselves in the same room were tense and unsatisfying. When Napoleon seemed to snub the director (trying to appear disinterested and circumspect), Sieyès supposedly remarked: "Do you see how that little insolent one treats a member of the authority that might have had him shot?" No doubt Bonaparte sensed the director's ambivalence about him. More fundamentally, to Bonaparte, Sieyès seemed opaque and given to abstraction. "He is a man of systems whom I do not like," he told his secretary Bourrienne, long before the hard negotiating began. But as Bourrienne claimed, "everything changed when skillful intermediaries [such as Talleyrand, Lucien Bonaparte, and Boulay de la Meurthe] engaged Bonaparte to join forces with Sieyès in overthrowing together a constitution that he dislikes."[23] Lucien Bonaparte's unique position as confidant of Sieyès and intimate of his brother made him invaluable in this delicate situation. Young and headstrong, yet ingratiating and popular, the deputy from Corsica was named president of the Council of 500 in October as a show of esteem by the chamber for the general. Far from being a mere token, Lucien became a dogged facilitator. He also worked to allay the worst fears of the Neo-Jacobins, some of whom he numbered as his friends.[24]

SIEYÈS, BONAPARTE, and their allies hatched a shrewd plan to cloak their constitutional coup in an aura of pseudo-legality. The parliamentary and oratorical skills of the plotters, not to mention their sangfroid, would be as crucial to the outcome as the deployment of military force. Indeed, the plot could not have proceeded at all without an effective bloc in the Council of Elders, where Sieyès had assiduously cultivated a circle of like-minded deputies. Although recruited by Sieyès, such deputies as Lemercier, Regnier, Cornet, and Cornudet would become Bonaparte's pliable servitors.

Almost all the officers of the two legislative houses elected in October joined the inner circle of the plotters, including Lemercier, president of the Elders; Lucien, president of the Council of 500; all five *inspecteurs de la salle* in the Elders; and most of their counterparts in the Council of 500. Ordinarily the *inspecteurs de la salle* performed routine housekeeping duties, but they would now be vital. Lemercier hosted a final preparatory meeting on the night of the 17th in his own home, attended by twenty or so deputies, including Lucien, Boulay, Chazal, Cabanis, and General Frégeville from the 500, and Regnier, Cornet, Baraillon, and Cornudet from the Elders.[25] Cornet, one of the *inspecteurs de la salle* charged with convoking his colleagues in the Elders for a special session on the morning of the 18th, admitted later that between sixty to eighty of the less amenable deputies were not notified in a timely manner. No unseemly debate would mar the scenario's opening act.[26]

The plotters capitalized on an obscure provision of the constitution that permitted the Council of Elders to shift the site of the legislature away from Paris temporarily, should popular turmoil in the capital threaten its deliberations. That minor prerogative meshed perfectly with the public pretext for the coup: to forestall an imminent coup by Neo-Jacobins and their terrorist allies in Paris. This vague allegation was entirely mendacious but not absurd, given the unpredictable behavior of political generals such as Jourdan, Augereau, and Bernadotte, and the historic ability of the Paris *sans-culottes* to mobilize. If nothing else, the psychological mechanism of projection bolstered the conspirators' conviction in making the charge. Preparing to overthrow the constitutional order without scruple, they might easily believe that their antagonists were ready to make a similar move themselves.

But the next step would discourage any effective response. Though nowhere stated in the constitution, it was a plausible corollary that if the Elders took the extraordinary step of transferring the legislature to Saint-Cloud, they should provide the military force to implement that constitutional decision in a safe and orderly fashion. Thus the second matter for the special morning session of the Council of Elders on 18 Brumaire was to appoint Napoleon Bonaparte commander in chief of all forces in the Paris region—not only the regular units of the 17th military division under General Lefebvre, but also the special guard corps of the legislative councils and the Directory.[27]

On 18 Brumaire, the Elders convened, duly voted to transfer the next day's session of both houses to Saint-Cloud, and named General Bonaparte commander of the region's armed forces. Then they immediately adjourned. Where normally the Council of 500 would be required not simply to approve but to initiate any decree, the concurrence of the larger house was not required for this special transfer decree, uniquely vested in the Elders by the constitution. On the morrow the legislature's session would be insulated from direct popular influence but under maximum psychological pressure from the revisionists and their military legions.[28]

INTO THE CRUCIBLE: FROM 18 TO 19 BRUMAIRE

In a whirlwind of activity Bonaparte touched all bases on the military side. Senior officers summoned to his home turned out with the greatest enthusiasm and virtually threw themselves under his orders. General Lefebvre prepared to deploy his troops in Paris, on the route to Saint-Cloud, and in Saint-Cloud itself, where Murat would be on hand as well, while Moreau agreed to supervise the sequestration of any obstinate directors. Bernadotte remained sullen and noncommittal, but finally indicated that he would not attempt to intervene.

The plotters hoped that all five directors would resign en masse to clear the way for a constitutional revision, but only two (Sieyès and Ducos) were ready to do so. Moulin and Gohier refused, despite Bonaparte's hectoring. But as rotating president of the Directory, a troubled Gohier did countersign the transfer decree on the 18th, which turned out to be his last official act.[29] (He would have to wait over twenty-five years to retaliate with the publication of his memoirs, a scathing attack on the high-handedness and hypocrisy of the brumairians.) Since the Directory could not legally act without the concurrence of at least three members, Barras held the balance. If Barras capitulated, Gohier and Moulin would be powerless to resist except through moral suasion, and the plotters intended to squelch that option by placing them under house arrest. Barras hated the prospect of abandoning his seat of power, and held out as long as he could against the veiled threats directed at him by Bonaparte and others. By the day of the coup, however, he recognized the personal risk he ran in resisting (given his history of corruption and double-dealing), and signed the face-saving letter of resignation that Roederer had prepared for him. That piece of paper would be a trump card.

On the 19th the conspirators were ready to argue in both chambers that the constitution had already expired, mortally injured by endless factionalism and by the unconstitutional actions of the Directory itself. As Lucien put it, "For a long time no one has understood the constitution to be anything more than the principles of popular sovereignty and national representation. . . . The rest is nothing but an arsenal from which each party attempts to draw weapons for its own use."[30] To salvage what citizens really cared about—the fundamental principles and gains of the Revolution—responsible representatives of the people had no choice but to scrap that dysfunctional charter. In its place, however, the plotters would not presume to offer a new one on the spot, but would install a provisional government.

Each component of this provisional government would have its roots in existing institutions, and would combine a new departure with a reassuring element of continuity. First, a provisional Consulate of three men—ex-directors Sieyès and Ducos, and General Bonaparte—would assume all executive responsibility, including local administration, vital for controlling reactions in the provinces. Secondly, the legislature would adjourn indefinitely after each house designated a commission of twenty-five reliable members to stand as surrogates. Empowered to enact any necessary decrees in the interim, the commissions' main task would be to draft a new constitution in consultation with the provisional consuls. At Bonaparte's insistence, the new constitution would be submitted to the people in a referendum. In substance, then, the Brumaire coup was a clearing operation, offering scant indication of what might actually follow. Bonaparte had told Sieyès that he would serve as a provisional consul—which for Sieyès assured the coup's success—but would reserve judgment about whether to join the definitive post-Brumaire government or remain as an army commander. That he might do both at once did not yet seem self-evident.[31]

Besides lacking a substantive blueprint for the future, the Brumaire conspirators had not even settled on the actual tactics to be followed at Saint-Cloud. After astutely orchestrating the first act on the 18th, they had run out of time and inspiration, and counted on improvisation and good luck to carry them through the next day. Boulay, Chazal, and Cabanis in the 500, Regnier, Cornet, and Cornudet in the Elders, among others, were primed with arguments, but they had no specific strategy for neutralizing the inevitable resistance.[32]

IN HIS NEW CAPACITY as commander in the Paris region and guarantor of the Council of Elders, Bonaparte informed his troops and the people of Paris about the transfer of the legislature to Saint-Cloud in public proclamations using vague but portentous language. Still within the bounds of legality, the decrees of 18 Brumaire announced that the revisionists were ready to act with military support. As the deputies converged on Saint-Cloud the next day, they knew it would not be business as usual.

Sieyès and Regnier (Bonaparte's future minister of justice) had wished to exclude preemptively from the session at Saint-Cloud "about twenty of the most hot-headed deputies" who were bound to agitate the Council of 500. The plotters could require special convocation cards instead of a deputy's permanent medallion for entry past the barriers into Saint-Cloud, then withhold the cards from the designated individuals. But Bonaparte and Boulay opposed this: "to exclude those twenty deputies would be to act as if we feared being disavowed by the nation," declared the general, while Boulay argued that it would mean "abandoning legal methods."[33] With or without the twenty, however, even if the Council of Elders remained cooperative, the Council of 500 presumably had to approve any revisionist project for it to have a semblance of legality.

For all the revisionists' allegations about Jacobin conspiracies, secret meetings, and mobilizations, the Neo-Jacobin deputies came to Saint-Cloud in a state of frustration and uncertainty. According to one neutral observer, the transfer decree came as thunderbolt that caught them by surprise. At Saint-Cloud, cut off from their familiar base and surrounded by three thousand troops, they appeared visibly upset. Like the brumairians, their opponents had no specific plan except their instinct to exhibit "a just defiance. . . . Our duties and our oaths obliged us to rally more strongly than ever to the constitution." Sizing up the long, narrow layout of their temporary hall, they sought to "surround the rostrum and take it over." By placing themselves in the front rows, they could physically control access to the rostrum, even though the presiding officers stood in the other camp.[34]

The first Neo-Jacobin speakers challenged the implicit premise of the whole plot: that one could in good conscience shed the constitution in order to shore up the republic. A republic, argued Grandmaison, could be anything—the United States was a republic and so was Venice; what we uphold is our own specific constitution. The speaker demanded a report from the Elders detailing its vague allegations about plots and factions, and then proposed that the deputies renew their oath to the constitution individually while awaiting that report. For how could his colleagues proceed to scrap the constitution if they had just taken a solemn oath to uphold it—unless, of course, they did so with "*un contre-coeur*," their fingers crossed, so to speak, under duress.[35]

It occurred to the Neo-Jacobin deputy Bigonnet "that it would be useful to extend this measure to the troops who surrounded us, and to require that their commanding general personally make the same act of submission." But a colleague talked him out of that notion and Bigonnet refrained from presenting it. Some moments later he came to regret his timidity and, he claimed, continued to rue the lost opportunity ever since. For who knows how the soldiers might have reacted or even how Bonaparte would have behaved had his hand been forced by that astute but solemn symbolic demand.[36]

After a good two hours for the individual oath taking, Lucien received Barras's letter of resignation ("depriving our adversaries of their rallying point") and read it to the deputies. This of course caused further consternation. They began debating whether to vote immediately on a list of replacement nominees for the three vacant directorial places, when suddenly everything changed. Up to that point, the Neo-Jacobins held their emotions relatively in check. Improvising, occasionally at cross purposes, they groped to find the stratagems for wresting momentum from the revisionists despite the long odds. "Never had unity been manifested with greater frankness and cordiality," Bigonnet nostalgically recalled; and they might have prevailed, he added, if only they could have continued to deliberate in relative calm. "Useful motions would undoubtedly have emerged," and perhaps a compromise could have been reached "favorable to the personal ambition of Bonaparte. . . . But the fatal blow was about to fall."[37]

Bonaparte loosed that blow personally and without the concurrence of his allies. Losing patience at the long delays and the lack of progress in either chamber, fearful of losing momentum entirely, he suddenly decided to speed things up. First, he entered the Council of Elders to exhort them. The Directory no longer exists, he asserted; the Council of 500 is hopelessly divided, and there are deputies "who wish to revive the Convention, the revolutionary committees and the scaffolds." The Elders must now act on their own. "And the Constitution?" shouted one deputy. To which Bonaparte replied: "The constitution . . . what is it at present but a ruin? . . . The constitution can no longer save the republic." To deputies who demanded to know the specifics of the alleged plots, he blurted out the unconvincing reply: "I tell you that Barras and Moulin have personally enlisted me to overthrow the government and to put myself at the head of affairs." Asked to elaborate further, of course he could not. Unskilled in public speaking (except when addressing his troops), the general became almost incoherent, contrary to later, air-brushed accounts. Having stirred things up without effectively justifying the coup, he withdrew, leaving it to his co-conspirators to take it from there.[38]

Cornudet rose to the occasion. Attacking a proposal that the Elders individually renew *their* oath of allegiance to the constitution, he demanded that

> we liberate ourselves from metaphysical abstractions. . . . What does one mean by the Constitution of the Year III? If it is the principles of liberty, representative government, the separation of powers, then I adopt them. . . . But let us beware of reestablishing a tyrannical Directory which kills that liberty. Thus in the name of the sovereignty of the people I invoke the order of the day on the proposed oath.[39]

Regrouping after Bonaparte's inept intervention, the conspirators in the Elders threw aside all reserve and the coup began there in earnest.

The general meanwhile moved across to the Council of 500, where the entry of armed soldiers other than its own grenadier guard was strictly prohibited. This reckless act appalled Sieyès: "That maneuver is going to ruin us . . . and undo all the plans prepared with such care," he lamented.[40] Bonaparte's unauthorized entry outraged the Neo-Jacobins. Immediately, cries of "*hors de la loi*" burst from all directions. As he made his way to the front in the company of several large soldiers, furious deputies surrounded him and harangued him with "clamors and vociferations." The towering Destrem rained down blows, which the grenadiers deflected, and Bigonnet at the front seized Bonaparte by the arms and shouted: "What are you doing? What temerity! Leave at once—you are violating the sanctuary of the laws." Scores of shouting deputies were on their feet threatening to avenge this brazen intrusion. Bonaparte never got to say a word, and quickly turned back with the aid of his escort.[41]

Lucien pushed to the rostrum to defend his brother, to recall his unparalleled services to the republic, but a voice interrupted: "He has just forfeited the entire price of his services; down with the dictator, down with tyrants!" With those words the commotion became "inexpressible," as Bigonnet recalled. "In vain did one propose measures of security in the midst of this disorder; it was impossible to get anything adopted." Cries of "*hors de la loi*" punctuated the din, with the distinct possibility that Lucien might have to preside over a vote to outlaw his own brother, in effect a symbolic death sentence without a trial. This he could not possibly do. Ceding the chair to the vice president, Chazal (a fellow conspirator), he left the hall in the company of soldiers sent by his brother to rescue him.[42]

Lucien's state of mind was at once more agitated than Napoleon's yet more focused, and it was Lucien who turned this chaotic moment to advantage. Outside, he addressed the assembled officers and troops. As president of the Council of 500, his appeal had immediate credibility. A faction of violent deputies, he claimed, holds the Council hostage. With their attack against Bonaparte, they are in rebellion against the Council of Elders. Their cries of "*hors de la loi*" were intolerable, but in fact, he adroitly countered, "those miserable offspring of the Terror have put *themselves* outside the law by their assaults on the liberty of this Council." Since some of its own deputies were endangering the republic, the soldiers must liberate the sane majority of deputies, "deliver them from stilettos with [your] bayonets" by clearing the hall.[43]

To galvanize the troops for the dubious mission of ousting the representatives of the people from their own hall, Lucien launched the myth of the *poignards*—claiming that Napoleon had nearly been murdered by the drawn daggers of irate Neo-Jacobins. Virtually every eyewitness, however, denies that mendacious embellishment. None confirms seeing any pistols or knives drawn, let alone anyone actually attempting, Brutus-style, to stab the would-be tyrant.[44] But as Lucien later observed, and as Bigonnet essentially confirms in his own account, the Jacobins were unable to capitalize on Napoleon's blunder. The raw emotionalism, the shouting, pushing, and shoving, the menacing cries of "*hors de la loi*" seemed to validate the image of the Neo-Jacobins that the brumairians incessantly retailed. Even without drawn daggers, this commotion seemed to confirm the Jacobins' reputation for violence and intimidation. "The excesses to which we saw the Jacobins carry themselves effaced the error committed by the General in violating our meeting place," Lucien accurately concluded. Boulay, an eyewitness who denied seeing any knives, still judged that "the movement against the General was an act of violence and an attack."[45]

Arguably a bellwether of the Brumaire conspiracy, Boulay prepared to follow Lucien out of the hall. But not before a brutal confrontation with a Neo-Jacobin deputy evoked the supremely high stakes that had now been established. Prudon cornered Boulay and shouted at him:

Do you believe that we don't know where you spent last night? We know . . . what you have done, what you have said, what you have resolved. But, brigand (he added, bringing fists up to his face), you will pay for that with your head. Remember, you scoundrel, that I am the one telling you this.[46]

No wonder Boulay concluded "that normal deliberation was no longer possible, and that the crisis would be resolved elsewise than by discussion."[47]

The climax now came—unplanned, tumultuous, and nasty. After Lucien's departure, the deputies debated whether to "leave en masse and proceed to Paris in search of protection and safety" or whether it was "more dignified to remain at our posts and brave the final outrages of tyranny." The appearance of armed troops headed by General Leclerc (Bonaparte's brother-in-law) put an end to this irresolution. "In the name of General Bonaparte, the legislature is dissolved. Good citizens must leave," Leclerc ordered. "Grenadiers, forward!" The Jacobins did their best to maintain their dignity, but "attacked like an enemy outpost," they had no recourse but to exit the hall in haste. Their worst moment, perhaps, came as many attempted to return to Paris, when they found the gates of Saint-Cloud closed, their egress barred and their fate uncertain for over an hour, until the sentries received orders to let them through.[48]

The parliamentarians now had to salvage a fig leaf of legality from the afternoon's debacle. The Elders, and a tiny rump of forty to fifty members of the 500, reconvened separately that night to enact the prearranged decrees for a provisional Consulate and two legislative commissions. Lucien addressed the Elders, brought them up to date on the collapse of the 500 and the assault on General Bonaparte by "those upholders of the constitution with daggers and *hors de la loi*."[49] Having broken definitively with the Neo-Jacobins, the rump of the 500 added one additional decree. After all their denunciations of the Directory's purges, they drew up a purge list of their own to expel sixty Neo-Jacobins from the legislature immediately because of their "excesses and attacks"—including Bigonnet, Destrem, Grandmaison, Briot, General Jourdan, and Prudon. No doubt reflecting on his own recent experience, Boulay told his remaining colleagues that their adversaries "opposed any kind of deliberation; tyrannized the Assembly; forced the sane and well-intentioned majority to leave this hall."[50]

Boulay did the heavy lifting in the rump of the 500 as *rapporteur* for the decrees abolishing the Directory, establishing the provisional Consulate, and proroguing the legislature. True, there was no longer any opposition to confront, but it would be his name on the official version of events. Cabanis likewise vouchsafed his reputation by justifying the coup in the Council's valedictory speech, which then became an official address to the French people. Finally, late that night, the Elders heard their select committee recommend the same measures and voted to approve them.[51] The interminable *journée* ended when the three new consuls swore an oath before the remaining deputies to uphold the sacred principles of the Revolution.

A spate of tailored press reports and proclamations papered over the ugly events of 19 Brumaire. They emphasized the impasse produced by the Directory, the corrosive effects of factionalism, the alleged violence of the Neo-Jacobins, and the need to sever republican values from a discredited constitution. "Wishing to retain the procedural elements of the constitution," declared Boulay, "would be to favor the dissolution of the body politic." The official addresses of Bonaparte, Boulay de la Meurthe, and Cabanis assured the French people that the events of Brumaire guaranteed the unity of the republic, the sovereignty of the people, liberty, property, and security, and that great prospects of renewal awaited.[52]

BONAPARTE, SIEYÈS, AND THE NEW ORDER

Brumaire had unfolded much like a military battle. Smoothly launched tactical plans went awry; noise and chaos permeated the field; unanticipated casualties were sustained (the pretense of legality); but in the end defenses were breached and the objective taken. Following the action, official communiqués downplayed the damage and extolled the achievement of victory. Accustomed to such turbulence and good fortune, Bonaparte must have been comfortable. Nor did the brutal turn of events in the Council of 500 alienate his co-conspirators, who showed little distress when he ordered the troops to clear out the enraged Neo-Jacobins along with all the other deputies. The cabal's planning, however, did not extend beyond the decrees of 19 Brumaire, which abolished the Directory, prorogued the legislature, established a provisional government headed by Sieyès, Bonaparte, and Ducos, and created out of thin air a mandate for the two self-selected legislative commissions to draft a new constitution.

With Bonaparte's military comrades now stepping back, one might have expected him to be enveloped by the politicians, lawyers, and intellectuals at the center of the coup. Most of the fifty parliamentarians who would ostensibly fashion the constitution had after all been recruited by Sieyès rather than Bonaparte. For their failure to contain or even dilute Bonaparte's looming ascendancy, the reasons are not hard to find.

In Brumaire's amalgam of the old and new, the new assuredly was what seized the public's interest. True, among small circles of veteran republican moderates, the names of Sieyès and certain legislative stalwarts were reassuring, but Bonaparte's presence created all the excitement.[53] According to an often-repeated though possibly apocryphal anecdote, the self-effacing third man in the provisional Consulate recognized this immediately. Having been Sieyès's faithful acolyte during their tenure as directors, Roger Ducos surprised his two colleagues when they convened their first meeting. "There is no point in voting on the presidency," he is supposed to have said, turning to Bonaparte. "It belongs to you by right." With astute timing and psychology, the general reportedly demurred and called for a rotating daily presidency, which became the practice.[54]

In this spirit, a veneer of collegiality persisted through the six-week tenure of the provisional government. The three consuls avoided issues of precedence and managed to agree on most personnel decisions—with the notable exception of Fouché, whom Sieyès wished to dismiss as police minister but whom Bonaparte insisted on retaining. Generally sidestepping contentious issues, they implemented measures that all brumairians endorsed. With the concurrence of the legislative commissions, for example, the provisional consuls repealed the law of hostages and the forced loan. In the realm of symbolic politics, they revised the calendar of official republican holidays to scrap polarizing anniversaries such as 10 August and 9 Thermidor, leaving only 14 July and the first of the year, 1 Vendémiaire, or the festival of the republic.

True, one of the provisional consuls' first acts did stir up a tempest, but they soon turned their misstep to advantage. Still insecure a few days after the coup, in a reflex action drawing on numerous precedents, the consuls ordered the penal deportation of about seventy former terrorists along with a handful of Neo-Jacobin deputies noted for their vocal resistance to the coup. They left it to Fouché to designate the individuals, and his bizarre melange was probably calculated to make the whole undertaking seem questionable. In any case some partisans of the coup deplored this kind of repression, all the more objectionable for including General Jourdan on the list of victims. (A whispering campaign by Fouché blamed Sieyès for initiating the deportations, and in his memoirs Napoleon later made the same claim, but the issue of responsibility remains moot. Such repressive instincts were foreign to neither man.)[55] Soon convinced that they had squandered some useful moral capital, the consuls enlisted Minister of Justice Cambacérès, a holdover from the Directory and a behind-the-scenes player in the coup, to extricate them from their precipitous act.

Two weeks having now passed, Cambacérès provided an edifying rationale for rescinding the deportation decree. Almost everywhere Brumaire has been received with enthusiasm, he optimistically claimed.

> That touching unanimity obviates the fear that some disorganizing force may provoke internal troubles. The [Jacobin] faction that would have wished to form a state within the State no longer exists. . . . Confidence surrounds the government. . . . To conserve public tranquility we no longer need to do anything but maintain a strict surveillance over those same individuals.[56]

This was only the first of innumerable occasions on which Cambacérès would provide the rationalizations, tactics, or draftsmanship to translate Bonaparte's wishes into policy. Invoking this report, the consuls immediately canceled the orders for deportation and placed the designated individuals under police ministry surveillance instead. Now the brumairians could in good conscience differentiate their coup from the succession of previous turns that ended with arrests, deportations, lynchings, or executions. Meanwhile, they had fired a strong warning shot across the bow of potential Jacobin dissidents.

WHILE the provisional Consulate functioned smoothly enough in public, a struggle for supremacy behind the scenes began with the drafting of the new constitution. Sieyès's fear of Bonaparte's inordinate popularity and ambition did not imply that he was ready to surrender. The fifty ex-deputies of the rump legislative commissions, brumairians almost to a man, had yet to be heard from. Presumably they shared not only Sieyès's resolve to eliminate Jacobin "demagoguery" but also to preclude any threat of despotism, whether from an entire legislature or one man. A united front behind Sieyès on the content of the new constitution might have curbed Bonaparte at this juncture. Ironically, it was Sieyès himself who made that outcome unlikely.

For years Sieyès had pondered the issues of sovereignty, representation, the separation of powers, checks and balances. In 1795 he had urged his colleagues to guard the integrity of their new constitution by creating a "constitutional jury," a third branch of government to mediate deadlocks between the executive and legislature and to interdict unconstitutional actions. (Vivid memories of political pretensions by the old regime's high courts or *parlements* ruled out the American solution of vesting such authority in the Supreme Court.) For all his prestige, however, Sieyès's ideas were largely ignored at the time, but the deadlocks, coups, and purges of the Directory years underscored their abiding relevance. But now that he had a second chance, Sieyès, it turned out, was not really prepared. His ideas, inordinately complex and of questionable practicality, had never been systematized or committed to paper in coherent form. Sieyès surprised and disappointed his comrades when he revealed to Boulay de la Meurthe that he simply did not possess a working draft of a constitution for their guidance. General notions about the principles of government abounded in his rough notes, along with a sheaf of institutional concepts, complete with new nomenclature: a *collège des conservateurs* or Senate, a Tribunate, a *grand elector*, consuls, lists of notability. But these notions remained vague and fluid; they had not been articulated or patterned in any convincing way. A belated attempt to marshal his ideas and dictate them to a patient Boulay produced a useful historical source but not a compelling constitutional draft.[57]

FOUR MAJOR ISSUES had to be settled in the new constitution: (1) The relationship of the French people to their government; (2) the nature of the executive power; (3) the scope of legislative power and its relationship to the executive; and (4) the "third force" mechanism for maintaining the integrity of the constitution.

Relentless denunciations by the brumairians of electoral instability and factionalism prepared the ground for a dramatic shift in the locus of sovereignty. The record of abuse and persecution brought on by factionalism, as Boulay later insisted when presenting the final draft to the legislative commissions, remained the overriding rationale for the coup: "It is finally time to deliver ourselves from factionalism forever. . . . The republic exists between those two extremes, the royalist faction and the demagogic faction. . . . Since they are in a permanent conspiracy, the government must have the consistency and the necessary force to prevent or thwart their efforts."[58] To this end, no longer having to placate the partisans of democracy, Sieyès proposed to sever political representation altogether from popular electoral control.

Back in 1789, Sieyès had espoused a narrow concept of popular sovereignty and a very strong, non-Rousseauian notion of representation: "The people, in its political activity, exists only through the national representation. . . . Outside of the representative elite, no one has the right to speak in the name of the people." Sieyès applied the division of labor, an animating principle of social organization, to political life. Government, in his view, was a specialized function requiring talent, education, and a degree of financial independence. In his republic of notables, one would distinguish clearly those who filled the governing function from the governed.[59]

Sweeping aside ten years of experiments in citizenship and electoral democracy, Sieyès now offered this remarkable postulate to his colleagues: "No functionary should be named by those over whom he must exercise his authority. Designation must come from those above him who represent the body of the nation."[60] Accordingly, parliamentary representation must be detached from its erstwhile constituents. Instead, a permanent, national electoral assembly or Senate would choose the nation's parliamentary deputies. Citizens would still convene in local assemblies but only to name slates of local "notables." These men would in turn choose a cohort of departmental notables totaling sixty thousand across the country, and a final cut by the latter would designate six thousand names for a national list of notables or *éligibles* from which the Senate could fill vacancies. Since none of these assemblies of citizens actually named anyone for any position, unqualified or dangerous individuals would no longer find their way into the halls of parliament.

Sieyès thus inverted the model of electoral selection. Large lists of nominees would percolate up from the bottom, but actual designations of legislators would be made from the top down. With minor modifications, the constitution of the Year VIII incorporated this scheme, adding the proviso that its cumbersome and largely empty mechanisms would not be activated for another year. Initially, a coopted Senate would simply choose all deputies for the new legislature. Bonaparte and most of the brumaire parliamentarians, with the vocal exception of the principled liberal Pierre Daunou, embraced this mystification of sovereignty by Sieyès that suppressed popular election.

On the other hand, Sieyès met complete failure with his convoluted and defensive approach to executive power. Weak executives and collective executives had been tried and found wanting during successive phases of the Revolution, but to his credit Sieyès still feared the concentration of power. Executive power, he believed, must be strong yet divided and layered. He therefore proposed to install as the ceremonial head of state a *grand elector*, designated for life and lavishly remunerated, whose sole governing function was to appoint—and at his unique discretion dismiss—the two chief executive officers of the state known as consuls. The latter would determine all policy decisions and appointments in their respective spheres: domestic affairs, and foreign relations and war. Sieyès thus advocated real but circumscribed power for each consul, along with a direct and definitive check upon their conduct should they stray.

This subtle amalgam, however, had obviously not been designed with Napoleon Bonaparte in mind. For which end of the stick could possibly satisfy the general? Confer on him the supreme honor and dignity of *grand elector* (which Sieyès had no doubt visualized for himself at one time), and the youthful man of action would be utterly stymied. When Bonaparte first confronted Sieyès over this plan, he remonstrated: "Have I heard you correctly? Are you proposing for me a position where I will name those who are given something to do, while I myself am to be involved in nothing?"[61] Not only did Bonaparte decline a future for himself as such a *roi fainéant*, but he memorably dismissed the whole concept as tantamount to *un cochon à l'engrais* (a fattened pig) making it appear ridiculous. On the other hand, if he were to become foreign consul, he would have no hand in regenerating French institutions, already much on his mind, and he would not be a veritable national leader. Worse yet, he would be subject to abrupt dismissal by the *grand elector* without recourse.

In hindsight, nothing should have been more urgent for the brumairians than the need to limit executive power, but the centerpiece of Sieyès's intricate design imploded under Bonaparte's withering criticism. After he swept it off the table, a void remained, with no viable alternative at hand to interpose against the general's brief for concentrated executive power. Taking up a suggestion from Boulay, Bonaparte proposed that supreme executive authority—more broadly defined than ever—be vested in a "first consul" for a ten-year term. He was happy to surround this figure with a second and third consul, who could proffer advice or be useful to the first consul in other ways but whose consent for any decision was not necessary; decrees need only be counter-signed by a minister, appointed and removable by the first consul.

Most of Sieyès's allies on the drafting commission accepted Bonaparte's critique of a divided executive power under constant threat of dismissal by some Olympian presence. Despite his intimate ties to Sieyès, Boulay, for one, had quickly converted: "It was evident (he recalled) that the national will had summoned Bonaparte to the head of affairs and that we had to invest him with sufficient power so that he could . . . employ his activity and his genius in the service of the fatherland."[62] In the end, although much of the nomenclature and machinery of the Consulate derived from Sieyès's thought, the spirit of the regime and its pivotal institution came from the other side of the room.

AFTER this outcome, the parameters of legislative power and the balance between executive and legislature took on added importance. Again, recent French experience narrowed the options. With the need to neutralize Louis XVI in 1789, the National Assembly had embraced an unalloyed doctrine of legislative supremacy. The behavior of the National Convention in 1793–94, however, traumatized the moderates, when no check of any kind existed to constrain the "representatives of the people" from the most radical actions. Without knowing exactly what to do about this problem in the constitution of 1795, the thermidorians divided the legislature into two houses to slow things down, but could not follow the American precedent of granting the executive a veto over legislation. Subsequently, the experience of the Directory suggested that mere bicameralism did not accomplish much; with two essentially co-equal but independent legislative houses, stalemates became common. Sieyès wished to infuse greater efficiency into the lawmaking process while still precluding precipitous actions. He proposed a new scheme for dividing legislative authority functionally. But in thereby weakening that branch, he actually played into Bonaparte's hands; his approach certainly promoted legislative efficiency but failed to offset an inordinate tilt toward executive power.

Overly obsessed, perhaps, with the division of labor as a model, Sieyès proposed a tripartite structure for lawmaking. A Council of State would equip the executive branch to offer drafts of proposed legislation at the behest of the consuls. A Tribunate would debate such proposals and take a non-binding vote; true to its evocative name, it would also receive petitions from the public and launch inquiries of its own. Finally, a Corps Législatif would have the dispositive voice in approving or rejecting legislation, but would not otherwise participate in the process. Like a criminal jury, it would listen mutely to the arguments (as presented by tribunes and counselors of state) and then vote in a secret ballot.

The emotive concept of a Tribunate implied for Sieyès a proactive role, a paternalistic sentinel for the people's rights and interests. But Bonaparte insisted that the Tribunate have no such powers of intervention or initiative. The latter should be vested entirely and unequivocally in the first consul assisted by his Council of State—a disinterested body of appointed experts on whose shoulders the hard part of lawmaking would fall, but always behind the privacy of closed doors. No doubt Bonaparte would have preferred to dispense with the Tribunate's debates altogether or at least keep them out of public view as well, for he loathed the clamor of open dissent and the demagoguery it ostensibly invited. For the time being he would have to endure the prospect of occasional public disagreement, but at least it would be strictly defined by what the government sent out for consideration. As it emerged from the drafting dialogue, Sieyès's notion of the Tribunate lost its proactive edge and was subtly flattened to the advantage of the first consul.[63]

The circle closed with the Sieyès's most novel creation, the Collège des Conservateurs, or the Sénat Conservateur, as it was finally called. The Senate, we have noted, would serve as a permanent electoral assembly to handpick the members of the Tribunate and Corps Législatif. It could thus provide positions for veteran revolutionary moderates and presumably assure a substantial degree of pliancy from future parliamentarians. But the Senate was also intended to be the "third force" that Sieyès had long advocated to guarantee the integrity of France's constitution. "This body is to be nothing in the executive order, nothing in the legislative order. That is because we need a constitutional magistracy, a regulator among the great independent authorities."[64] Named for life, generously remunerated, and barred from holding any other position, the senators in Sieyès's scheme were the counterparts of the *grand elector* in their Olympian and largely passive role at the pinnacle of the political order; in fact, he would have given them the power to remove the *grand elector* and "absorb" him into their own ranks should he prove derelict. To Bonaparte, the whole notion of a Senate was suspect, an ideal setting for conspiracies, as Roman history suggested, but it was too integral to the brumairian "republic of notables" to be resisted outright.[65]

As the political theorist Marcel Gauchet argues, however, relative to Sieyès's long-standing and somewhat mystical vision for this "third force," the Senate of the Year VIII was essentially stillborn. On paper it did receive an extremely vague mandate for constitutional adjudication. (Article 21: "It maintains or annuls all acts that are referred to it as unconstitutional by the Tribunate or by the Government; the lists of eligibles are to be counted among those acts.") But its nature was problematic from the start, when Sieyès and Ducos, named as the first senators in the text of the constitution itself, chose the next twenty-nine, who in turn co-opted twenty-nine more men to fill the initial complement of sixty. An emanation of the ruling group, a lofty vehicle for distributing spoils, with its own lavish perquisites, the Senate was not calculated to foster independence or moral courage, especially with its exceptionally vague mandate. And if the opposite became true, if the Senate capitalized on this vagueness to thwart the first consul or the legislature, who could limit its potential to abuse its own power? Who, in other words, would watch the watchers, as Daunou demanded to know in the drafting sessions.[66] But few of his colleagues feared that the Senate would initiate mischief under any circumstances, while for the opposite problem of spinelessness there was no obvious antidote.

As it emerged from the constitutional deliberations, the Senate had two real functions in 1800: first, to designate some four hundred suitable tribunes and legislators, a task that did not interest Bonaparte very much; and second, by its distinguished collective profile to adorn the Consulate with prestige and lend it gravity. Later, Bonaparte would realize that the Senate's nebulous role as conservator of the constitution could be harnessed not to block his moves but on the contrary to sanction or even initiate the changes he desired in the constitution to enhance his power.

THE CONSTITUTION of the Year VIII had been hammered out in about a dozen tense negotiating sessions between Sieyès, Bonaparte, Daunou (who had been enlisted as redactor), and a small group of parliamentarians led by Boulay who mediated the differences among those three principal figures. Boulay presented the final version for the pro forma approval of the legislative commissions. Two days later, Dominique Garat (shortly to be named as a senator) brought the process to closure with an address celebrating their achievement as they prepared to submit the constitution to a national referendum.

Now fifty years of age, Garat before the Revolution had been a lawyer, intimate with the last generation of *philosophes* such as Marmontel, and a writer of comparable mediocrity. A member of the National Assembly of 1789; minister of justice at the time of the September massacres of 1792; minister of the interior in 1793 during the purge of the Girondins, who were his friends; a member of the republic's new learned academy, the National Institute of 1795; a deputy in the Council of Elders in 1799 who joined the circle of conspirators before Brumaire. Garat, in sum, was a well-connected intellectual in politics, a stalwart revolutionary across the 1790s, a man of liberal convictions yet an opportunist of the first order, or in the words of a detractor, a "political eunuch."[67]

According to the bitter memoirs of Garat's friend, the ousted director Gohier, Bonaparte personally asked Garat to deliver this important address precisely because he knew of Garat's misgivings about the new charter. "At first Garat hesitated," writes Gohier, "but upon reflecting that the revolution [of Brumaire] had been consummated, he concluded that the sole recourse left to those who loved their country and who wished to render it less noxious (*funeste*) was to march sincerely along with it, in order to guarantee France against an opposition as dangerous as it is futile. Garat could not refuse for very long . . . he whom no one had yet known how to resist."[68]

Having agreed to do this (thus no doubt ensuring his designation to the Senate), Garat left all reservations behind. The ponderous locutions, inept similes, and flights of optimistic fancy make this speech a chore to read, but it did the job. Here is the apologia for concentrated executive authority. ("An executive power which, by its unity, is always in action and in accord; by its speed, reaches everything; by having initiative in lawmaking, can assimilate into the republic's code all the fruits of experience and all positive enlightenment about government; by its irresponsibility [*sic*] is an immutable fixed point, around which everything becomes solid and constant.") Here is an evocation of senatorial grandeur surpassing even Sieyès's fondest images. ("You have constituted a senate of men who have reached the age when all great movements cease or moderate themselves, where one has nothing more to acquire. . . . Like tutelary divinities, they scrutinize the acts and conserve the laws of a world that has become a stranger to their passions.") Here is praise for the foolproof if fraudulent method for choosing the representatives of the people. ("By means of a direction as predictable as if it were mechanical, the elections of the French people, so often misled in the past, will now fall almost always on those with talent and virtue.") And here, finally and inevitably, is the encomium for Napoleon Bonaparte. ("The brilliant success that everything points to is further assured by that extraordinary man on whom you have principally conferred power . . . by raising him to that function, the leading position in the world, which his genius will render even more eminent. . . . Bonaparte can have no ambition other than becoming ever greater among all the peoples and down through the centuries.")[69]

When Gohier read this cloying address, he understandably reproached Garat, and not for his stylistic deficiencies. Garat reportedly replied very simply and in the saddest of tones: "My friend, we must prevent civil war!"[70] Perhaps he was thinking of the military enthusiasm for Bonaparte, which made rejection of the constitution seem unthinkable, or of Jacobin and royalist factions waiting in the wings. In any case, with the complicity of men like Garat, the ascendancy of Bonaparte was now a fait accompli. With or without misgivings, his collaborators from the crucible of Brumaire anticipated a vast improvement in government and were eager to serve.

II

Organizing Power

*I*F THE WEAKNESS of France's political culture in the 1790s did not lead inexorably to Bonaparte's ascendancy, it certainly contributed to the enthusiasm of his collaborators for the Consulate. Now all but forgotten in the annals of the Revolution, the Fructidor coup of 1797 is a particular key to explaining the success among the political elite of the Brumaire formula: generous patronage and government without the hazards of democratic politics.

HEALING THE FRUCTIDOR SCHISM

By definition the men forced out of public life by the Fructidor purge did not participate in the Brumaire coup, and those who were ordered deported overseas (fifty-three prominent opposition deputies along with Carnot and Barthélemy, the two directors on the losing side of the struggle) assuredly did not. Most targets of the deportation decree (including Carnot) evaded arrest and hid out in France or abroad; seventeen were apprehended and deported, including Barthélemy, who was too proud to run, and four subsequently died from the rigors of the tropics. Who, then, were the victims of the Fructidor coup and why should it matter in regard to Brumaire?

Elections in the spring of 1797 (Year V in the revolutionary calendar) had changed the balance of power in the legislature by returning a solid phalanx of new deputies who, combined with the "new third" from the previous election, now formed a majority on the right. What exactly that portended for the future of the republic is impossible to say with certainty. As a first step, the right clearly wished to eliminate all vestiges of the Convention (a step denied them until now by the "two-thirds decree" of 1795), including in due course the original regicide personnel of the Executive Directory itself. The legislature, especially the Council of 500, now treated the Directory (still anchored to the republican center) with an open hostility that created a perilous stalemate. At one point the lower house voted to cut off all new funds for the government, which could have produced an unmanageable crisis. Meanwhile, both houses began to roll back the exclusionary legislation against émigrés and refractory priests that had formed a cornerstone of the thermidorian settlement.

Beyond that, however, the anti-directorial right was a shaky and ambiguous coalition. It comprised a number of hard-core royalists (some in contact with British agents, Bourbon emissaries, or both) eager to overthrow the Directory and effect a Bourbon restoration. But it also contained a large bloc of conservative constitutionalists not inclined to go that far, and certainly not to use force. The latter group valued the achievements of the Revolution but felt that it had gone terribly wrong; they wished somehow to return to 1791, to welcome back the republic's victims, and to efface every residue of the Jacobin experience. The lack of coherence and solidarity on the right gave the Directory its opening, for in the end many anti-directorials shrank from acting decisively under the leadership of veritable royalists plotting to overthrow the republic, some literally subsidized by Pitt's gold.[1]

Consider the example of Boissy d'Anglas, a lawyer from the Vivarais and a deputy to the Estates General. "The Revolution was not made by a few men, but by the whole nation," he wrote in early 1791, expressing the optimistic credo of the patriot majority in the National Assembly.[2] Elected to the Convention in 1792 from his department of the Ardèche, he voted against the execution of the king, sidestepped the Girondin-Montagnard conflict, withdrew from active participation during the Terror, and emerged after Thermidor as one of the Convention's leaders. As president of the Convention in May 1795, when an insurrectionary crowd of enraged Parisian *sans-culottes* invaded the hall demanding "Bread and the Constitution of 1793," Boissy stood his ground even after the crowd murdered one of his colleagues and paraded the head on a pike. This *journée* became the pretext to scrap the

Jacobin constitution of 1793 (which had never been implemented), and Boissy became the *rapporteur* for the constitutional committee's new draft. He presented the constitution of 1795 to his colleagues with a famous remark that government would now be returned to the best elements of society, meaning the propertied.

Along with other architects of the Directory regime, Boissy thus shaped a second chance for the Revolution to recover its veritable principles and equilibrium. But in the rancorous political struggles during the next two years, his sense of those principles brought him ever closer to the royalist militants. His commitment to the republic had been entirely pragmatic—it manifestly lacked the resonance and sacrality that it had for the directorials.[3] When the directorials struck in Fructidor, they included Boissy and several conservatives of the same ilk, along with a number of committed royalists, among those to be deported overseas. Boissy escaped to England, where he remained until Brumaire, and like the rest of the targets of Fructidor he had no part whatsoever in bringing Bonaparte to power. But if they had done nothing for Brumaire, Brumaire would do a great deal for them.

For the hard-core royalists—implacable enemies of the republic who despised Bonaparte and his revolutionary allies—Brumaire was a joke. In turn, the Brumaire parliamentarians regarded certain ex-deputies purged in Fructidor as irredeemable enemies, such as General Pichegru, whose collusion with royalist agents was proven by documents that had fortuitously fallen into General Bonaparte's hands in 1797, and which he had forwarded to the Directory.[4] But allied with the true subversives before Fructidor had been men less doctrinaire, less incendiary in their rightward drift, and more hesitant. Even if little seemed to separate them from veritable royalists, men like Boissy d'Anglas regarded themselves as moderate liberals, similar in that respect to their erstwhile directorial colleagues. They were no longer enthusiasts of revolution (as the directorials seemed to be) but neither were they outright counterrevolutionaries.

Above all, they had presided for a time over the new civic world of government, legislation, and administration created in 1789. From several perspectives they were the natural allies of their directorial adversaries, both camps having survived the Jacobin tempest. For them to be brutally shut out of the political elite by the Fructidor coup despite their electoral victories must have seemed an outrageous travesty, although in the heat of the struggle some were prepared to show as little quarter to their opponents. Similar to the pattern in Brumaire, we can see a certain amount of projection in the confrontation of 1797: in Brumaire, revisionists and Neo-Jacobins each feared plots by their opponents, as did directorials and the right in Fructidor. In the end, however, the right could marshal neither tactical unity nor sufficient armed force, whereas the Directory's controlling "triumvirate" in 1797 did summon the will to act decisively and the requisite troops, thanks to support from Generals Hoche and Bonaparte.

Was it really necessary for the Directory to carry out a coup in 1797 with military force, massive purges, and brutal deportations to thwart an imminent royalist plot? Directors Carnot and Barthélemy did not think so, although the former would certainly have resisted an overt movement to restore the Bourbons.[5] But their colleagues believed that behind the prolonged and increasingly rancorous deadlock there did indeed lie a conspiracy in collusion with the British and the Bourbons, which Pichegru's maneuvers seemed to prove. Indeed, the successful royalist electoral effort in 1797 had been secretly subsidized in part by British funds. One historian of Fructidor, who studied it specifically through the lens of British agents working in France, concluded: "There can be no doubt that a plot to overthrow the Directory did in fact exist. That it was confined to a minority [of the right] does not alter the picture materially. . . . The leaders of the anti-Directorial group did their utmost to convince the majority of confused and frightened royalists that a blow against the Directory was necessary."[6] In any event, the conflicts and tortuous alignments of 1797 had finally produced a wrenching schism that fractured the moderate elite of 1789 yet again.

It is easy enough to see continuities in Brumaire with the arbitrary practices of the Convention and Directory. The brumairians too perpetuated themselves in office and in effect nullified recent elections—indeed, the future of the electoral process itself—ostensibly to protect the Revolution's fundamental achievements. Even more relentlessly than the Convention or the Directory, the Consulate stigmatized organized opposition as illegitimate; like the *constituants*, the Montagnards, and the directorials before them, the brumairians claimed that they—in the person of their anointed leader—were the authentic voice of the people. Furthermore, the Neo-Jacobins who vainly opposed the coup on 19 Brumaire at Saint-Cloud immediately found themselves outside the pale of the new regime, along with anyone known as a violent, unregenerate terrorist. (And a harsh personal reckoning with certain reputed ex-terrorists lay in the future, as we shall see.)

But the new government also made a serious effort to mend the wounds from earlier schisms. Reluctantly, General Bonaparte had lent public support and military muscle to the Fructidor coup of 1797. But Fructidor was water under the bridge to him, an unfortunate event whose ramifications made his own future more difficult if left to stand. The Brumaire coterie provided the core of Napoleon's servitors and supporters, but it was too narrow a foundation upon which to construct a new regime.

BEFORE the Consulate slammed the door on free political expression, an anonymous tract appeared in Paris entitled *Dictionary of the Great Men of the Day, by a Society of very small individuals*, reminiscent of old-regime and revolutionary *libelles* in its biting sarcasm and personal vilification.[7] The "big men" in question—most of them reviled and a few admired by the author—included intellectuals and political veterans recently coopted into the Consulate's Council of State, Senate, and Tribunate. The pamphleteer scorned as mediocrities most of the new regime's favored savants and writers now ensconced in the National Institute, but its bitterest sallies recalled the schism of Fructidor, and it might well have been written by someone purged in that coup. Offering knowledgeable if exaggerated comments on prominent figures recruited into the Consulate's institutions, the *Dictionnaire* did not simply attack individual reputations but made a case about inclusion and exclusion.

One hero of the author was Barthélemy, the newest member of the Directory in 1797, who was deported in Fructidor for his alleged royalist leanings: "One of the most capable diplomats in Europe. His mission to Switzerland showered him with honor. But . . . they *proved* that he was a traitor and he was proscribed. The triumvirs [the three majoritarian directors] and their base valets [in the legislature] Bailleul, Boulay, Chénier, and Chazal, would never pardon him his love for peace, his hatred for the brigands and the factious." The first consul apparently agreed; for as the entry concludes, "Bonaparte has just presented Barthélemey as a candidate for the Senate."[8]

Several architects of the Fructidor coup, meanwhile, reappeared among the most active participants in the Brumaire coup two years later. Boulay de la Meurthe, for example, emerged as one of the earliest, ablest, and most devoted collaborators of Bonaparte, who appointed him president of the legislative section of the new Council of State. The author of the *Dictionnaire*, however, pilloried Boulay as a "harbinger of upheavals and proscriptions" for his role in Fructidor, and for his "unjust and atrocious report" in support of Sieyès's motion a few months later to deny civic rights to ex-nobles.

"Shouldn't one fear conferring into his hands the weapons of Thémis? . . . He has not been very economical in proposing revolutionary laws."

While the author denounced the terrorist past of his subjects when they qualified for that accusation, few of the brumairians had a terrorist past. Nor was mere membership in the National Convention prejudicial in and of itself. Ex-*conventionnels* Boissy d'Anglas, Cambacérès, Carnot, and Daunou, for example, were treated with respect. The harshest abuse of all, it is true, fell on Merlin de Douai, newly appointed by Bonaparte as commissioner to the Tribunal de Cassation, the nation's highest court. A noted jurist and leading figure in the National Assembly, Convention, and Directory, Merlin is depicted in the *Dictionnaire* as cruel and sanguinary, a vain opportunist and *fripon*, and above all as the author of the "monstrous" law of suspects of 1793. Yet notwithstanding this diatribe against Merlin de Douai, the fault line that preoccupied the author dated not from 1793 but from 1797, when the "tyrannical" purge of Fructidor made a mockery of liberty.

The *Dictionnaire* relentlessly attacked the men associated with Fructidor who were now visible in Bonaparte's entourage such as Bailleul, Berlier, Boulay, Chazal, Chénier, Debry, François de Neufchâteau, Merlin, Riouffe, and Sieyès. At the same time it lauded Benézech, Boissy d'Anglas, Carnot, Mathieu Dumas, Dumolard, Emmery, Fleurieu, and other victims of Fructidor for their courage and integrity. The author was implicitly praising Bonaparte for repatriating such men, while urging him to think twice about the character and reliability of his closest Brumaire allies. Inadvertently, then, he points us to the effort of the Consulate to bridge the Fructidor rift in the revolutionary elite.[9]

A SERIES of police reports from the months after Brumaire illustrate the same point in recounting how the new government tried to sort out the targets of Fructidor's deportation decree. The hard-core royalists would be left to their fate for the moment and excluded, while others would be rehabilitated. The reports classified fifteen deported ex-deputies, along with six convicted royalist conspirators and journalists, as *non-rappelé*, outside the pale. The others, allowed back or emerging from hiding after Brumaire, were initially placed under police surveillance. But that surveillance lifted almost immediately for a number of figures slated for integration into the new governing circle, including Barthélemy, Boissy, Carnot, Cochon, Gau, Muraire, Pastoret, Portalis, and Vaublanc, and it would shortly be lifted from others such as Barbé-

Marbois, Mathieu Dumas, and Siméon who would later rise to prominence in the regime. Meanwhile, the government immediately coopted several ex-deputies purged in Fructidor without deportation.[10]

When the Council of State convened a year into the Consulate, it would look as if Fructidor had never happened. Around that table, the new hub of lawmaking in the French state, sat Barbé-Marbois, Benézech, Emmery, Fleurieu, Pétiet, Portalis, Roederer, and Thibaudeau—targets to one degree or another of Fructidor—side by side with Berlier, Bernadotte, Boulay de la Meurthe, Français de Nantes, and Réal—enthusiasts for the Fructidor purge. They would shortly be joined by Treilhard and later by Merlin de Douai, two of the directorial architects of Fructidor, but also by Mathieu Dumas, Muraire, and Siméon, three other anti-directorial legislators ordered deported at that time.

Among other targets of Fructidor, Carnot was appointed Bonaparte's minister of war, Barthélemy was made a senator, Boissy and Siméon became tribunes before moving on to higher positions, while Vaublanc and Dumolard were named by the Senate as members of the Corps Législatif. On the other side of the divide, directorials Creuzé-Latouche, François de Neufchâteau, Lenoir-Laroche, Garat, and Lambrechts became senators, while three leading pro-Fructidor deputies—Bailleul, Chazal, and Chénier—entered the Tribunate. In this respect, then, the Brumaire regime reversed the revolutionary practice of "unity by partition." Alongside a group of relatively non-political or technocrat types, the Consulate conducted activists on both sides of the Fructidor divide into an obligatory reconciliation.

As Bonaparte's minister of the interior Chaptal put it, with only slight exaggeration, "When Napoleon arrived at the head of the government, he conceived the project of reuniting all the parties. . . . He attempted to rally to his person all the men who had shown some talent during various phases of the Revolution. He attempted to extinguish all the germs of dissension, and he succeeded." Joseph Bonaparte, whose views carried some weight in these early years, reinforced his brother's instincts by forcefully counseling that the émigrés be allowed to return and that the regime utilize the talents of all Frenchmen, from ex-aristocrats to ex-Jacobins.[11]

The results of this approach are described by François-Nicolas Mollien, a financial expert much valued by Napoleon and eventually his minister of the treasury. Mollien's bland memoirs, while expansively self-justifying on his record in financial matters, still constitute one of the least tendentious accounts that we have of the era. He understood the psychology of both Napoleon and his servitors. By striking at the extremes, Mollien reasoned, Napoleon "wished to astonish and defy all the parties, and say to them: 'despair of relying on yourselves and count only on me.' . . . In the government he established, each person was occupied only with the particular area that he was authorized to deal with, and with the benefits that he could expect from it. Not only did no new opposition arise, but everywhere dissension dissipated." With great insight Mollien concluded that the revolutionaries of the 1790s among Napoleon's servitors "were astonished to regain a kind of security that they had not known when they themselves governed."[12] The purged and depor- tees of Fructidor must have been particularly grateful to recover their place in the corridors of power alongside directorials who had driven them out in 1797.[13]

As for individuals on the left, Bonaparte remained cautious about who merited his confidence, and, prodded by the most conservative of his servi- tors, shunned most "first line Jacobins." As the Jacobins' self-styled patron Fouché put it in his memoirs: "His biases fell particularly against those whom he called the obstinate ones (*obstinés*), either because they wished to remain tied to the popular party, or because they were forever exhaling complaints about dying liberty."[14] Clearly an invisible wall of sorts existed on that side of the spectrum. One of the few democrats to make it into the new Legisla- tive Corps sensed this and complained directly to the first consul. "The sys- tem of fusion that you have adopted in the choice of public officials has undoubtedly produced very good effects," he acknowledged. "But, I tell you frankly, you seem to me much too inclined toward those who openly or secretly [are partisans of the old order] and with whom I am sure you cannot coexist. . . . Yes, citizen first consul, your unshakable partisans, the true and disinterested patriots, are being shunted aside little by little. You are being isolated. . . . Little by little the majestic tree of liberty is being uprooted."[15] Still, Bonaparte did reach out to certain men of the left (as we shall see), the best known being Réal, Berlier, and François Lamarque, who welcomed the chance to remain in public life instead of joining the protesting Neo-Jacobin deputies of Saint-Cloud in the desert.

ANTOINE THIBAUDEAU, a young member of the National Convention whose political course had taken several dizzying turns—regicide, momen- tary Jacobin enthusiast, stalwart of the thermidorian reaction—was recruited early on into the new government. In his memoirs, he fondly recalled the

early years of the legislative section of the Council of State, arguably a micro-
cosm of the entire Council. Thibaudeau had nothing but admiration for
every one of his colleagues, starting with the two most conservative members
and victims of Fructidor: Emmery, described as a "patriot of 1789" in the
National Assembly, a moderate of independent character, who lacked all pretense and lived a quiet life; and Portalis, described as talented, self-effacing,
at bottom a royalist but one willing to listen to all sides ("He extended his
hand to the patriots and received the caresses of the royalists with pleasure").
Uniting simplicity and gravity, religion and philosophy, Portalis would later
prove his worth on the drafting committee for the Civil Code and then serve
as Napoleon's first minister of religion.

But Thibaudeau also lauded the two men to his left in the section. The ex-
regicide Berlier (in Bonaparte's eyes the house Neo-Jacobin) he portrayed as
a learned lawyer; a good man at the rostrum and in committee; independent,
sincere, truthful, and (like Emmery) a man of admirably simple habits. Then
there was Réal, an active Jacobin in 1793, who held important administrative
posts in Paris on and off during the 1790s, and who gained particular notoriety in 1796 as a defense lawyer for Babeuf and other militants of the left.
To Thibaudeau, Réal was a spirited presence in the government. Presiding
over this amalgam as president of the section was a man whom Napoleon
had immediately singled out for leadership. Boulay de la Meurthe in turn
impressed Thibaudeau as a fine organizer with a philosophical turn of mind
and an aptitude for legislation. In this account, what comes across most
strongly is the goodwill and camaraderie that prevailed in the section. Talented men of varied ages, experience, and political persuasions could work
together in good faith, deploy their considerable expertise and persuasiveness
in debate, and generally reach consensus among themselves and with the first
consul on a succession of issues.[16]

THE SENATE'S SELF-IMAGE

In the annals of political spoils it would be hard to find a cozier or more blatant case than the French Senate of 1800. Within a few years, to be sure, that
body would become Napoleon's Senate—an appendage of Napoleon's will
and the pliant handmaiden of his dictatorship. At the outset, however, the
brumairians intended their Senate as a "third force" between a strengthened
executive and a much weakened but still conventional legislature. As such it

held little interest to the general, who if anything initially regarded the Senate as a potential source of cabals in the style of its Roman ancestor.

Post-Brumaire negotiations between Sieyès and Bonaparte, as we saw, blurred the Senate's potential constitutional role with a mandate so vague as to border on inconsequentiality. As Senator Cornet put it in his sour memoir of 1824, "The Senate had the appearance and not the reality of a great power."[17] Even so, its original manner of selection, its perquisites, and its patronage powers left little to be desired for the Consulate's favored collaborators. At the moment of its inception, the Senate members confirmed that the Brumaire coup remained a joint venture between themselves and the first consul. Despite its nebulous governmental role, the Senate stood as the brumairians' visible trophy, their special preserve and source of security, both political and financial.

Having relinquished their roles as provisional consuls, Sieyès and Roger Ducos were named textually in the new constitution as the first two senators, with the power to designate the next twenty-nine, in consultation with the new consuls. They did so with relatively modest input from Bonaparte, who merely endorsed a few senior generals and his favorite savants—chemists Berthollet and Monge (who had accompanied him to Egypt), the naturalist Lacépède, and the mathematician Laplace—while vetoing the liberal legislator and constitutional bishop Grégoire. The first cohort then coopted an additional complement of twenty-nine senators for a total of sixty. With two additional senators to be named annually in the years ahead, the body was eventually supposed to comprise eighty members.[18] Lifetime tenure and an annual stipend of 25,000 livres for limited duties made a senatorial designation among the most coveted rewards the regime could confer on its adherents who met the minimal age of forty. As the fount of all parliamentary appointments without the inconvenience of elections—one hundred tribunes and three hundred members of the Legislative Corps waiting to be named at the outset—the Senate immediately became a prime locus of political patronage beyond its own ranks.

The social origins of the new senators exemplified the amalgam of *notabilité* that inspired Sieyès's vision of the French Revolution in 1789. They included nine ex-nobles, thirteen ex-barristers, twelve generals and admirals, nine men from commerce or banking, and as many as fifteen intellectuals, savants, or professors (including four from the circle of *idéologues* or latter-day *philosophes*: Cabanis, Destutt de Tracy, Garat, and Volney). Politically, the majority of senators were moderate revolutionary veterans, men who had rallied to the cause in 1789 and in many instances had helped to forge the Brumaire coup ten years later. Of the senators named in the first cohorts, thirty-eight had sat in a revolutionary legislature, often in successive bodies, including twelve from the National Assembly of 1789 and eleven who began their careers in its successor, the Legislative Assembly of 1791. Twenty-one of the new senators sat in the legislature at the time of the Brumaire coup, the allies par excellence of Sieyès.[19]

Apart from the two functions of rewarding themselves and selecting members for the new Tribunate and Legislative Corps, the brumairians visualized the Senate as the collective embodiment of the Consulate's political and social values, its supreme form of self-representation. Particularly interesting in this respect was the cooption of certain distinguished citizens beyond their own circle. Reaching out to such individuals, Sieyès and his comrades seemed to be qualifying the Revolution's mythic break from the past with a new note of continuity. They encouraged a bonding of veteran revolutionaries with Frenchmen whose major achievements had come before 1789, as long as these men had signified their support of the Revolution in some manner. As it honored such renowned figures from the past, the regime preserved but softened its revolutionary heritage.

DURING the Senate's first year, five senators passed away, and like the old royal academies the Senate arranged for formal eulogies later enshrined in a special leather-bound register. (The register then ceased to be used, for reasons unstated.) Those five necrologies—on first glance little more than formulaic encomia—resonate with the Senate's values and state of mind at its inception. While embedded in generally bland texts, their nuances are helpful in grasping the self-image of the new senatorial elite.

The Senate's most senior member, Louis Daubenton (b. 1716), attended its first session, only to be felled by a stroke and die a few days later. This ill-starred event had a beneficial side effect for the process of self-representation, since it yielded exceptional publicity to his presence in the Senate. The educated public perhaps recalled this physician and naturalist as a close collaborator of the celebrated Buffon earlier in the century. With expertise in human and animal morphology as well as rural economy, Daubenton had been a member of the Royal Academy of Sciences, a professor of natural history at the Collège de France, and head of the mineralogy section at the Museum of Natural History. In 1789, prevented by his age from taking an active part in

the Revolution, claimed his eulogist, "Daubenton could not have been indifferent to the triumph of the grand principles of justice and humanity,
whose proclamation was the French Revolution's veritable manifesto."[20]

Still, it was incumbent that such a prominent old regime savant had signified his adherence to the Revolution in some fashion. This Daubenton did
(alongside future senators Volney and Berthollet) by his public lectures of
1795 at the short-lived Ecole Normale. With this new teacher training institute, the Convention had intended to produce a new generation of elemen-
tary schoolteachers or *instituteurs* by leavening the republican enthusiasm of
its recruits with lectures by noted scholars in various disciplines. Although
this amalgam proved utterly ill-suited to the Ecole's novel mission, since
the lectures went completely over the heads of its untutored students,
Daubenton's eulogist did not fail to underscore his act of devotion to the
republic.

Next in line as the *doyen d'age* of the Senate's first cohort stood M.-F.
Dailly (b. 1724). Where Daubenton had been a colleague of Buffon's, Dailly
was remembered for his long association with Louis XVI's finance minister
Necker (as *premier commis des finances*, director general of direct taxation, and
planner of the experimental provincial assemblies of the 1780s). Unlike his
mentor, however, Dailly vaulted into the Revolution as a deputy to the
Estates General (although he soon resigned for ill-health) and later served as
an elected administrator of the Seine department in 1791–92. Now called
back from an honorable retirement, he adorned the Senate as a living example of distinguished service under the old regime and support of the Revolution in its early stages.

As a younger son (began his eulogist), J.-M. Darçon (b. 1733) had been
earmarked for an ecclesiastical career but had balked and insisted on study-
ing mathematics—a decision manifestly to his credit in the value system of
the Senate, for why include that long-forgotten detail if it were not? After a
stint at the select Ecole de Meziers for military engineers, Darçon embarked
on a stellar career as a field officer (noted for his innovation with floating
artillery batteries at the siege of Gibraltar during the Seven Years War) and as
an influential author on fortification and sieges.

Darçon's career hit a rough patch during the Revolution—which, in his
eulogist's view, redounded to his moral credit—when he was forced to leave
military service temporarily in 1793 because of the "absurd denunciations" of
Charles Hesse, a notorious revolutionary militant. Darçon later returned to
duty as a general for the first Dutch campaign, after which he retired from

active service. He then lectured on fortifications at the new Ecole Polytechnique, where he developed a theory of defensive warfare based on fortified bastions whose use, he argued, could create the conditions for a durable peace. A peerless example of meritocracy and service, "the most esteemed officer in the corps of army engineers," Darçon finished his days as a lustrous adornment to the new Senate.[21]

Natural history, financial administration, military engineering, and now, as if central casting rather than providence had struck down this succession of elderly senators, came the turn of mathematics and physics. The necrology for Jacques-Antoine Cousin (b. 1739) began with a swipe at pre-revolutionary social values. This young man had aspired to a military career, according to his eulogist, but "that career was closed to him by a blind and unjust exclusion of those whose only nobility was that of virtue." Such social prejudice and inequality was the face of the old regime that the brumairians would always deplore. Cousin turned instead to a career in education with the study of philosophy and mathematics. His laurels included a chair of physics at the Collège de France; recognition as a celebrated teacher of mathematics at the Ecole Militaire; and appointment as an associate of the Royal Academy of Sciences. For his contributions to physical astronomy, he drew royal pensions worth 1200 livres annually.

At the peak of his career in 1789, Cousin rallied enthusiastically to the Revolution, which changed his life. As his eulogist put it: "Already the impact of the French Revolution on all men of good faith had caused Cousin to suspend his philosophic meditations and to focus his attention on matters of immediate utility." Elected as a municipal official in Paris in 1791, he busied himself with public assistance and subsistence issues, and "more than once he confronted death in order to fulfill his duty." Cousin became that ideal brumairian: a surviving victim of the Terror who returned to public service after Thermidor. Imprisoned in the Luxembourg during the Terror, "along with a multitude of excellent citizens whose talent and courage were feared," he avoided execution only by a fortuitous mix-up at the last minute. After his release Cousin resumed his administrative duties in the Seine department, where he faced mortal peril yet again during the Parisian uprising of Prairial Year III (May 1795) for bread and the constitution of 1793—"when an insane faction wished to reestablish the reign of terror"—then served as one of the Directory's three commissioners on the Paris Central Police Bureau. Elected in 1799 to the Council of Elders, he of course supported the Brumaire coup. "Elevated to the Senate, Cousin would no doubt have profited from the honorable leisure that he enjoyed in order further to enrich science," his eulogist concluded, but tragically illness soon afflicted him and took his life.[22]

The untimely death of J.-A. Creuzé-Latouche (b. 1750) elicited the first senatorial necrology emphasizing service in the Revolution more than distinction during the old regime. Indeed, this senator was the quintessential *perpétuel* so detested by hard-line royalists, a fixture in the legislative establishment between 1789 and 1799. Creuzé-Latouche also exemplified the classic path by which many revolutionary leaders emerged from successful careers as members of the old-regime bar: "a profession that by the nature of its studies and the liberalism of its principles has molded so many useful citizens," as his fellow barrister Garran-Coulon unblushingly put it in his eulogy. Creuzé-Latouche's governmental experience as a royal *sénéchal* official in Poitou became his springboard for election to the Estates General. Since the Constituent Assembly had barred its members from succeeding themselves in the next legislature, his constituents honored him in 1791 with election to the nation's highest court, the Tribunal de Cassation, and the following year returned him to the National Convention.

Distancing himself from all factions in that body, his labors were notable for their utility rather than their brilliance, recalled his eulogist, but his moderation did not exclude courage. His fellow senators remembered him especially for a notable speech "in which he forcefully opposed that disastrous law of the Maximum" (the contentious Jacobin program of price controls). To his necrologist, this speech was one of the last free acts in a Convention that soon became "subjugated" until liberated by Thermidor. During that unfortunate period Creuzé-Latouche also sheltered the daughter of the Rolands following their execution with the Girondins. After Thermidor he continued to fight "against the antithetical efforts of Royalism and of demagoguery," thereby upholding the centrist values of the future brumairians.

Creuzé-Latouche served in the directorial legislature continuously, and also (characteristically) as a member of the 2nd Class of Moral and Political Science in the National Institute, the republicans' answer to the defunct royal academies. Finally, he took his place in the inner circle of the Brumaire cabal as a member of the rump legislative commission that provided its legal cover. In lamenting the loss to the republic of this moderate paragon, his eulogist offered the thought (similar to the allusion about Darçon's youthful turn from the church) that Creuzé-Latouche "never believed that morality required the frail support of superstition."[23]

A collaborator of the great Buffon; a close associate of the legendary

Necker; "the most esteemed officer in the army corps of engineers"; an accomplished physicist under the old regime and a Parisian official under the new; an ex-barrister and centrist legislative stalwart for the entire revolutionary decade—such were the five senators whose passing provided moments of reflection for their colleagues during the Senate's first year. Only the last two participated in the Brumaire coup, with Creuzé-Latouche epitomizing the revolutionary veterans of Brumaire. Instead, the departed senators evoked a broader collective image: the prestige of science, scholarship, technical military prowess, government service, and legislative experience. Exemplars of meritocracy, they had risen to eminence in the bosom of the old regime without benefit of noble privilege—the youthful Cousin having indeed been thwarted by such practices. Although it was not a burning issue, they seemed immune to the undue influence of organized religion, and to a man they had served the Revolution at least symbolically in some fashion, although two had been victimized during the Terror. As they bade successive farewells to these deceased colleagues, their eulogists burnished the Senate's sense of a Revolution fulfilled, of consensus and social equipoise.

A NEW PATRONAGE MACHINE

The cascade of patronage flowing from the Brumaire coup coursed down two parallel tracks from their respective sources in the Senate and the first consul. Once the Senate had been coopted, it designated one hundred tribunes and three hundred members of the Legislative Corps (with the proviso that there be at least one representative from each department). In the future the Senate would continue to fill legislative vacancies as they normally occurred, although after 1802 the pool of nominees would be chosen by departmental electoral colleges of local notables. From the first consul, meanwhile, came ministerial, diplomatic, and senior military appointments, as well as designations to the Council of State. Within three months, the government enacted its new system of local administration for which the first consul appointed a prefect in each department, a subprefect in each arrondissement (usually four to six per department), and the mayors of large and medium-sized towns. In due course he also named all kinds of judges who had previously been elected.

The German historical sociologist Werner Giesselmann has drawn a collective portrait or prosopography of the "Brumaire elite," as he calls it: the combined original membership of the Senate, Tribunate, Legislative Corps, and Council of State—altogether about five hundred individuals. Successful men of the old regime for the most part (including 65 nobles), 136 had been royal officials, 233 members of the professions (mainly lawyers), 63 intellectuals, and 30 priests on the eve of the Revolution. With solid, albeit middling careers in the professions or government service before 1789, they had vaulted to the top through the opportunities opened by the Revolution for elective public service. Most important, they had moved from relatively circumscribed provincial orbits to membership in a new national governmental elite in Paris. Along the way, with some exceptions, their social status rose and their personal finances generally improved, often from the purchase of *biens nationaux* (former church and émigré land nationalized by the revolutionary state and sold off to private citizens). As Giesselmann puts it in somewhat dated terms, the Brumaire elite were men "who climbed with the bourgeoisie and within it" during the Revolution. They shared a decidedly moderate collective mentality, distinguished by a self-conscious centrism, a commitment to the trappings of legality, and a sense of danger dating from 1793 that never left them.[24]

Their rapid rise to national public office during the Revolution entailed an extremely precarious hold on status and power that seems to explain their willingness to overthrow their own constitution of 1795 and to embrace General Bonaparte on his own extravagant terms. The Brumaire coup did not simply mark Bonaparte's rise to power but confirmed a trend toward oligarchy within the republican political establishment that Neo-Jacobins had long feared and denounced. The Revolution, with its frequent elections and political battles, may have been the source of their ascent, but by the end of 1799 the brumairians craved a tranquil post-revolutionary future without the hazard of elections. For this usurping group, the Consulate promised that elusive security.

It stood to reason that the Consulate's legislative bodies would be filled with former revolutionary politicians. In fact, the continuity of personnel from the Directory era was striking, apart from the excluded Neo-Jacobins who had resisted the coup on 19 Brumaire at Saint-Cloud. Seventy-seven percent of the "Brumaire elite" had sat in directorial-era legislatures, and they adapted to the new order without missing a beat. Most of the Consulate's legislators were not quite the "perpetuals" that royalists liked to deride; only 21 percent had been members of the Convention and a mere twenty individuals had been unambiguous regicides. But 240 of the 300 members of the Legislative Corps came straight from the last directorial legislature, while only 21 had never sat in any revolutionary assembly. Similarly 69 of the 100 tribunes had been deputies in the directorial legislature, although a dozen or so Parisian intellectuals now embellished their ranks.[25]

OVER TIME the prefectorial corps more than any institution came to be synonymous with Napoleon—the hallmark of his centralizing drive, and his prime instrument for pacifying the country. Neither the idea nor the term, however, originated with the first consul, but rather from such brumairians as Sieyès, Roederer, and Chaptal. The figure of the prefect was in some measure a logical response to previous experience and to the decision to eliminate elections at all levels of government. The prefect melded into one individual the attributes of the elected departmental administrations of the Directory plus the Directory's appointed commissioner to each department. The division of power between those two positions had always been murky and subject to abuse, but was justified by a concurrent need for local self-government and a measure of supervision from Paris. Now that the Consulate had eliminated elections, it made sense to have one man with power and responsibility in each department, who would in turn oversee a pyramid of subalterns (sub-prefects, employees, and appointed, unpaid mayors in each commune) while reporting directly to the minister of interior and receiving instructions from him.

The creation of the prefectorial corps opened up a substantial line of patronage, but its recruitment posed a greater challenge than simply shifting former deputies to new legislative venues. The government could turn in several directions for prefects, sub-prefects, and the appointed, unpaid members of departmental advisory councils (*conseils généraux*), who gave a veneer of local participation to an otherwise centralized system of local administration. For ten years, countless citizens had passed through local administrative and judicial positions in departments, districts, and municipalities, most by election, some as employees, and some by appointment from Paris as commissioners of the Directory attached to departments, cantons, or courts. In addition, hundreds of deputies to successive revolutionary assemblies had returned home after failing to be reelected or after being purged.

Good information of local provenance was vital for making these appointments. Many newly coopted legislators mobilized informally in ad hoc departmental "deputations" to pool their recommendations and maximize their influence. Initially, some of their interventions went astray since they were unaware that the government had decided to insulate its new prefects from local pressures by "the rule of avoidance." Like top local officials in the Chinese Empire or the *intendants* of the Bourbon monarchy—and contrary to revolutionary practice—prefects would not serve in their native departments. Nor could legislators from the same department always agree, and in some cases they forwarded contradictory recommendations to the interior ministry. Moreover, the "deputations" had to compete with prominent civil and military notables who wrote hundreds of letters supporting individuals of their acquaintance, especially as the department in question came closer geographically to Paris.[26]

As but one example of the attempt to influence patronage, four newly appointed members of the Legislative Corps from the Aveyron presented long, annotated lists of recommendations covering all positions to be filled in the department. Touting their choices as impartial republicans, they played skillfully on the Consulate's announced desire to depoliticize the country. The candidates they supported were "men against whom the only reproach of the Royalists could be that they were Republicans, and whom even the most suspicious Republicans could not suspect of royalism." The names included a complement of ex-legislators and ex-departmental administrators, most described as being of independent means and experienced in public service. These paragons were depicted as enlightened, moral patriots untainted by either terrorism or reaction. And somehow this translated into the assertion that they "have the rights and the claims to new administrative positions" greater than other possible candidates.[27]

J.-A. Dulaure, supported by Berlier among others, offers one illustration of this addiction to public office. Dulaure, a man of letters and journalist, had been in the legislature continuously from 1792 to Brumaire. Although a regicide, he had suffered greatly for fifteen months during the Convention when he fled an arrest decree for his Girondin sympathies. His fellow citizens had shown confidence in him repeatedly thereafter—indeed, in 1798, in a departmental electoral assembly that split apart in partisan conflict, both sections named Dulaure to their slates. "Those eight consecutive years in the legislature have eliminated [my] means of procuring a living," he claimed. All he asked for now was a sub-prefecture in his native department of the Puy-de-Dôme. Similarly, a former administrator of the Seine department who had petitioned in vain for a sub-prefect's position in his department, wrote to the ministry repeatedly. "I have a moral need to work, and I can do so only in the administration. It is there that I have made my vocation (*état*)." Under the circumstances he was now willing to go anywhere: "Give me any post that it pleases you to confer on me," he pleaded.[28]

The man who rose instantly from obscurity to celebrity when he identified and detained the fleeing king Louis XVI at Varennes in 1791 presents another variant on this story. Jean-Baptiste Drouet's notoriety had brought him election to the Convention, a period of Austrian captivity, unwarranted arrest as an accomplice of Babeuf's in 1796, and acquittal at the ensuing trial. Drouet remained politically active throughout the Directory, and now sought a sub-prefecture in his hometown of Sainte-Ménehould (Marne). By April 1800, however, he had heard nothing, although he claimed that Cambacérès had assured him of the appointment. "My existence is so closely identified with that of the Republic," he plausibly argued to the ministry, that if he was being passed over, "the enemies of the Republic will conclude from that fact that the overthrow of the Republic has been decided, and from then on I will become the starting point for the persecutions that they in their rage are contemplating against the republicans." In fact, his appointment soon came through and he remained in the post of sub-prefect for fourteen years.[29]

The interior ministry's oversized worksheets for collating this information, and the mass of supporting letters and petitions either recommending individuals or soliciting positions in one's own behalf, would be difficult to analyze in any systematic way. But in and of themselves they constitute compelling historical artifacts. For they demonstrate, in the very assumptions of the petitioners, how the Revolution had created a class of people (not to be confused with a twentieth-century *nomenklatura* of party members) long involved in public service on one level or another and by now dependent on public employment for their livelihood, their sense of well-being, or both.

AT THE OUTSET the first consul did not have the knowledge or interest to take command of this patronage machine. He relied primarily on his brother Lucien, his misguided first choice for minister of interior, and it is estimated that Lucien was responsible for about sixty-five of the initial nominees, with input from Cambacérès, Talleyrand, and perhaps Fouché accounting for several others.[30] But when it came to sub-prefects and other local appointments, the recommendations from the ad hoc legislative "deputations" and other prominent individuals probably carried more weight.

In the initial cohort of about one hundred prefects, forty were revolutionary politicians, members of at least one legislative assembly. The number of such men reached its maximum of fifty (or 46 percent) in 1802, which is to say that unlike the Napoleonic legislature, the prefectorial corps was never entirely dominated by ex-deputies. The initial cohort came from previous local administrations, the legal profession, and the army, as well as the ranks of ex-legislators. J.-J. Marquis exemplified such revolutionary veterans. A noted barrister in Lorraine, he was elected to the Estates General in 1789, and in 1792 the citizens of his department of the Meuse sent him to the Convention, where he voted to spare the king and kept a low profile during the Terror. Reelected to the Council of 500, he resigned in early 1797, but was later enlisted by the Directory to help organize four new departments on the left bank of the Rhine. Appointed as the first prefect of the Meurthe, his successful tenure lasted eight years until failing eyesight obliged him to resign.[31]

During the course of the Empire a growing trend of professionalization marked the prefectorial corps, an emerging career track in which younger aspirants trained first as *auditeurs* in the Council of State, then as subprefects, and perhaps as prefects in a lesser department before appointment to a choice prefecture. The pool of ex-revolutionary politicians and administrators that formed the first cohort of prefects soon sorted itself out in regard to competence, and then gradually aged. With retirements, deaths, promotions, an occasional dismissal, and the geographic expansion of the Empire, new openings drew on a more diverse group of men, with particular opportunities for the scions of old regime nobles who rallied to Napoleon. Socially, men of bourgeois origin always constituted a majority of the prefectorial corps, but the proportion of ex-nobles increased over time from 23 percent at the outset to 43 percent by 1814. Yet this did not imply any repudiation of the revolutionaries tapped in 1800, some of whom served long and effectively.[32]

DEPOLITICIZATION

While Bonaparte clearly succeeded in depoliticizing and stabilizing the government in Paris, the prefects became his point men in the more daunting effort to pacify the provinces. The official line held that past conflicts should be forgotten, and the new government did its part by suppressing the elections that ostensibly rekindled them. The tranquil image that the Consulate promoted was evoked by Beugnot, one of the more successful prefects: "The Seine Inférieure has an excellent public spirit," he reported, "because there reigns here a great political immobility and a great movement toward domestic concerns. When a people has made a wise and serious delegation of public powers [i.e., to Bonaparte], it has nothing better to do than to occupy itself with other matters."[33] But depoliticization was of course an ideal rather than an accomplished fact. In many, perhaps most, departments, a kind of low-intensity warfare smoldered. Certain prefects helped damp down the recriminations and rivalries of the past decade, but others turned out to be partisan themselves or at least insensitive to one camp or another.

Delve into the local sources for the Napoleonic era, and the embers of revolutionary conflicts are not hard to detect. On a surveillance mission for Bonaparte in the Year IX, Counselor of State Lacuée analyzed the difficulties of depoliticizing public life in the provinces. "Every individual who was previously attached to any kind of party and who was frequently injured by the rival party, often sees in what is merely a political measure dictated by prudence a favor accorded to the party he dreads. . . . Believing the enemy party to be recovering under the protection of the government, notions of vengeance and oppression terrify him. His zeal and patriotism are impaired, his confidence chilled by fear."[34]

General Rampon, a senator and local notable in Ardèche, reported in 1804 from Argentières that "I found the two parties equally exasperated with each other. . . . They call each other by the same names they have always used, *Jacobins* and *Chouans*." The government has little to fear from the first group, he added, and both are under active surveillance by the sub-prefect. His colleague Senator Jacqueminot, a vehement anti-Jacobin, visited the Pas-de-Calais department around the same time, and found intense acrimony in Arras between "anarchists" and royalists. "The two parties there are envious and suspicious. They detest each other." But, he added, "neither the one nor the other are declared enemies of the current order."[35]

And that was the government's bottom line. It could not get into people's heads and extinguish their hatred or distrust of local antagonists from the revolutionary decade, but it could work to preclude such animosities from undermining support or at least submission to the new regime. The Consulate officially strove to balance the hopes and fears of rival "parties," to placate each up to a point, and occasionally to make a bold gesture against the "extremes"—whether by deporting a cohort of notorious ex-terrorists or by abducting and executing a Bourbon prince, the duc d'Enghien.

Consistent with his desire to end persecutions and win over all but the most irreconcilable factions, Bonaparte held an indulgent attitude toward émigrés who wished to return, which grew stronger over time. "They were victims, in his view, of their devotion to a principle that he shared, the monarchical principle. . . . He flattered himself that he was inheriting it, and did not fear the Bourbons," observed his counselor of state, Pelet de la Lozère. A notion that the emperor expressed in 1806 may well have reflected his view even in 1800: "The émigrés had the courage to make war then and to make peace now."[36] Bonaparte thus welcomed back all émigrés willing to submit to the new order, although on Fouché's urging he placed them under police surveillance in their communities.[37] At the same time he repeatedly reassured the purchasers of *biens nationaux* (former church and émigré land) that their acquisitions were inviolate despite the designs on them by their former émigré owners.

This was asking a lot from both sides. During his surveillance tour of the Paris hinterland, Lacuée, like all of Bonaparte's emissaries, addressed this problem. The returned émigrés "are firmly convinced that possession of their sold property will be returned to them," he reported, and the purchasers were understandably worried. Yet he believed that most people "who would have considered the return of the émigrés dangerous under a weak government and in the midst of factional conflicts, do not believe it dangerous at all under a strong government that knows how to contain all parties equally."

This reflected Bonaparte's conviction about the benefits of strong leadership when he allowed the émigrés back en masse. In the long run his policy succeeded, but not without serious local tension and numerous ugly incidents. Lacuée's colleague on mission in Normandy, for example, reported that several purchasers of *biens nationaux* in the Orne, Calvados, and Manche departments had been murdered, their throats cut. In another region: "no purchasers of *biens nationaux* have been attacked directly, and no property has been ceded as a result of intimidation; but there is a great deal of obsession and factitious opinion."[38] Prefects were supposed to promote an accommodation between these natural antagonists, but a conciliatory approach did not guarantee results, as the prefect of Deux-Sèvres in Brittany learned to his dismay: "At a dinner he brought together some émigrés with those who had acquired their property; that démarche did not produce a good result." Perhaps he was pushing too hard. Or perhaps it was a hopeless task in that region.[39]

AS THE INTERIOR and police ministries continuously monitored "public spirit" in the departments, the prefects naturally became their prime source for local information. But the prefects' performance was in turn scrutinized from time to time by counselors of state or senators sent out on inspection missions and by Fouché's network of police informers. The appointed departmental advisory councils, which the prefects convened annually to discuss budgetary matters, also drafted annual reports for the interior ministry outside the prefect's presence. In such reports for 1803, well over half these *conseils généraux* offered unconditional praise for their prefects. From about thirty departments, however, came reservations and complaints, and by the time these commentaries were collated, four prefects had already been recalled.[40]

In most cases, criticism focused on the character more than the politics of the prefect. While almost always attesting to his probity, some councils found their prefect to lack stature, finesse, or capacity, or taxed him with haughtiness, a "lack of affability," or "weakness." Such men lacked the distinction and public esteem that Paris valued above all else. Amazingly, the veteran legislator Jean Debry managed to retain the prefecture of the Doubs until 1814 despite his obnoxious personality: "He is reproached for his lack of knowledge and capacity, for haughtiness and rigidity, for his stingy and isolated living style." Conversely, the aforementioned Marquis, prefect of the Meurthe, enjoyed a sterling reputation as a modest, gracious, caring, and fair-minded administrator, who took seriously his inaugural proclamation to his constituents, where he promised "to deal with your inquiries expeditiously, to listen impartially and with interest to your requests and complaints."[41]

In about twenty departments, however, the advisory councils criticized the political atmosphere in the prefecture. In the Loire and the Loiret, they complained that the prefect was "surrounded by men who were too conspicuous in the revolutionary regime." More commonly the opposite tendency provoked their censure, as in the Jura, where Prefect Poncet de la Cour was said to be too favorable to returned émigrés and refractory priests, while excluding "men known for their sage loyalty to the Republic." In the Lot the prefect allegedly "surrounded himself with enemies of the Revolution . . . made bad choices for mayors . . . and allowed republican institutions to be debased." Faucheux, the prefect in the Vosges, seemed to combine all manner of negative qualities: "He is reproached for a great haughtiness and pretension, for making access difficult, for surrounding himself with enemies of the Revolution," and for excessive solicitude for émigrés and refractory priests. Faucheux was eventually recalled and ended up in the Legislative Corps, where he would presumably do less harm.[42]

IN OR OUT? TWO JACOBINS OF THE DORDOGNE

François Lamarque was the leading light of a resilient Neo-Jacobin circle in the department of the Dordogne during the Directory. A former barrister first elected as a district court judge in 1790, then to the Legislative Assembly of 1791, and finally to the Convention, where he voted to execute the king, Lamarque had a terrible piece of luck that later became a political blessing. While on mission to the front in April 1793, he and three colleagues were handed over to the Austrians by the traitorous general Dumouriez. For thirty-three months the deputies languished in captivity, meaning that Lamarque sat out the entire period of the Jacobin dictatorship in an Austrian prison. While this experience affected his health adversely, it left his passion for democratic republicanism unsullied by any association with the Terror. With this moral capital, Lamarque returned to the new Council of 500 as a standard-bearer for the democrats of his department, defending their newspapers and clubs and advocating an indemnity for Babeuf's co-defendants who were acquitted after a lengthy incarceration and trial.[43]

In the Neo-Jacobin resurgence of 1798, the majoritarian assembly of Neo-Jacobin electors in Paris chose Lamarque as a deputy, but he declined that honor in order to accept reelection in the Dordogne along with another regicide ex-*conventionnel*, his friend Roux-Fazillac. Lamarque's lack of a terrorist past, however, did not shield him from the Directory's anti-Jacobin animus. In the purge of Floréal Year VI (1798), the government annulled the entire slate of deputies chosen in the Dordogne. Elected yet again in 1799, Lamarque supported Jourdan's Neo-Jacobin motion to declare the fatherland in danger (see chapter I), and had nothing to do with Brumaire. Although he himself had been victimized by the Directory, he was rightly assumed to be unsympathetic to the coup.

Lamarque immediately left the capital under a cloud after Brumaire. A letter from a friend in Paris evokes the ex-deputy's uncertain situation: "Cabanis [a respected intellectual and a key parliamentary player in the coup] has led me to believe that he and several others were responsible for your not being included on the proscription list"—a reference to the provisional Consulate's abortive move to deport potentially troublesome Jacobins. Quinette (a colleague who had shared Lamarque's Austrian captivity, and the Directory's last minister of interior) and Joseph Bonaparte were both solicitous about Lamarque, according to this correspondent: "you see, my friend, that you are well regarded. And you would do well to leave as soon as you can [for Paris]." This was sound advice, echoed by none other than Cambacérès. Lamarque had written to the second consul for help in finding a low-profile, non-political position, but Cambacérès "persisted in thinking that his former colleague can be more actively and usefully employed than as the director of a library, which is where citizen Lamarque seems to have set his sights." In fact, within three months Lamarque vaulted from the prospect of being deported as a leftist dissident to appointment as a prefect in the Consulate's new administrative system.[44]

While waiting for his situation to clarify, Lamarque drafted a vigorous memorandum that he intended to send to Bonaparte, although whether he actually did so is unclear. One part sensible analysis, one part partisan pleading, and one part wishful thinking, it epitomized the uncomfortable situation of men on the left who opposed the Brumaire coup, but who hoped that its outcome might yet be positive, providing that the brumairians reached out to them.

Lamarque discerned three and only three "parties" in France: the pure royalists; "the half-hearted or equivocal Republicans who tend toward aristocracy or oligarchy" (a standard Neo-Jacobin view of their "revisionist" adversaries before Brumaire); and finally his own party, whom he described as "the strongly committed liberal Republicans." With a touch of disingenuousness he maintained that members of the first two groups, "fearing General Bonaparte more than they desire him," had denounced the general in the past for various reasons, whereas most Neo-Jacobins had considered General Bonaparte an heroic carrier of republican values, "persuaded that he has acquired the glory that envelops him by fighting for them and with them." But Lamarque worried that the second group, which now surrounded the first consul as a kind of court, constituted a "corporation" seeking to monopolize public employment and government service. Though he recognized estimable individuals among them, taken as a whole the group, he warned, was greedy, prone to intrigue, and isolated from the great mass of the nation—the army, artisans, cultivators. Not to put too fine a point on it, Lamarque lamented that they all but monopolized the Senate, Tribunate, and Legislative Corps, and were girding up to dominate the new prefectures and judgeships: "that same corporation thus wishes to constitute all the new columns in the social edifice." And, misjudging the veritable balance of power in the new regime, he added, "If they succeed, the genius of the first consul will have to accomplish miracles each day to avoid being constrained to govern in the sense that the corporation will have determined." In short, Lamarque retained his faith in Bonaparte but distrusted the consul's political partners of Brumaire.

These warnings formed one half of his brief, the other being a plea in behalf of his own "party," the *patriotes prononcés*. To begin with, he insisted that his camp did not include the veritable demagogues, "those mendaciously energetic and truly atrocious men who, under diverse labels and in different ways, were all proscribers (*proscripteurs*)." Rather, his party simply comprised men who, by principle (if educated) or by instinct (if uneducated), "have shown themselves consistently to be sincere and ardent defenders of liberty."

> But the men of that class, even those who were faithful to the principles then in force and therefore opposed 18 Brumaire, prefer in the Republic's current situation the constitutional government of a single chief such as General Bonaparte to government by the corporation. . . . Political wisdom as well as justice demand that [our] party not be oppressed. It is not a party strong enough to dominate by itself; nor is it a party so weak as to be harmless if it is rigorously excluded. . . . The necessary condition is one of reciprocal tolerance and a complete forgetting of the past.[45]

Moving beyond past conflicts; showing good faith and tolerance; sharing patronage—such was the political coin of the realm in this new post-electoral era.

With the support of Cambacérès and perhaps Berlier (whom he knew well and resembled in political coloration), Lamarque was appointed to the less than choice prefecture of the Tarn. When he finally made his way to its capital, Albi, he found a heartwarming reception. "I was received as in the great days of the Revolution. That is to say, with the same enthusiasm . . . and by citizens of all classes," he wrote to his friend Roux-Fazillac. To another ex-*conventionnel*, former Neo-Jacobin and native of the Tarn, General Lacombe Saint-Michel, he exulted: "The manner in which I was received in your department has allowed me to forget a good many troubles and to taste a veritable joy."[46]

News coming from the Dordogne, however, prompted him to complain bitterly to Minister of the Interior Lucien Bonaparte. After supplying the confidential evaluation of "public spirit" in the Tarn requested by the minister—little disaffection, confidence in the government—he added a blistering postscript about the reaction in his native department, whose military commander, he had been told, refused even to use the title of *citoyen*. He pleaded with Lucien to instruct the prefect in Périgueux "to have some regard for those patriots who are all my friends." Thus far, the names of the subaltern appointments in the department

> are enemies of you and the first consul as much as mine. They are counterrevolutionaries in the sense of the right wing of the constituent assembly. Why is the department of the Dordogne the only one in which that happy amalgam of parties, so strongly recommended by all political wisdom, is not receiving its application? Why, at the moment that the Government is honoring me with its confidence . . . can I not bring it about that a single one of the citizens I have recommended has been named? The reason is that Senator Beaupuy [a former directorial commissioner and nemesis of the Dordogne's Neo-Jacobins], and Malleville of the Tribunal de Cassation, supported by Lacuée and Treilhard, are trying to proscribe in my department all the patriots who have had any liaison with me. I tell you frankly, my faith in the Government is limited to you, the first consul, and Cambacérès.[47]

Meanwhile, he was fighting on other fronts. To Didot *jeune*, publisher of the reactionary newspaper *Le Mercure de France*, he protested an article referring to an escape from barbarism in the Year VIII. One would have thought, he retorted, that this had occurred in 1789. "I pride myself in thinking that the ten years of Revolution that destroyed royal despotism, feudal tyranny and religious fanaticism, that instituted trial by jury and gave counsel to the accused, that advanced the progress of science, law and political economy . . . were hardly years of barbarism!" To the end of his days Lamarque struggled to write a history of the French Revolution embodying such views, but he never mastered the endless skein of notes that he generated for this project.[48]

As the months went by, neither his spirits nor his health improved, and he was soon asking Lucien to be relieved of the prefecture in favor of a "tranquil post" as director of a library. To Roux-Fazillac he lamented, "I see that the insolent and perfidious faction that surrounds the Bonaparte family, and that hates and misleads it, conserves its eminence and continues to govern within France. I see the return of the émigrés. . . . I want nothing more now than my library and my garden." Lucien replied that "It is not yet time for us to relax. I enlist you to continue serving the Republic in your department by holding back all the resources of the factions." But Lamarque was impatient to resign even if he could not secure a less demanding post, and told Roux that if necessary he would manage on his private income of 2,400 livres while he wrote his memoirs.[49]

Still, Lamarque did desire an appointment of some kind, both for its income and for his self-esteem, and he campaigned for months among his contacts in Paris for assistance—Lucien himself having been ousted from the interior ministry in November 1800. Finally, plagued by ill-health and the harsh environment of the Tarn, he resigned in April 1801 and departed. Eight months later he was appointed as deputy state commissioner to the Tribunal de Cassation in Paris, perhaps with the help of his regicide colleague in the Convention Bordas, now a high functionary in the ministry of justice.[50] In 1804, Lamarque at last secured the undemanding post that he coveted, when he was presented by the emperor as one of three candidates for a vacant judgeship on the Tribunal de Cassation and was chosen by the Senate. As he acknowledged in his application, a judgeship on the high court would be "a kind of honorable and active retirement . . . the fulfillment of my ambition," for which he would willingly take a 2,000 franc cut in salary.[51]

HIS FRIEND Roux-Fazillac found it much harder to work his way back into public life after Brumaire. A long-serving military officer before his election to the Convention, Roux's tenure in that body had been more contentious than Lamarque's. Among other things, his reputation was dogged by his personal responsibility while on mission for apprehending the fleeing Girondin deputy Valady and sending him to his death. Appointed to local positions in the Dordogne for brief periods during the Directory, elected but purged from the legislature in 1798 before he could take his seat, he was called in as a division chief in the interior ministry under Quinette in the Directory's last months, but was out even before Brumaire. Like Lamarque he considered Cambacérès to be sympathetic, and solicited his help at the beginning of the Consulate and again in May 1804, days before the second consul's elevation to archchancellor. In this second letter, Roux briefly recapitulated his post-Brumaire experience:

At the time of your installation in the Consulate, I expressed to you my wish to occupy a public function under a Government that inspired my confidence. (Could I have regretted the passing of the directorial government—I who more than once was a victim of its tyranny?) Although I was disposed to accept the functions that you would have liked to confer on me—pardon my frank words—I thought that it would be appropriate neither for my character, nor for the dignity of the functions I had exercised during the Revolution, nor to your own personal dignity, that I go chasing about to obtain employment by importuning solicitations. And with peace seemingly established with our enemies abroad, with calm reestablished in the interior, I made the decision to finish my days peacefully in retirement.

My hopes, however, were deceived. The perfidious English broke all their engagements [in the Treaty of Amiens]. Unable to vanquish us except by criminal acts, they conceived the assassination of our first magistrate, and as a logical consequence no doubt, the assassination of all like ourselves who can expect no indulgence from the Bourbons. Under the circumstances, Citizen Consul, I permit myself to ask you once again to help put me in a position where I can be of some use to the fatherland. One of your *arrêtés* appears to announce the creation of new *commissaires généraux de police*. Confer one of those posts on me, and you can trust to my zeal, my fidelity, and my gratitude.[52]

Roux forwarded a copy of this faintly embarrassing letter to Lamarque, adding that he would be willing to go anywhere in greater France to serve in such a post. But his covering letter to Lamarque emitted a bittersweet if indomitable tone:

Here I am, my friend, launched on a career of solicitations. I enclose a copy of my letter to Consul Cambacérès. Now it must pass through the crucible of friendship, and in judging better than I can the timing, circumstances, propriety, and possibility of success, he will make what use of it he deems most appropriate. [His remarks to Cambacérès might seem rather free, he tells Lamarque, but] In the Convention I had rather close relations with him; he and I maintained a kind of trust in each other. Of course I know that those days are long gone and circumstances today are very different. . . .

And if one is willing to take on a "Jacobin" who never set foot in the Jacobins [Club]; a "terrorist" who never acted without the direction of the constituted authorities and always in strict conformity with the laws;

finally an "anarchist" who reestablished discipline in one of our most important armament manufactures—If, I say, one would like such a person as a *commissaire généraux* . . . I would be the man for Réal [an ex-Jacobin in the Council of State whose bailiwick was the police] and ready to take up my post.[53]

Roux also wrote to Berlier and Réal for assistance, apparently to no avail. He does not seem to have gained the position, for which he was well qualified, and continued to vegetate in private life, where he is said to have spent some time teaching local peasants to read and write.[54] With his long record of service and manifest patriotism offset by his reputation as a terrorist, Roux could not gain a foothold in the early days of the Consulate, and by 1804 the door had all but shut on such men, once the new amalgam hardened. The help of such contacts as Lamarque, Berlier, Réal, or even Cambacérès could only go so far. And perhaps, in the final analysis, Roux had misjudged his bygone rapport with the second consul.

III

Early Warning Signs

*O*N THE EVENING of 3 Nivôse Year IX (24 December 1800), the first consul and his party departed as scheduled for the Opéra, accompanied by a squad of mounted grenadiers. Swerving to avoid a seed merchant's cart awkwardly blocking the rue Saint-Nicaise, the coachman continued on at his usual gallop. Seconds later, as he was entering the rue de Malte, a deafening explosion rocked the coach and nearly threw the troopers from their horses amid a cascade of hurtling glass. Behind them at least eight people were killed, twenty-eight wounded, and dozens of houses damaged. The horrendous explosion on the rue Nicaise shattered more than hundreds of nearby windows. This assassination attempt and unprecedented terrorist act exposed the vulnerability of the entire Brumaire settlement. For the first time since 1789, assassination loomed as a practical political weapon of frightful potential.

Prominent revolutionaries had been assassinated before, but those punitive acts produced limited consequences. In 1793–94 a sentimentalized cult of revolutionary martyrs arose briefly around a trio of slain Jacobin leaders: the incendiary journalist and member of the Convention, Jean-Paul Marat; the Lyonnaise Jacobin leader Châlier; and the regicide deputy Louis-Michel Lepeletier.[1] Failed attempts to assassinate Robespierre and Collot d'Herbois had followed, but even if successful they would not have ended the Terror. In the republic's political culture, which discouraged any cult of personality or dominant individual leader, assassination could barely have altered the current balance of power, let alone toppled the government.

With the unique political and psychological ascendancy of General Bonaparte, however, the murder of one man could decapitate the regime and cause it to unravel. While there had been nothing inevitable about Bonaparte's role, once he became first consul it was obvious that no individual among his collaborators could fill his shoes. The post-Brumaire regime remained a joint venture, to be sure, but as provisional consul Roger Ducos observed at the outset, it now had only one possible leader.

By a matter of seconds, Bonaparte survived the bomb. Before the attack the general had always been fatalistic about his personal safety, whether away on campaign or out on the streets of Paris. This intrepid streak made it easier to impose his will, since he never acted from a sense of weakness or panic but only from impatience or contempt. And act he did. The "infernal machine" in the rue Nicaise failed to bring down the first consul but ricocheted against his long-standing bête noire: the remnants of the Jacobin interregnum.

THE LINGERING SHADOW OF JACOBINISM

The Consulate's depoliticization stranded the most fervid Jacobins and *sans-culottes*. With their parliamentary cadres excluded from the new legislature, and with oratory now restricted in its precincts anyway, they lost their bearings. While liberal principles could still find voice in the Tribunate's debates, democratic and egalitarian sentiments vanished from that body, as they did from the newly muzzled press. Most important, the suppression of political clubs deprived local Neo-Jacobins of their accustomed forums and rallying points.

Only a private kind of fraternization remained, a sociability in homes, taverns, or cafés. Such gatherings occasionally produced a satiric song or a clandestine broadside against Bonaparte, such as the poster that appeared in Perpignan and other communes in the Pyrénées Orientales. This *affiche* harangued French citizens for their "criminal repose" in tolerating the annihilation of liberty, the reestablishment of despotism, and the revival of religious fanaticism. "Awake from your slumber! Rouse yourselves . . . combat these vile people coming to slaughter you under the pretext of religion, with a rosary in one hand and a crucifix in the other. . . . Long live the Republic!

May the tyrants and the ambitious ones perish!"[2] But the circulation or impact of such dissident provocations was usually negligible. Besides, every moderate or reactionary official knew just where to find the local *exagérés*, and warily followed their activities, real or imagined.

These officials might well have agreed with historian Richard Cobb, who argued that the militant *sans-culottisme* of 1793–94 was more a matter of temperament than class or ideology.[3] In those heady months, more pragmatic colleagues might have constrained the most hot-headed *sans-culottes*, but as the former withdrew into prudent acquiescence to the Consulate, the passionately irreconcilable were left to feed on their own emotions. Bereft of any protective covering, barred from engaging in accustomed political activity such as club meetings or electoral campaigns, they remained isolated and frustrated.

Still, the Jacobins' adversaries did not regard them as harmless. For their hallmark had always seemed to be the sheer will to dominate, and there was no reason to believe that they had relinquished such ambition. They remained a threat, in this view, because the republic's retribution against ex-terrorists had aborted in 1795. Apart from the direct settling of accounts by violence in the South of France, where bodies of murdered Jacobins regularly washed up on the banks of the Rhône, the amnesty of 1795 that inaugurated the Directory regime opened the jail cells of incarcerated Jacobins and put them back on the streets.[4] In the electoral campaign of 1798 they regrouped on a broad front, turned republican institutions to their advantage, and won election as deputies and local officials. Purged that spring, they rebounded again during the war crisis of 1799, when they attracted particular notoriety for several intemperate speeches at the Neo-Jacobin Manège Club of Paris.[5]

A local incident encapsulates the raw emotions aroused by this last Neo-Jacobin revival. Some weeks before Brumaire, a man named Bossuelle was prosecuted for incitement to murder against certain members of the Manège Club. The charge had enough plausibility to produce a conviction in the criminal tribunal of the Seine department. But Bossuelle appealed, as was his right, to the tribunal in the neighboring department of Seine-et-Oise, where the court reversed his conviction, much to the approval of the local newspaper. Under the prevailing circumstances, the court did not regard the defendant's threat—"that he would personally kill the first terrorist who came to arrest him"—as a provocation to murder but as an appropriate warning.[6]

The official version of Brumaire demonized the left yet again by retailing the image of Neo-Jacobin deputies as violent men immune to the appeals of reason and moderation. Even if certain deputies had not unsheathed their knives against Bonaparte, as the legend claimed (and almost all the evidence suggests that they had not), their cries of "*hors de la loi*" against him could be deemed the equivalent of a knife blow. Ironically, Guyot, an anti-Brumaire deputy, gave weight to this view when he allegedly boasted back home that on 18 Brumaire "I exhausted myself in crying *hors de la loi*, and if my colleagues has not been such cowards, Bonaparte would have gotten nowhere at that point." (For his repeated allusions to Bonaparte as a usurper, and such comments as "I now abhor the Tuileries more than I did Versailles," Guyot was denounced repeatedly by the prefect of Lozère until he threatened to sue the official for slander.)[7] Without prompting, the Brumaire parliamentarians had purged about sixty Neo-Jacobin colleagues immediately after the coup, but the provisional consuls went further, as we saw, by ordering the deportation of an assortment of notorious Jacobins and Parisian *sans-culottes*. Since this arbitrary act blatantly contravened the regime's precarious claim to be law abiding and non-violent, the consuls soon rescinded it, but the gauntlet was down. While the decree no doubt intimidated the more temperate Jacobins, certain former revolutionaries, Cobb's quintessential *sans-culotte* hotheads, convinced themselves that against the new tyrant only an act of *tyrannicide* could serve.

For months, Fouché's police spies reported the vows by such men to dispatch the first consul personally. Such braggadocio (or drunken bluster) was not limited to Paris. In Langres (Haute Marne), for example, Denis ("*Coup-tête*") Didier was indicted (and eventually acquitted) for seditious remarks, the best documented being his comment shortly after Brumaire that "If I had found myself in Paris I would have disemboweled Bonaparte like a pig, along with the grenadier who protected him."[8] But vehement mutterings and scheming were most abundant in Paris, where Fouché's *mouchards* claimed more than once to have overheard in a café that "everything is ready to blow up Bonaparte." Fouché later commented that "far from dampening the anarchists' spirit, the vigilance of the police seemed to arouse even more nerve and audacity."[9]

Two cabals went beyond bluster and imprecations, though whether the plotters would have actually killed Bonaparte remains moot, since the police easily penetrated their small groups. On 10 October the sculptor Ceracchi and Aréna, the brother of a purged deputy, were arrested along with several others on the eve of an alleged plot to murder the first consul in his box at the Opéra. About a month later, while arresting two other "*tyrannicides*"—

Chevalier, a sometime chemist and former employee in the armaments workshops of the Committee of Public Safety, and his accomplice Veycer, a shoemaker—the police seized the materials for a large bomb. Locked away in the Temple prison, Chevalier in fact had nothing to do with the explosion on the rue Nicaise, but the government immediately stressed the coincidence.[10]

On the day after the blast, the quasi-official *Moniteur* published a brief account, along with this suggestive comment: "Two months ago the government was warned that thirty or so of those men who covered themselves with crimes during all phases of the Revolution, especially during the *journées* of September [the prison massacres of 1792], had conceived the very same project. Since that time, twelve have been under detention in the Temple prison." There followed a notice from the prefect of police about the arrest several weeks earlier of Chevalier, and the "infernal machine" found in his possession. Notwithstanding the fact that these men were behind bars, the coincidence directed attention to the left.

THE LEADING PROPONENT of this view was Bonaparte himself. After showing remarkable sangfroid while he completed his visit to the Opéra that evening, once back at the Tuileries he erupted in fury at the ex-terrorists whom he blamed for the bombing. Before a throng of counselors of state and others who converged to congratulate him on his narrow escape, the first consul raged against the *septembriseurs*—an epithet of choice which evoked the Parisian mobs that slaughtered over one thousand prisoners (royalists and common criminals) in September 1792 after the fall of the monarchy.

> So long as this handful of conspirators were content to plot against myself alone, I desired to leave their punishment to the ordinary course of the law; but when it comes to so unexampled a crime as this [bombing], which endangers the lives and property of the citizens at large, the punishment must be prompt and exemplary. A hundred or so of the wretches who have disgraced the name of Liberty by the crimes they have perpetrated in its name shall be deprived of the power of doing further evil.[11]

In a conversation with one of his prefects some years later, Napoleon recalled his thinking about such men, as he likened local *sans-culotte* leaders to the NCOs who formed the backbone of the army:

A *sous-officier* comes from the same class as the soldier and thus while commanding he sympathizes with him and persuades him. He exercises a moral influence over the soldier that carries him along; he knows what to say and never shocks him because he is his equal. . . . At the time of 3 Nivôse, I seized the occasion and deported the *sous-officiers* of the Revolution, the *septembriseurs*, the leaders of the faubourgs. Since then I began sleeping tranquilly because, you see, I have no fear of conspirators who rise at nine o'clock in the morning to put on their fine white shirts.[12]

With this notion fixed in Bonaparte's mind, Fouché ran into a stone wall when he suggested that royalists had probably set off the bomb. Bonaparte railed at his minister of police and insisted that the "anarchists" were to blame. Since Bonaparte had almost been killed on his watch, despite Fouché's supposed mastery over the world of intriguers and plotters, the minister was temporarily stymied. The shaken, tight-lipped Fouché quietly maintained that he would in due course prove who had really done the deed.

In fact his associate, Counselor of State Réal, shortly produced forensic evidence that eventually led to the culprits. Back at the scene, Réal retrieved the leg of the horse that had drawn the explosive-laden cart, all that remained intact of the carcass, and noticed that it had been newly shod. Calling in Parisian blacksmiths, the police soon found the artisan who had done the job as well as the seed merchant who had sold the cart and mare, and received from them a description of their customer. Using his dossiers on presumed royalist agents in Paris, Fouché began rounding up several suspects on 28 Nivôse, although others managed to elude him, including one of the ringleaders. In the course of his investigation Fouché learned that the plotters had considered the even more terroristic tactic of planting the bomb "under the very foundations of the auditorium in the Opéra, in such a way as to blow up in a single coup Bonaparte and the elite of his government."[13]

By April, the domestic servant Carbon and the former naval officer Saint-Régent, who had actually detonated the rue Nicaise bomb, were tried and executed, while five other royalists were condemned in absentia. But that resolution came far too late to save the Jacobins from paying for this deed as well, since the government had already moved against the incarcerated Jacobin plotters such as Cerrachi, Aréna, and Chevalier. Instead of languishing in prison—for they had not actually passed from talk to action—the "opera" plotters were immediately tried for attempted murder by the criminal tribunal of Paris, while five men implicated in the Chevalier affair went before a military commission. A total of nine were executed, paying an appalling price for their "café conspiracies."[14] Yet even that severity did not appease Bonaparte's wrath against the "anarchists."

AN OUTPOURING OF ANGER

No doubt taking their cue from the *Moniteur*'s implication that Jacobin "anarchists" had planned the bombing, Bonaparte's supporters across the country responded with letters expressing their shock, immense relief at his escape, and lingering fury. The general always claimed to rule in accord with public opinion and here was one occasion where an authentic groundswell of elite opinion reinforced his own convictions. The sentiments in this outpouring of anger appear genuine; we are not dealing here with the "manufacture of consent" at which Napoleon excelled on other occasions. Prefects, subprefects, mayors, municipal counselors, and the like registered anxiety and frustration alongside genuine outrage and indignation. The bombing—shocking enough simply by its destruction of life and property in the capital—stirred a deep sense of vulnerability.

This backlash meshed perfectly with Bonaparte's reaction, since most of these officials blamed the "anarchists." They knew as a moral certainty that Jacobin cadres remained irreconcilable. Their language demonized and marginalized "that impure horde of anarchists"; "that handful of madmen, of scoundrels"; "that impious sanguinary faction"; "that odious sect, enemy of all social order"; "those men (in reality a small number) who want no government because they wish to bring back the anarchy that protects the crimes they have committed and that fosters their vengeance and ambition." As the mayor of Bourges put it in a veritable frenzy: "Why are these furies, covered with the blood of their victims, still breathing? Why are they not gone? May those monsters with a human face be consigned to perdition!" These "monsters"—a commonly repeated epithet—had now attempted the most monstrous crime of all. For as numerous letters observed, "the nation was attacked in the person of its chief."[15]

Since these relentless enemies of order could now wreak complete havoc with one blow, draconian measures were imperative. The writers and petitioners frequently criticized the first consul for his previous acts of indulgence, the *funeste clémence* that he had extended in the past, and the consequent impunity that his enemies had enjoyed. Now, prompt and exemplary punishment must be served. Indulgence, amnesties, rescinded deportation decrees, second chances must be replaced by vengeance and severity as well as continuous prevention thereafter: tight surveillance, further purges, whatever it took.

The bombing became a pretext for another settling of accounts not only in Paris but in the provinces. Certain officials declared that their local "anarchists" knew about the plot, anticipated it, and applauded the prospects of such attacks. "Public comment all around town accuses a certain number of well-known individuals of having been informed in advance of the crime that has just been committed," claimed the municipal council of Angoulême (Charente). "The relations of these men with an individual arrested in Paris has aroused in the entire town a sentiment of horror and indignation."

"There are in this department irreconcilable enemies of the government and of the *journée* of 18 Brumaire," warned the prefect of the Lot. "For almost a month they have been holding secret meetings, and have been announcing that soon one would hear of a great event. . . . The joy that they displayed [at that time] compared to the sorrow which they cannot hide today all lead me to believe that they were not strangers to what was being hatched in Paris." The police commissioner in Bordeaux alleged that "certain men who never cease complaining about despotism, about the loss of liberty—because they themselves do not administer or govern—have manifested sentiments which . . . prove that they knew about that horrible plot." His counterpart in Lyon similarly reported "menacing remarks openly pronounced; one of them did not shrink from designating the day of vengeance. In another assemblage it was stated that of eight projects to bring about Bonaparte's death, the least likely one was chosen."[16]

To be sure, a few who wrote to celebrate Bonaparte's survival struck a different chord by blaming the cowardly act on royalist agents supported from across the Channel: "England has no doubt vomited up these monsters." As Imbert, prefect of the Loire, reminded the first consul: "England well knows that if the Republic lost you it would disintegrate into the abyss of revolutions. That is England's veritable system of waging war. . . . It knows not how to vanquish, but it is fully acquainted with the art of assassination." And in the Breton department of Côtes-du-Nord, the prefect had good reason to connect the bombing with English-sponsored royalists. Conspiracies in Paris, he believed, "coincide with the movements that have occurred for some time in our department and its neighbors. . . . Here as in Paris the English government is still playing the leading role."[17]

To a few former revolutionaries, the bombing on the rue Nicaise portended not just Bonaparte's demise but an attack on "all men who had loyally served the Revolution" (Merlin de Douai) or even "the extermination of the last friends of liberty" for whom Bonaparte was now the standard-bearer (La Chevardière). From his prefecture in the Tarn, François Lamarque joined the chorus of relief, but assured Bonaparte, "it is impossible that you should ever have anything to fear from the friends of liberty." At this early date without any proof at hand, he understood that either of the two extremes could have set off the bomb, but as always he tried to distance honorable Neo-Jacobins like himself from the most compromised fanatics on the left. "Only the vile scoundrels for whom crime is a habit and disorder their element, or the ignominious tools of the foreign enemy could be capable of conceiving the horrible thought of cutting short your days." Lamarque concluded with the wish that "the impartial hand of Justice strike rigorously at the criminals"—words that were anything but formulaic, since he had witnessed previous waves of repression to settle accounts against the left.[18]

Blaming England and royalist agents or calling for a calm and lawful investigation, however, proved a distinctly minority opinion in the outpouring of relief, anger, and exhortation. On the contrary, the dominant and intense anti-Jacobin sentiment in reaction to the bombing of 3 Nivôse only stoked Bonaparte's animus against the lingering demons of the Terror.

EXORCISING THE TERROR

Bonaparte immediately consulted his Council of State on how to punish the presumed culprits and deter future conspiracies. At first, the Council had no trouble responding. It proposed to expand the jurisdiction of the special tribunals without juries already under consideration for dealing with endemic brigandage. But the first consul rejected this as unresponsive to his intention of "delivering the country from a certain number of terrorists in a permanent conspiracy against society and its laws." Réal later recalled Bonaparte erupting into a tirade calculated to put everyone on edge: "The tribunals you talk about would be too slow in action. More drastic vengeance is needed, something as rapid as gunfire. Blood must flow! As many culprits must be shot as there were victims. Two hundred more must be deported where they can do no further harm!"[19] Sanitizing his words, perhaps, another counselor recorded that Bonaparte insisted on "rendering what is due to 100 or 200 scoundrels, *septembriseurs* and murderers who cannot abide any government. . . . Paris and France will not have peace of mind until they see 100 or 150 villains who cause a general terror killed or deported. We are invested with the power to do that."[20]

If the special tribunals were inadequate to the task, what then? The choice seemed to be either enacting a new repressive law aimed retroactively at the ex-terrorists or striking at them with an extraordinary decree under the government's police powers. Like Bonaparte, most of the Council understood that proposing a new law meant delay and possibly a show of resistance in the Tribunate and consequent embarrassment to the government. Moreover, some apparently believed that the regime's integrity would be badly served by a new law of exception; a repressive law of dubious character adopted in haste could do more damage to the Consulate's aura of legality than a swift act under a one-time emergency decree.

Bonaparte demanded a decree deporting without trial 150–200 former terrorists and *sans-culotte* militants. The euphemistic language of the draft decree—"[they] will be placed under special surveillance outside the European territory of the Republic"—scarcely disguised their likely fate in Guyana or the Seychelles Islands in the Indian Ocean. Avoiding a direct linkage of this measure to the bombing itself (since the evidence was beginning to point toward the royalists), Bonaparte justified such deportations to distant French possessions as a long-overdue retribution combined with preventive deterrence. The targets, he believed, would be people who had committed all sorts of crimes in the name of the Revolution that went unpunished; people notoriously prone to violent methods; the kind of people known to have advocated and even planned the first consul's murder. In short, they were virtually or morally guilty of the explosion on the rue Nicaise even if the actual bomb had been detonated by an entirely different set of foes. Bonaparte instructed Fouché to draw up a list of such "anarchists."[21] Certain that he faced summary dismissal if he balked, Fouché complied even as he pursued the suspected royalist perpetrators. In the process he shielded a few likely victims by creating a second list of about fifty men to be exiled from Paris and placed under surveillance in the interior.[22]

Ready to move by executive decree, Bonaparte wanted his collaborators actively involved. Accordingly, he welcomed a suggestion from Roederer that "the Senate should be called upon to determine if the exceptional means being used by the Government are or are not in conformity with the Constitution." But even if the Senate would now be asked to provide official cover for this act, the first consul still wanted the maximum complicity from his most intimate advisers, the Council of State. With Fouché's list in hand, Bonaparte therefore convened another plenary session of the Council on 11 Nivôse. Here is an account of that tense meeting by Thibaudeau, the former revolutionary whose memoirs are generally reliable and insightful:

> The names were read out of those designated in Fouché's report for transportation or exile.
>
> *Bonaparte:* "The subject of discussion is whether all these people should be subjected to one general measure."
>
> A somber silence ensued.
>
> *Bonaparte:* "I shall put the question to the vote."
>
> *Thibaudeau:* "I have listened with amazement to the list of names which has just been read. It is not possible for us to judge and condemn a number of individuals on whom we have no information whatever. This is not within our province. The only questions we have had before us are whether extraordinary measures are necessary, and if so whether the Executive Government should ask the Corps Législatif or the Senate, or should itself assume the power to punish persons who have been proved guilty." *Boulay* supported my objections.
>
> *Bonaparte:* "I am not such an idiot as to propose that the Council should pronounce judgment on each individual."
>
> *Roederer:* "The Minister in his report does not speak of the crime of 3 Nivôse. He says only that he has discovered some clues. We must be careful lest we punish one party for what may have been done by another."
>
> *Bonaparte:* " . . . The Chouans and the émigrés are simply skin diseases, while the Terrorists are an internal disease. The Minister has not spoken of the crime of 3 Nivôse because the measure before us is not directed against that outrage; it merely gives us an opportunity for the action we propose to take. It is our duty to profit by the present feeling of indignation. . . ."
>
> *Roederer:* "We must not be suspected of reactionary motives, the fear of which has already been expressed in the Council."
>
> *Bonaparte:* "The Government is convinced, but in the absence of legal proofs it cannot proceed against these individuals. We transport them for their share in the September massacres, the crime of the 31st of May

[the purge of the Girondins], the Babeuf conspiracy, and all that has happened since."

Cambacérès: " . . . It would be misleading to speak of the crime of 3 Nivôse as being the motive for this measure, which is one of general utility. It will be carried out neither by the Council nor by the Consuls, but by the proper responsible authorities, the Minister and the Prefect of Police."

Bonaparte: "No doubt. The list has been read only in case anyone wishes to make any observations. I am now consulting the Council as to whether an extraordinary police measure is necessary." (Decided in the affirmative.) "Next, ought we to have a law?"

Lacuée and *Defermon* [who in earlier sessions had argued in favor of a law] maintained that since the measure was to be referred to the Senate, no law was necessary. *Truguet* [who had joined them in opposition previously, and remained the only one to persist] insisted on the necessity of a law. (Decided that there should be no law.). . . .

Bonaparte: "The Senate can neither add to nor alter [the decree]; its duty is only to declare that it is, or is not, in accordance with the preservation of the Constitution."[23]

In the end, the Council of State posed no objection to a decree deporting without trial one hundred thirty men accused of no specific crime in the present but of past behavior and future threats. As Fouché's accompanying report put it, "they are not the enemies of a particular government but of any kind of government. . . . Everything they have undertaken for the past year has had assassination as its object. . . . It is an atrocious war that can be terminated only by an exceptional police measure. . . . It is not a question today of simply punishing past acts but of guaranteeing the social order in the future." The decree then went over to the Senate, which observed that indulgence toward such individuals in the past had only emboldened them: "The presence of such men of blood in the Republic is a continual cause of alarm and of hidden terror for peaceful citizens, who fear the fortuitous success of one of their plots and the return of their vengeance." Therefore, the Senate formally declared, the deportation decree indeed "serves to conserve the constitution."[24]

Bonaparte had successfully finessed the whole matter—he had used the explosion as his pretext, but in the end did not explicitly link the deportations to the bombing, aware by the time he introduced Fouché's deportation list that responsibility for that act probably lay elsewhere, although the first royalists were not actually arrested until 28 Nivôse.[25] But even if ex-terrorists had not carried out the bombing, the Council shared Bonaparte's detestation of "anarchists," and hence "took care not to show the smallest sign of sympathy with the condemned," as Thibaudeau added. While on mission in the provinces a short time later, Counselor of State Lacuée found that public opinion condoned this indifference. In the aftermath of the bombing, he reported, the Jacobins were widely blamed and a cry went up for summary action against them. "Later, when it was learned officially that some *chouans* were the veritable authors of this crime—it pains me to say this, but it is the truth—the fermentation suddenly quieted. . . . Public indignation was no longer stirred as it had been previously."[26]

Looking back decades later, Boulay de la Meurthe affirmed that he would have preferred a legal route to prosecution and trial, "but such was the horror inspired by the names inscribed on the lists prepared by Fouché, that no protest was raised in their favor, even after the discovery of the truth."[27] Berlier, more closely associated in the past with the Jacobins, struck a more defensive and critical note in his terse comment about this affair in the 1830s, yet he had behaved no differently from the others: "I was certainly not the partisan of such men, of whom scarcely two or three were known to me; but the low regard that was their due did not efface the *arbitrariness* exercised against them." All well and good, but even after the royalists Carbon and Saint-Régent were executed for the crime, no one in the Council of State formally proposed to rescind the deportations, although Berlier did lobby vigorously in private with Bonaparte for indulgence toward one victim, his former colleague Talot.[28]

Individually and collectively, the members of the Council of State clearly hoped to minimize their involvement in this whole matter. While most counselors initially reacted to the bombing as Bonaparte had, and were not averse to a prophylactic punishment of notorious "anarchists," the gratuitous nature of the deportation decree, not to mention the arbitrary selection of its victims, was too blatant for comfort. The Council engaged in a dance of denial as it sought to avoid a direct confrontation with the first consul. When Bonaparte decided to use the Senate for his constitutional cover, one can almost hear a sigh of relief rising from the assembled counselors. The pretense of constitutionality would be preserved (by others) and the first consul could have his way. Only a few members offered a mild show of resistance

when Bonaparte first revealed his intentions. His naked use of power evoked
no "exit" and only a restrained "voice" of opposition from the Council. By
the end of the final deliberation, only the gruff Admiral Truguet stubbornly
opposed the tide, for which he earned a humiliating tongue-lashing from
Bonaparte after the session adjourned.

The pliancy of liberals such as Thibaudeau, Réal, Boulay, and Berlier, who
plainly disliked this measure yet went along with little ado, is perhaps best
explained by the passage in Berlier's memoirs immediately preceding his
laconic reference to the 3 Nivôse affair. During the first year of the Consulate,
he observed, before the bomb exploded, "no persecution had been carried
out for past deeds, nor because of past opinions; access to public employment
was opened to all the talented who were either friends of the new government
or disposed to rally to it. Finally order had been reestablished; the constitution was respected. . . . Then a terrible attack occurred that disturbed for a
certain time the fortunate situation that France was beginning to enjoy."[29] At
bottom the Council of State was deeply grateful to Bonaparte, immensely
relieved that he had survived the attack, and therefore disinclined to chal
lenge him. The fact that they could hand off formal responsibility for endors-
ing the decree to the Senate evidently helped ease their misgivings, but it did
nothing to offset the brutal impact of the act.

FOR THE VICTIMS, deportation without benefit of a trial was a catastrophic
blow, tantamount in most cases to a slow death sentence in some barren
wilderness thousands of miles out to sea. (What bittersweet pleasure they or
their bereft families might have taken in foreseeing how Napoleon would end
his days!) After a brief flurry of desperate maneuvering by the targeted individuals, a few managed to avoid or evade arrest, but a surprisingly large number of those named in the decree were apprehended and transported to the
coast. While some remained in confinement on the island of Oléron or the
Ile de Rhé off the coast, most were shipped out to the colonies.[30] A few of
those sent to Guyana later made their way back to France when the British
overran the colony and repatriated its garrison. But the seventy deported to
the Seychelles Islands in the Indian Ocean drew the worst lot. By the end of
1807, thirty-eight had died, nine had escaped to an unknown fate, and twenty-
three remained on the islands.[31] Early that year, the survivors on Mahé sent
certificates of good conduct from the authorities on the island to buttress a
poignant appeal to the emperor for clemency:

When word of the magnificent victories that you have carried off made its way as far as our mournful place of exile, hope was revived in our hearts. What!, we said to ourselves, when the French and all of Europe are ready to form a single family; when united by the most tender ties they abjure all spirit of party; when hatred and vengeance give way to amity and concord, will we remain abandoned, separated from our fatherland? . . . what an appalling notion! No, Sire . . . you could have believed us to be guilty but surely time has enlightened you on our account. . . .[32]

It was of course to no avail. Napoleon's frequent indulgence to perceived dissidents found no application here. Even the men who made their way back to France were barred from Paris and placed under strict and confining surveillance. In 1813 a number were rearrested and imprisoned.[33] Clearly Bonaparte regarded these men as ineradicably evil.

WHILE Bonaparte gave his supporters exactly what many seemed to be clamoring for after the frightful bombing on the rue Nicaise, the deportation decree of Nivôse IX became, from the standpoint of legality, his first truly transgressive act as first consul. In turn, this arbitrary and brutal repression affected the spirit and equilibrium of the consular regime. In the Council of State, it subtly altered the atmosphere and constricted the zone of candor that Bonaparte had encouraged from his counselors at the outset. More starkly, the episode transformed the Senate's role, turning it into Bonaparte's handmaiden rather than a potential check upon his will. As Barante, a young, royalist-leaning servitor of the Empire, accurately recalled in his memoirs, the deportation decree, "neither a law nor a judicial finding, . . . was an act of absolute power with which the first consul associated the Senate, a Senate which would later lend itself with such docility to every violation and mutation of the laws and the constitution."[34] As Bonaparte hectored the Council of State and maneuvered the Senate into complicity, the joint venture of Brumaire was becoming a forced merger.

BONAPARTE INVADES THE SENATE

Well before the advent of the Empire the Senate slid from being the proud third force of Sieyès's vision into an instrument of Napoleon's ambitions, as the first consul interfered with the selection of new members and sapped the Senate's hypothetical autonomy. Bonaparte's preliminary masterstroke in taming the Senate was to compromise Sieyès's future influence by endowing him (on behalf of a grateful nation) with a munificent estate from the pool of unsold *biens nationaux*—a more conspicuous payoff than anyone's reputation for independence could survive. Thereafter, an enervated Sieyès largely withdrew from active involvement in the Senate's affairs, although he did venture an occasional foray into oppositional intrigue. The loyal second consul Cambacérès filled the void as Bonaparte's liaison and the Senate's guiding hand.

Initially, the Senate chose its new members (two a year plus replacements for deceased senators) from three nominees for each vacancy submitted respectively by the first consul, the Tribunate, and the Legislative Corps. For two years the process resembled a "normal" if extremely rarefied politics. The two parliamentary houses balloted without obvious constraint to designate their respective choices, while the Senate seemed to act freely when it chose among successive trios of nominees. Indeed, its somewhat contentious selection of the legal scholar and liberal ex-deputy Lanjuinais and the liberal bishop and former member of the Convention Grégoire, rather than the first consul's nominees for those vacancies, brought into the Senate two of the rare members who would oppose Napoleon's willfulness in the future.[35]

The situation changed dramatically in December 1801. In the course of that year Pierre Daunou turned forty and thereby became eligible for the Senate. One of the most esteemed parliamentary veterans of the Revolution, Daunou had not favored the Brumaire coup, since the constitution of 1795 had largely been his own handiwork. Yet he agreed to serve on the rump legislative commission of the Council of 500 after 19 Brumaire, and from there was invited into the smaller group preparing the Consulate's constitution. In part to offset Sieyès's influence, Bonaparte solicited a constitutional draft from Daunou, which he then ignored, and designated Daunou as the commission's redactor. Although Daunou often found himself a lone discordant voice, as in his advocacy of genuine elections, his participation lent the entire process a measure of precision and credibility.

With his keen eye for talent, Bonaparte readily forgave Daunou his dissenting comments and invited him to the join the Council of State, the real hub of the new government. Daunou demurred, since he preferred a less dependent role in the Tribunate, which subsequently showed its respect by choosing him as its president by 76 out of 78 votes cast. Daunou did not wish to be in the position as a counselor of state of defending government bills before the Tribunate or Legislative Corps that he personally opposed. In due course—alongside such independent-minded tribunes as Constant, Ginguené, and Chénier—Daunou did not hesitate to criticize proposed laws submitted by the government. Even so, at a private dinner Bonaparte once again tried to lure Daunou into his Council of State, but the two men ended up in a hostile exchange. The first consul blurted out that he sought Daunou not because he liked him but because he needed him: "For me men are instruments whom I use according to my pleasure," he declared. To which Daunou is said to have replied simply, "As for myself, I care for the Republic."[36]

In December 1801, both the Tribunate and the Legislative Corps nominated Daunou by close votes as their respective candidate for a senatorial vacancy. Bonaparte dispatched the second consul to alert the Senate of his anger at this affront: "His designation by the Senate would be regarded as a declaration of war against the first consul," Cambacérès warned. Bonaparte also used a reception at his home to inform certain senators directly that he regarded Daunou's nomination as a personal affront. "And you know," he threatened, "that I have never tolerated any insults." The senators must have realized that Bonaparte was confronting them with his most dangerous psychological imperative, and they prudently shrank from testing the general's combustible sense of honor. When the intimidated senators balloted, they chose Bonaparte's candidate, General Lamartillière, by a vote of 52 out of 54. Bonaparte had successfully invaded the Senate, and would gradually annex this stronghold of the Brumaire politicians to his own domain.[37]

WITH the two constitutional modifications that accompanied his promotion to consul for life and then to emperor, Bonaparte not only preempted the Senate's power to coopt new members but shrewdly increased its prerogatives. After the life consulship in 1802, he alone would propose the three candidates for any vacancy, drawing on a pool of names submitted by new departmental electoral colleges. More important, the first consul was now empowered to name up to forty additional senators directly, extended in 1804 to an indefinite number. Conversely, the original stipulation that senators could not serve in other functions disappeared, so that Napoleon could use (and reward) senators at will. Thus, he appointed Roederer and Fouché as senators in 1802 to distance them from the hub of government, but later recalled Fouché as police minister and authorized Roederer to assist brother

Joseph Bonaparte in his kingship of Naples. Over time dignitaries of the Empire, retired generals, and foreign notables gained Senate seats alongside the original cohort of Brumaire politicians.

The vast majority of senators either cheered Bonaparte's every move or resigned themselves to grudging acquiescence. The *idéologues*, by habit and conviction advocates of intellectual freedom, found themselves in an uncomfortable position. Enthusiastic supporters of the Brumaire coup and of the enlightened general who led it, they grew increasingly disenchanted as the regime's authoritarian streak unfolded. On his side, Bonaparte occasionally scorned their circle as useless metaphysicians and obstructionists, and kept them under an oppressive police surveillance. Of the four *idéologues* coopted into the original Senate—Cabanis, Garat, Volney, and Destutt de Tracy— only Garat (who had once called Bonaparte "a *philosophe* who has appeared for a moment at the head of the armies") ventured occasional criticism and cast negative votes in senatorial deliberations. But generally these disillusioned Brumairians turned away from public life to private scholarship, and confided their anguished comments only to their intimate friends—all of which allowed them to remain in Napoleon's good graces.[38] The liberal physician and philosopher Cabanis, a severe critic of popular democracy and a prime apologist for the Brumaire coup, incurred one disappointment after another, but essentially stopped arguing after 1802. When he died of a cerebral hemorrhage in 1808 at the age of fifty-one, Cabanis was interred in the Panthéon with Napoleon's blessing.[39] Destutt de Tracy and Volney also lapsed into public quiescence. Volney, a respected scholar who at one time had close personal ties to Bonaparte, reportedly considered resigning from the Senate but was dissuaded by Napoleon himself. Perhaps Volney shared the view expressed by Senator Cornet that resignations would not serve the public interest: they "would be the mark of a faction, and could lead [Napoleon] to take measures against it."[40]

In fact, no one resigned from the lucrative sinecure of a senatorial seat, although that gesture would have been a notable act of opposition. Over time the dissidents who persisted in roiling the Senate's bland consensus proved to be not the members of the *idéologue* circle, but two veterans of the National Assembly and Convention, the Breton legal scholar Lanjuinais and the liberal cleric Grégoire, along with the Belgian jurist and directorial minister of justice Lambrechts. Unlike Cabanis or Volney, they seem to have anticipated what Adam Michnik recommended in Poland of the 1980s: one strives for freedom simply by acting as if one were already free, regardless of what the government forbids or encourages. A well-paid, lifetime seat in the Senate might have seemed an ideal place to practice that maxim, but if too many senators had done so there is no telling how Napoleon might have reacted. In the event, after 1802 very few senators had such inclinations.

For the rank and file, the behavior of Senator Cornet seems typical. A member of the Council of Elders who overcame his customary reticence by taking a prominent part in the drama of 18 and 19 Brumaire, Cornet was rewarded with a Senate seat. No great liberal, he nonetheless soured on the regime over the years but kept a consistently low and conformist profile. Yet one day in 1813 he felt compelled to speak out against a proposal giving Napoleon power to name the president of the Legislative Corps without benefit of nominations from that body. By his account, his extremely circumspect and modest note of dissent astonished his colleagues and made them uncomfortable; they responded, he claimed, with warnings and chastisement.[41]

IN SIEYÈS'S original vision of a Senate or "constitutional jury," the Senate would be able to facilitate necessary changes in the constitution. Like Bonaparte, he believed that a constitution must be viewed as an organism and therefore required "a capacity for unlimited improvement, which can bend to and accommodate the necessities of each epoch." The constitutions of 1791 and 1795 had been too detailed and too rigid, the process of amendment too cumbersome and protracted to permit smooth accommodation to changing circumstances. This led to upheavals that destroyed or discarded these constitutions altogether. For the sake of stability, then, the Senate could be empowered to enact amendments to the constitution or organic laws on its own authority.[42]

This idea disappeared in the vague formulations of the constitution of the Year VIII, but Bonaparte implicitly revived it when he submitted the deportation decree of Nivôse IX for the Senate's approval. Finally, it became explicit in the constitutional transformations realigning various institutions with the life consulship in 1802 and the hereditary Empire in 1804. The constitution of 1802 empowered the Senate to modify the constitution by issuing an "organic" senatus-consulte "to establish whatever was not foreseen in the constitution and is necessary for its functioning . . . or to explicate articles of the constitution which give rise to differing interpretations." In addition, the Senate could issue "ordinary" senatus-consultes or decrees under specified conditions. One fundamental proviso, however, limited both kinds of action: the Senate could act only when the executive took the initiative, only when the first consul or (after 1804) the emperor presented the measure in question.

Conscription became the main area in which the Senate routinely used the "ordinary" *senatus-consulte*. Since sessions of the Legislative Corps were few and far between, Napoleon shifted authorization of troop levies to the Senate in 1803, thereby increasing its complicity with his international expansion in a fundamental if roundabout way. As hopes for a lasting peace imposed by France waxed and waned, conscription calls grew increasingly onerous. Yet never until the end of 1813 did the Senate raise the slightest objection to ever larger and more frequent levies. Napoleon squelched any criticism of this unpopular imposition on French citizens by offering a primitive theory of deterrence. Any questioning of conscription levies in the Council of State or Senate, he insisted, would be taken abroad as a sign of weakness and would harden the enemy's determination to fight. A manifest willingness by France to build up its armed forces, on the other hand, would intimidate potential foes and might well win France's diplomatic objectives without the need for war. "A conscription call resolutely announced without hesitation . . . will cause the weapons to fall from Austria's hands," he maintained in 1808. "The least hesitation, on the contrary, will induce Austria to take up its arms and use them against us. No objections, but an immediate and punctual execution of the decree that I am sending you—there is the way to secure peace."[43] In reality, of course, it did not work that way. And with the strong hand provided by his remarkable conscription machine, Napoleon rarely settled for anything less than victory through battle. But how could any senator risk opposing such logic, no matter how often it proved specious?

TAMING THE TRIBUNATE

The one hundred original tribunes—legislative veterans garnished with a sprinkling of Parisian intellectuals—came to their positions as men of Brumaire and collaborators of Bonaparte par excellence. But the first consul's extravagant demand for unity in his regime made their role problematic. Willing enough to entertain debate over laws in the private confines of the Council of State, he viewed with overpowering irritation the occasional public displays of hyperbole and self-righteousness coming from certain tribunes as they discharged their constitutional role to debate proposed laws. Since the tribunes had no initiative and no input whatsoever in drafting those laws, nor any power to propose amendments, their sole recourse was to attack perceived deficiencies publicly. For each draft law submitted by the executive, the Tribunate formed a committee to study the proposal, debated its recommendation, and took a purely advisory, non-binding vote. The house then designated three members to present its view to the Legislative Corps, alongside three counselors of state representing the government. The legislators, it will be recalled, had no prerogative of debate but simply listened to the speakers and then voted by secret ballot to adopt or reject the proposed law.

Bonaparte reacted furiously whenever the Tribunate recommended that the Legislative Corps reject a proposal, rare as such occasions were. During its first two years the Tribunate actually treated most measures submitted by the government respectfully—eighty-seven won favorable votes while only seven drew a recommendation for rejection. But at least a third of the tribunes voted against eight additional bills, while several others encountered some degree of opposition. In the few cases where the Tribunate rounded aggressively on a proposed law—such as one authorizing special tribunals without juries for certain crimes—Bonaparte considered such opposition not only a challenge to the integrity of his government but demagogic and even conspiratorial.[44] When his most important legislation to date, the first two titles of the Civil Code, went before the Tribunate the following year, a real crisis ensued. Chagrined at being excluded from the consultation that preceded the drafting, and perhaps hoping to increase their leverage in the future, the tribunes tore into certain relatively minor provisions and in the end voted twice to recommend rejection of whole sections. At that point Bonaparte lost all patience and pulled the entire Civil Code back from consideration.[45]

COULD the Tribunate be intimidated into cooperation? The means lay readily at hand with the prescribed annual renewal of one-fifth of the parliament's membership by the Senate. Since no constitutional stipulations specified how this should be carried out, the government urged the Senate to designate the tribunes and legislators to be retired rather than resorting to the customary drawing of lots. In the most literal sense this would not be a purge, since it could be construed as a legal and practical way to accomplish an assigned task. But in reality Bonaparte, operating through Cambacérès, made it per-

fectly clear that dissident and obstructive tribunes as well as unreliable legislators must be purged.

In January 1802, while Bonaparte conferred in Lyon with Italian notables
on their constitution and prepared to accept the presidency of the Italian
Republic, Cambacérès deftly managed the affair in consultation with friendly
senators. His point man turned out to be Senator François-Denis Tronchet,
a distinguished jurist of the old regime, influential member of the National
Assembly, lawyer for Louis XVI at his trial, and most recently one of three
principal architects of the Civil Code. Tronchet was a fortunate choice to
head the Senate committee chosen to report on this matter, since the Tribunate's opposition to his handiwork had probably offended Tronchet. He
duly proposed that the Senate carry out its renewal of the parliament by
reviewing the entire membership of each house and designating four-fifths of
the members who would retain their seats. Those who failed to make the cut
would of course lose their seats, although their names would not be officially
mentioned one way or another.

Tronchet's report sparked a serious debate with many interventions on
both sides of the argument, but in the end by a vote of 44 to 15 the Senate
adopted his plan and rejected the non-partisan method of drawing lots. The
Senate also declined to divide the members of parliament into five cohorts so
that each deputy would know in advance how long his term would last. In
the resulting state of insecurity, the remaining parliamentarians would presumably be more cooperative.

Going one by one down the alphabetical list of the 300 members of the
Legislative Corps in order to retain 240 proved an exceedingly laborious way
of eliminating 60 others. And given the virtual anonymity of these deputies,
who never debated and who voted by secret ballot, it is hard to fathom the
criteria employed by the senators to make their cuts. But in some cases they
apparently struck at men known to associate with presumed dissidents such
as the circle of Germaine de Staël or the salons of the widows Condorcet and
Helvétius in Auteuil, which overlapped with Sieyès's coterie and the circle of
Parisian intellectuals know as the *idéologues*.

Greater interest lay in the renewal of the Tribunate, where Cambacérès
enjoined the senators "to separate out . . . the dissident members." Bonaparte
had designated only five such figures by name (Chazal, Chénier, Thiessé,
Garat-Mailla, and Daunou), but the obvious targets included three other
intellectuals: Mme de Staël's special friend, the outspoken liberal Benja-

min Constant; the *idéologue* editor of the *Décade philosophique*, Pierre-Louis Ginguené; and the political economist Jean-Baptiste Say, who rarely spoke but had advocated stricter budgetary controls than Bonaparte was ready to accept. (When Say published his influential *Treatise on Political Economy* in 1803, with its claims for the science of political economy as a check on government policy, he must have confirmed Bonaparte's belief that such intellectuals had no place in his parliament.)[46]

Cambacérès conveyed Bonaparte's demand that "the dignity of the Government" must be bolstered in the face of its critics, as well as the first consul's threat to withhold all legislation for at least a year if he did not find a friendlier climate in the Tribunate. With many admirers in the Senate who had already been forced to rebuff him for election to that body, Daunou posed a particular problem. But Cambacérès insisted that senators "well disposed" to the government must remove Daunou, unappealing as that might be. In the end the most nettlesome tribunes lost their seats.[47]

To fill the twenty vacancies in the Tribunate, the Senate selected obscure individuals for the most part, along with Daru (a first-rate military administrator), Lucien Bonaparte, Boissy d'Anglas, and Carnot (a designation they would come to regret). Now placated, Bonaparte could afford to be indulgent toward the ousted parliamentarians. Most of the purged tribunes, and some of the former legislators, received compensatory state employment, including a prefecture for Chazal, directorship of the Bibliothèque Nationale for Daunou, and even a post as an educational inspector for the much reviled Chénier. Benjamin Constant, however, lost favor completely and went into internal exile, supported for a time by Mme de Staël, that "veritable plague . . . whose métier is intrigue," in Napoleon's eyes. When the emperor ordered her into permanent exile in Switzerland in 1807, Cambacérès stated that he agreed completely, yet cautioned that "one must not ignore the fact that Mme de Staël and Constant have many friends and partisans in Paris."[48] But by this time Napoleon's aversion to her knew no limits, and the reaction of public opinion (or posterity, for that matter) no longer deterred him.

In due course the organization and constitutional status of the Tribunate was modified to make it more tractable. Henceforth, most of its work would not be done in public plenary session but in three sections (finance, legislation, interior), meeting privately and consulting from time to time with members of the Council of State. After 1803 the Tribunate was allowed to atrophy, since no new members were added, and it disappeared altogether by decree of the Senate in 1807, with its remaining fifty members folded into the Legislative Corps. That same year the *Décade philosophique* ceased publication.

Meanwhile, Bonaparte telegraphed his impatience with intellectuals who meddled in government by dissolving the Class of Moral and Political Sciences of the National Institute. Far more than the Senate or Tribunate, the section of this class devoted to "the analysis of ideas" had been the institutional bastion of the *idéologues*. Rooted in a materialistic philosophical discipline, their innovative if ponderous social science supported a certain style of liberalism and fostered secular republican values and education. Bonaparte genuinely admired scientists and scholars, but he drew the line when intellectuals became mired in a wordy and useless "metaphysics." He did not purge these individuals from the Institute, but scattered the members of the Class of Moral and Political Sciences (both the majority of traditional scholars and the minority of *idéologues*) among two large, reconstituted classes devoted to Literature and Modern Languages and to History and Ancient Languages. By thus reorganizing the National Institute, the Consulate brought it closer to the old regime model of the former Académie Française and its counterpart for historical scholarship, the Academy of Inscriptions.[49]

ON THE EVE of the Empire, then, Bonaparte had moved against a variety of perceived dissidents by arbitrary or highhanded methods. He inflicted extralegal retribution against purportedly unreconstructed Jacobins and *sans-culottes*, and symbolically exorcised the Terror's memory with his deportation decree of Nivôse IX. When he turned to the obstreperous tribunes, he did not confront Jacobins but only liberal moderates who shared his anti-Jacobinism yet who took their role seriously and thereby collided occasionally with his government. The dissident tribunes, in turn, were linked in Bonaparte's mind (and, up to a point, in reality) with the salons of certain influential women and other coteries. While he occasionally erupted in scorn against liberal intellectuals as phrasemongers and metaphysicians, it may well be that on a deeper level he recognized them as serious antagonists, as dangerous with their words and pens if left unchecked as *chouan* rebels or Jacobin *tyrannicides* with their daggers and bombs.

IV

From Consulate to Empire

O N 25 MARCH 1802, Joseph Bonaparte and Lord Cornwallis concluded their arduous negotiations and signed the Treaty of Amiens that ended a decade of European war. Public enthusiasm for Bonaparte in France was never higher: the first consul had achieved peace and international preponderance through military victory, the restoration of traditional Catholic religious practice, and the repatriation of most émigrés—all without jeopardizing civil equality, the abolition of seigneurialism, or the transfer of the *biens nationaux*. Bonaparte seemed to be sustaining the most tangible interests created by the Revolution while soothing its most aggrieved victims.

In an exultant mood, the first consul chafed at the restraints on his initiative from the Consulate's web of institutions, the residue of Sieyès's "metaphysical" concern for the balance of powers. Several important collaborators reinforced his belief that France now required a return to monarchical forms. Constitutional monarchy, in this view, was the veritable form, the original intent, of the Revolution of 1789. Bonaparte explained to his minister of interior Chaptal that the Revolution had stirred the people and taught them to understand their rights, but "the fall of the monarchy was merely a consequence of the difficulties that were encountered; it was not at all the intention of the revolutionaries."[1] As Bonaparte increasingly concentrated authority in his own hands—behind the watchwords of order, stability, efficiency—he could be seen as progressing toward the early Revolution's lost point of equilibrium, with the added attraction that he would owe his crown not to his birth but to his personal merit. Those inclined to resist this drift with talk about public liberty Bonaparte stigmatized as "ideologues."[2]

A FIRST STEP: CONSUL FOR LIFE

After the Treaty of Amiens, the Tribunate and Senate vied to proclaim the nation's gratitude to the first consul. The president of the Tribunate moved that "the Tribunate express its desire that a reward worthy of the Nation's gratitude be presented to General Bonaparte." But what form this should take remained unclear. Financial rewards or symbolic gestures would not constitute a sufficient response, given Bonaparte's personality. A vote of confidence extending his mandate seemed more promising, but how far should this be carried? To Thibaudeau, a member of the Council of State whose revealing account of these months is unsurpassed, the Tribunate's vague gesture merely hinted at the intrigue afoot. To his uneasy friend Josephine he warned: "schemes are ripening in the dark. . . . The more power Bonaparte grasps, the wider does the breach become between him and his best supporters, the Men of the Revolution. They will submit, no doubt; but they will no longer be attached to him."[3]

Certain collaborators, on the other hand, assuredly wished to see Bonaparte's power enhanced: notably brother Lucien, Foreign Minister Talleyrand, and Roederer and Regnaud, two original participants in the Brumaire cabal, presently hardworking members of the Council of State. With perhaps less zeal, second and third consuls Cambacérès and Lebrun were in their camp as well. Yet Bonaparte, sensitive to timing and public sentiment, would not publicly endorse his preferred option, designation as consul for life. He therefore left his supporters in the Senate—where the initiative lay—somewhat in the dark.

This confusion led Bonaparte's slavishly devoted follower Lacépède, *rapporteur* of the Senate's committee, to misplay the hand. Since the constitution empowered the Senate to designate a consul for a ten-year term, Lacépède proposed that the nation's gratitude be expressed by extending the first consul's tenure here and now for an additional ten years. Another senator then proposed as an amendment Bonaparte's appointment for life, the response that he actually desired. Senators Lanjuinais and Garat spoke in opposition; then a senator requested a vote on the two alternatives. President Tronchet, however, would only entertain the first, official proposition, and the Senate duly voted 60 to 1 for a prolongation of Bonaparte's term of office for an additional ten-year term—the lone dissenter being Lanjuinais, the redoubtable Breton legal scholar and liberal veteran of several revolutionary assemblies.

Tronchet—an eminent jurist, influential member of the National Assembly, architect of the Senate's purge of the Tribunate that Bonaparte had demanded not long before, and member of the small drafting committee for the Civil Code—was seemingly an ally and servitor par excellence of Bonaparte. Yet according to Thibaudeau, while Tronchet ("neither a republican nor a courtier") admired Bonaparte, he also feared him. "In a private meeting of senators he [reportedly] said: 'He is a young man still, but he has begun like Caesar, and he will end like him. He is too fond of talking about mounting his horse and drawing his sword.' "4

Tronchet's maneuver slowed down the juggernaut only briefly. Since Bonaparte considered a ten-year renewal meaningless, he now launched a devious stratagem to secure the consulship for life. Responding evasively and with feigned modesty to the Senate, he declared: "I was invested with the supreme Magistracy by the vote of the people, and I cannot feel myself assured of their continued confidence in me until the act that prolongs my term of office shall have been ratified by the whole nation." He then instructed Cambacérès to convene the Council of State for an act of political alchemy—to convert the Senate's proposition for a ten-year extension into a plebiscite on a life consulship.

Thibaudeau again provides light where the public record is obscure. Cambacérès convened the Council: "The questions before us are how, when, and in what terms the necessary vote shall be put to the nation?" Bigot de Préameneu (another architect of the Civil Code) maintained that the vote of the nation could not be restricted merely to the ten years fixed by the Senate. Roederer agreed that ten years did not provide the necessary stability and that the vote of the sovereign people need not be limited to that option: "The Senate confined itself to ten years, under the impression that it had no authority to do more; but the people's authority is unbounded, and the question to be submitted to it must be whether or not the First Consul shall be elected for life."5 Then someone added to the mix the right of Bonaparte to name his successor, which Roederer and Lucien had been urging for months.

When the Council finally took its vote, all members present voted yes except for five who pointedly abstained (Bérenger, Berlier, Dessolle, Emmery, and Thibaudeau).

Cambacérès appointed a committee to draft a formal opinion (*avis*) from the Council of State, which it produced in short order. But sometime between that evening and the next morning when the Council's *avis* was made public, the right of Bonaparte to name his successor disappeared from the proposition to be submitted for a plebiscite. Bonaparte considered this power to be awkward and unnecessary at the present time, and declined to accept that "duty." Thus Bonaparte countermanded the official views of both the Senate (which had proposed a ten-year extension) and his Council of State (whose advisory opinion he altered to his liking). Behind the facade of the Senate and Council of State, Bonaparte personally framed the brief proposition to be voted on by the French people: "Shall Napoleon Bonaparte be named first consul for life?"

This turn of events distressed certain "men of the Revolution" but not enough to desert the first consul's camp. Bonaparte's ardent servitor Boulay de la Meurthe, for example, was on a medical leave of absence from the Council of State at the time and took no part in its deliberations, but he was not pleased. His son's memoir-cum-biography briefly describes Boulay's reaction this way: "They spoke of the Republic, they conserved the outward forms, but at bottom they were thinking of monarchy. . . . This rapid return toward the past was not without disadvantages or dangers in the eyes of Boulay."[6] For his colleague on the Council of State Théophile Berlier, a dedicated republican, the discomfort level was greater:

> It was difficult for me not to see retrograde tendencies in this, which grieved me all the more since I carried a sincere attachment to the first consul, and since, in the first year of the Consulate, he seemed to me to be the man sent by providence to consolidate our republican institutions and make them respected in all of Europe. . . . It was painful for me to feel that we were drifting from the goal. However . . . the name [Republic] still remained, and the reality could still bring a recovery of some of its rights.[7]

In addition to such retrospective comments, we have from Thibaudeau a bit of direct repartee with Bonaparte. After the plebiscite and the subsequent *senatus-consulte* revising the constitution, Bonaparte patiently explained to him that the new arrangements assured the stability and durability of the

Consulate and placed the first consul on a level with foreign sovereigns—a consideration of paramount importance in Bonaparte's view. To Thibaudeau's comment that "the impression of the Revolution is still too fresh and this transition too abrupt," Bonaparte replied with his standard refrain: "For the Men of the Revolution I am the best guarantee"[8]—a mantra that liberals such as Boulay, Berlier, and Thibaudeau evidently internalized and from which they could never free themselves. The more so since Bonaparte's steps toward monarchy were spaced apart, gradual, and embedded in avowals of fidelity to the Revolution's underlying achievements, garnished with the reminder that the general himself owed his career to the Revolution, although in truth that notion held little meaning for him by this time.

THE PLEBISCITE OF 1802

When Thibaudeau, in the same conversation, expressed regret to Bonaparte that the Senate should at least have initiated the life consulship for the sake of legality, he candidly replied: "if they had originated it I should have always been dependent on them; for obviously those who elect can dismiss. The plebiscite has the advantage of legalizing my extension of office and placing it on the highest possible basis."

This was to be the first veritable plebiscite in French history. Though reminiscent of the three referenda in which voters had approved the Jacobin constitution of 1793, the directorial constitution of 1795, and the constitution of the Consulate in 1800, the coming vote concerned only Bonaparte's title and personal power. Related constitutional modifications would come in due course through an act of the Senate without consulting the citizens.

Back in 1800, with eligibility to vote approximating universal male suffrage, about 1.6 million citizens had voted yes on the constitution of the Year VIII (1800). But wishing to bolster the Consulate's image with a stronger mandate than the 2 million votes recorded for the Jacobin constitution of 1793, the government falsified the results of the referendum by announcing 3.1 million "yes" votes. Minister of Interior Lucien Bonaparte supervised the conflation of cantonal returns into spurious departmental totals (that no one could check), which added 900,000 fictitious "yes" votes, and then created around 500,000 military "yes" votes out of thin air.[9]

In 1802, by contrast, the announced result of about 3.6 million "yes" votes was essentially honest and accurate. The wait-and-see attitude that many

French citizens prudently adopted in 1800—the *attentisme* that had become a habit after so many abrupt political changes—had yielded to genuine acceptance. But as historian Claude Langlois suggests, the falsification of 1800 inhibited the regime's public relations in 1802, since the number of veritable "yes" votes had actually doubled rather than increasing by a mere 20 percent over the (falsified) official results of the previous vote. The real number of votes revealed an impressive, dramatic advance in popular acceptance of Bonaparte's power that could not be exploited to full advantage.[10]

Turnout was the crucial variable in all these votes. Bonaparte had named Roederer to an ad hoc position with responsibility for "the direction and surveillance of public education and public spirit." An aide-mémoire in Roederer's papers suggests that the issue of "public spirit" caused misunderstandings and recriminations between them. But when it came to promoting the plebiscite of 1802, Roederer's zeal matched Bonaparte's intention, since the life consulship was as much Roederer's idea as anyone's. On stationary carrying by his full and ponderous title, Roederer hectored the prefects: "It is vital, citizen prefect, that public spirit be stimulated in execution of this decree [for the plebiscite] . . . that the voting registers are opened and available to everyone . . . that no one neglects to express his view in the belief that it is superfluous. . . ."[11]

The ministry of interior expected enthusiastic and concrete steps to assure favorable results locally, including prefectorial circulars to mayors that showed some spirit and finesse. A dry, matter-of-fact reaction from a prefect drew a negative assessment in Paris, while flattering encomiums for Bonaparte and pledges that everything possible would be done gained high marks. Ministerial notations on this correspondence ranged from a laudatory "He neglected nothing in implementing this" to a censorious "this is the driest of responses."[12]

Government concern did not center on the prospect of "no" votes—in 1802 they numbered only 8,374, including Lafayette's, which he explained in a letter to Bonaparte. With individual voting by inscription in 45,000 open communal registers (rather than the 1790s method of voting in primary assemblies), it would take an extraordinary commitment and sangfroid to pronounce publicly in writing against the life consulship. Rather, it was the extent of abstention and its implication of passive opposition that kept the government on edge.

An illuminating report by the minister of interior evokes that concern. With results complete except for a handful of departments with only partial results, Chaptal observed that the "yes" votes were running in the overwhelming ratio of 442 to 1. "But it seemed to me appropriate to compare this also to the mass of citizens who have the right to vote. Their number, established by way of registrations conducted by the municipal councils in execution of the law of 13 Ventôse Year IX, totals 7,147,561." With over 3,653,000 "yes" votes recorded, there was already an absolute majority, and extrapolating the votes yet to be tallied, that margin would be even higher.

> Thus, if it is claimed, against all likelihood, that all citizens who did not vote should be counted in the negative column, it would nonetheless be valid to regard the affirmative vote as the express and unequivocal will of the majority of the French nation. But if we suppose, more reasonably, that the minority that remained silent was leaving it up to the majority that did express itself, one must conceive among the non-voters the same distribution of opinion as among those who did vote.[13]

Even without this delusional gloss, the results were comforting and did indeed surpass an absolute majority of eligible voters. "Men of the Revolution" such as Thibaudeau and Berlier had to be impressed by this resounding quasi-democratic rite and could consider it a further reason to go with the tide.

A SUCCESSOR TO BONAPARTE?

When Bonaparte excluded from the plebiscite on the life consulship the clause specifying his power to name a successor, he was rebuffing those brumairians who fretted incessantly, perhaps with good reason, that if Bonaparte suddenly died, their entire political edifice might crumble. The Italian campaign of 1800 had sorely tested their nerves already. After the first consul disappeared over the Alps and closed with the enemy, days went by without any word from the front. Rumors of French defeat and of Bonaparte's death in battle swirled around Paris. (The battlefield death of a great general proved to be true, but the victim was Desaix, the real hero of Marengo and a military comrade dear to Bonaparte.) Despite his consternation, Second Consul Cambacérès ignored these rumors as best he could, but out of fear or ambition others began to credit them and to act.

The extent of the ensuing intrigue remains obscure, but Sieyès certainly animated some of it, while Fouché and Talleyrand, despite their mutual animosity, were likely participants at meetings out in Autcuil, where Talleyrand and some of the regime's disenchanted intellectuals resided. Fouché and Sieyès in particular feared that Bonaparte's demise might unleash momentum for a Bourbon restoration that could prove fatal for regicides like themselves. Sieyès seems to have convoked certain members of the Brumaire legislative commissions (minus men who were now too close to Bonaparte, such as Boulay de la Meurthe) in the hope of creating a veneer of legality for any improvised solution. According to some sources, they agreed with difficulty that Lazare Carnot should fill any void at the top.

Bonaparte cleared the air with his *bulletin* about the great victory at Marengo—in reality a near disaster, save for Desaix's heroic intervention. But once he returned to Paris, word of these "conspiracies" naturally reached him and irritated him deeply. Fouché, playing his usual double game, tried to mollify the first consul while eliding his own involvement and minimizing the role of others. Bonaparte made a show of fury nonetheless. "So they thought I was done for, and they wanted to try another Committee of Public Safety!" he stormed. "I saved those men, I spared those men! Do they take me for a Louis XVI? Let them dare and they'll see! . . . I'm not afraid of anything; I'll drive those ingrates, those traitors, into the dust heap."[14] Carnot in particular lost favor and would soon be eased out of the war ministry. In contrast, Cambacérès's relative imperturbability and lack of involvement in this intrigue validated Bonaparte's confidence in him.

Even without such dramatic reminders as the close call at Marengo or the royalist bomb of Nivôse Year IX, which barely missed annihilating the first consul, the question of a successor continued to haunt his collaborators. Bonaparte himself, on the other hand, could not bear to think seriously about the succession, despite the threat of assassination plots and exposure in combat. Before 1804, he pushed aside the issue in various ways. After the plebiscite on the life consulship, he told Thibaudeau: "No one likes to name his successor while he himself is alive; it is a thankless task, in face of the jealousies and factions which such a nomination would cause."[15] In more candid moments Bonaparte maintained that at present no one could succeed him.

When forced by his interlocutors to discuss this, he threw up another obstacle: suppose he did have the right to name his successor, or to nominate one to the Senate—whom could he choose? Cambacérès, for all his loyalty and manifest virtues (of which more in the next chapter), would not do and no one ever suggested otherwise. The Bonaparte brothers—Joseph, Louis, or Lucien—even less so. Napoleon believed that his brothers owed their standing entirely to himself and had earned no consideration whatever on their own merits—perhaps a plausible view of his two younger brothers (although Lucien's value to him on 19 Brumaire cannot be overstated), but a condescending one of Joseph that ignored his older brother's wide personal appeal and proven diplomatic talents.[16]

Napoleon could be goaded into idle speculation about other possible successors in the pre-empire days, but only to prove how silly the whole matter seemed. While he once told Roederer that Carnot "is perhaps worth more than another," he had long since removed Carnot from the hub of power, and probably agreed with Roederer that "the French nation will never believe itself free and honorable under a member of the Committee of Public Safety." Bonaparte also allowed that General Moreau, his one-time rival, deserved consideration, only to dismiss him with this *mot*: "If only Moreau were another man! [Si Moreau était un autre homme!] And besides, he has no friends at all." [17]

Bonaparte initially played the good son of the Revolution by scoffing at the notion of an hereditary succession. The Revolution had obliterated heredity and the first magistrate could not be chosen on that basis, he told Thibaudeau in 1802—music to the latter's ears. To the monarchically minded Roederer, he put his objections in different and more obscure terms: "My natural heir is the French people," he declared. "Heredity has never been instituted by a law . . . it has always been established by fact. . . . No one has any interest in overthrowing a government in which everyone who possesses merit finds a place. . . . The French at this moment can only be governed by me." With such narcissistic evasions Bonaparte temporarily stymied Roederer, Talleyrand, Lucien, and others seeking to fix the Brumaire settlement with the cement of an hereditary succession.[18]

Ironically, however, Bonaparte's personal desire to take the title and powers of an emperor necessarily forced the succession question onto the agenda as well. With Bonaparte already consul for life, the wish to solve the succession problem in the clearest and most traditional fashion by heredity provided a solid justification for the creation of a new dynasty. Yet even if the linkage between an imperial title and hereditary succession seems entirely logical, it remained problematic from Napoleon's perspective.

One can almost sympathize with him as he assessed his family situation and saw a mare's nest of complications rather than an obvious solution to anything. Napoleon had no natural sons and would not have any while he remained married to Josephine, as he fully intended at this juncture. Since he had no confidence in any of his brothers, that left the option of adopting an heir. But the adoption route too had its pitfalls. Joseph, the eldest brother, had no sons as yet, and while brother Louis did, they were too young at this time to offer any certainty. The paradox in all this is obvious: Napoleon's lack of a son coupled to his commitment to Josephine ran up against his disdain or exasperation with the rest of his family—brothers, sisters, and their spouses—whose maneuvering he resented mightily, especially when it came at Josephine's expense. The most blatant offense to her interests was of course the advice constantly being pressed on him that he should divorce her immediately and remarry a fertile princess—advice which Napoleon adamantly rejected at this juncture as he affirmed his loyalty to Josephine.[19]

Notwithstanding such complications, Bonaparte's determination to acquire the cachet and powers of a monarch meshed with his collaborator's obsession over the succession issue and their concomitant desire to return to monarchical government. France would become an empire under a new dynasty, with the imperial dignity hereditary in the Bonaparte family. The specter of a first consul assassinated in a royalist plot provided the catalyst or pretext to consummate this scenario.

It began with the arrest of two royalist agents acting for Bonaparte's nemesis, the irreconcilable *chouan* chief Georges Cadoudal. Under interrogation, the agents implicated General Pichegru (a royalist deputy who escaped deportation after the Fructidor coup of 1797 by fleeing to England) and General Moreau (Bonaparte's foremost rival in military success and public esteem, whose politics had always been somewhat enigmatic). Moreau was soon arrested, Pichegru run to ground and apprehended, Cadoudal himself finally seized; later the duc d'Enghien, a Bourbon heir living in Baden at the time, who was thought to be implicated in the plan, was kidnapped and brought to France.[20] But even before those arrests or the ensuing trials, Minister of Justice Regnier issued a preliminary report sketching the outlines of this latest plot to assassinate Bonaparte. Where gratitude to the first consul had touched off the intrigue that ended in the life consulship, it was the imminent danger to him from this counterrevolutionary conspiracy that became the pretext for establishing the Empire. The transition reflected a consensus—enthusiastic or grudging—within the Napoleonic elite; some remarkable notes of dissent from the same quarters; a panoply of interesting rationalizations; and an intimidating mobilization of military opinion that gave this event a particular flavor.

THE LAST STAND OF THE OLD REVOLUTIONARIES

The Council of State had no official role to play in the turn to Empire, but Bonaparte assuredly sought to include those valued collaborators in the preliminaries. Second Consul Cambacérès, who usually chaired the Council in Bonaparte's absence, informed its members that the first consul wished them to discuss this matter without the usual formalities and with complete candor. Not only would Bonaparte absent himself, but Cambacérès and council secretary Locré would withdraw as well to give them maximal freedom.

Most members could not have known that Cambacérès himself did not favor the transition. According to his unpublished apologia of 1818, he had two misgivings. First, there was the question of public sentiment: "I was certain that the idea of the Republic still lived in the hearts of a large part of the Nation." Shattering the fiction that Bonaparte remained the head of state in a republic might create a needless provocation. This opinion Cambacérès certainly conveyed to Bonaparte. His second reservation he no doubt kept to himself: "Besides, I feared that the active inclination of the first consul, which was sometimes contained by republican forms, would no longer have any restraint as soon as we will have returned to monarchy." And who, as we shall see in the next chapter, would have better reason to know.[21]

Cambacérès could also be taxed with a purely self-interested motive for opposing the transition, since the proclamation of an empire would necessarily abolish the post of second consul, possibly leaving him to a less exalted or less secure future. But Bonaparte took no offense at Cambacérès's tactful reservations and did not claim to see in his reluctance a display of self-interest. On the contrary, Napoleon's very first act upon assuming the title of emperor was to name a small group of men as imperial dignitaries, with Cambacérès ranked immediately below brothers Joseph and Louis Bonaparte under the apt title, "Archchancellor of the Empire."

While Cambacérès did not take the lead in promoting the hereditary empire he certainly did nothing publicly to oppose the tide, least of all by attempting to influence the Council of State. His withdrawal from the room in any case left the initiative to Regnaud de St. Jean d'Angély, one of Bonaparte's closest subordinates since 1797, and currently president of the interior section of the Council. A proposal fashioned by Regnaud and the presidents of the Council's four other sections emphatically linked the move to an hereditary dynasty with a reaffirmation of the Revolution's basic gains. After enumerating the benefits that would flow from making the head of state an hereditary office in the Bonaparte family, Regnaud insisted that

> the stability and effectiveness of hereditary power and the rights of the nation that will have voted for it must be inseparably guaranteed in the same act. . . . [These rights consisted of] individual liberty, religious freedom, the inviolability of property, the irrevocability of the sale of the *biens nationaux*, the political equality that opens all positions to all citizens, the civil equality which assures that all citizens are judged according to the same laws, and the approval of those laws and of the annual levels of taxation by a national representation.[22]

This same sentiment would be invoked in the Senate and the Tribunate, and it raised no argument. The real question before the Council of State was: "Is it desirable to base the Government of France on the hereditary principle?" According to Thibaudeau's credible account, Regnaud echoed Bonaparte in arguing that it was indeed "the only hope for preserving France from the disorders that an elective Government must bring upon the country. It was equally necessary, he said, to the success of our foreign relations." But when the chemist Fourcroy proposed that the Council go on record to approve the principle of an hereditary empire, a prolonged silence followed. Several members murmured that this should be put to a vote, but then Berlier, arguably the staunchest republican in the Council, broke the silence. His intervention never reached the public at the time but it has long resounded in the historical record. As transcribed by Thibaudeau,

> Berlier began with a short preamble stating that his conscience imposed upon him the painful duty of combating with all his powers a measure that was approved by many enlightened and able men. He then said: "If the hereditary system is now to be adopted, not a trace will remain of that Republic for whose establishment and preservation France has sacrificed untold treasure and human lives. I do not myself believe that the French people are prepared to renounce what remains of an advantage so dearly purchased. The arguments deduced from our foreign relations do not seem to me to apply at all to a State the head of which [already] has a life tenure in his office. . . ."
> Berlier had not, in fact, been in favor of the Consulate for life, but in

the present state of affairs he was content to entrench himself behind that measure to ward off further changes. He laid special stress upon the false position in which an hereditary and monarchical system would place all those who had contributed in any degree to the success of the Revolution; a large and important class who were now to be used in reconstructing, amid the jeering contempt of their enemies, the very edifice which they had demolished.

This reflection was met by Regnaud, who said: "Have no fear on that point. The man who governs France has an arm strong enough to protect one party from triumphing over another. He is himself the child of the Revolution."23

After Berlier's intervention a debate began around the question of whether, when all seemed to be going so well, this was an opportune time for such a change. As Thibaudeau summarized the argument (which reflected his own view): "At the present moment the world at large will see in it ambition rather than patriotism. It is both ill-timed and premature. To these considerations the partisans of the hereditary system replied that a period of calm was the best possible time to prepare for the storm and to give France the best constitution possible." Within its narrow terms, the debate became highly animated and required four sittings, after the Council finished its ordinary business, to wind down. Finally twenty members endorsed the adoption of hereditary rule while at least six voted for postponement (Bérenger, Berlier, Boulay de la Meurthe, Dauchy, Réal, and Treilhard).24

More significantly, the dissenters refused to sign the address drawn up by Regnaud, claiming that they had been expressly invited to offer their individual opinions. And if the majority signed Regnaud's address, the minority would draft a counter-address, which might leak and embarrass the government. When Bonaparte heard of this impasse, he asked that each member simply submit his opinion in writing individually. As with Cambacérès, he showed no resentment against the members who opposed his plan since they had played by his rules, had kept their arguments in house, and no doubt framed their reservations tactfully.

Decades later, when Berlier composed a political memoir intended for his descendants, he referred his readers to Thibaudeau's published account of that debate in the Council of State. (Since Thibaudeau himself was presumably no longer present, having been appointed as prefect in Marseilles a year earlier, perhaps his notes came from Berlier to begin with.) But Berlier lingered with pride over his act of dissent. He knew that resistance in the Council would be fruitless, he recalled, "but it was impossible for me not to render this last homage to the Republic that I had loved so much, that I had served with such good faith in the midst of so many vexations, and whose disappearance down to its very name I could not witness without experiencing the most painful feeling."

All the more necessary, then, to explain his continued collaboration with Napoleon after the Empire became a fait accompli. Berlier's exact words give us the most explicit glimpse into the sentiments of a once ardent republican in the service of Emperor Napoleon I:

> The Empire having been decreed and consecrated by the national will [in a plebiscite], it was of course necessary that I submit to it. And it was a consolation to me to think that I had done everything that my conscience prescribed to defend in legal fashion the remnant of republican government.
>
> On the other hand, looking around me I saw a host of good citizens who, initially partisans of the republic but now fatigued by the oscillations suffered for several years, ended up being persuaded that in the heart of an old and monarchical Europe, the best France could reasonably hope for definitively was a representative government under a new dynasty, whose power would be limited by liberal institutions.
>
> [Personally, Bonaparte still retained Berlier's confidence]. . . . His ambition satisfied by his arrival at the acme of constitutional power, victor abroad, he would make it his principal concern to govern the interior in a liberal fashion. Finally, at bottom the man was a child of the Revolution, who could not forget his origin and who—offering every guarantee to the legal interests born of the revolution—also presented a sure support for patriots concerned about order.
>
> There was in this view plenty of plausible grounds for hope. And I was prevailed on to consider it a duty dictated by liberalism not to abandon positions from which patriots could still render service to the state and to liberty.[25]

In addition, Berlier acknowledged that personal considerations helped keep him in the Napoleonic fold, and the historian must be grateful for such candor. "I was without any patrimonial fortune," he noted, and while he now enjoyed an annual income of 25,000 francs as a counselor of state, recently supplemented by 15,000 francs and free lodging as president of the *conseil des prises* (the national commission that dealt with maritime seizures), he had commanded such income for only a short time and had not as yet amassed the capital necessary to support his family. Nor was the prospect of returning to the practice of law at the age of forty-five appealing. Berlier felt both too old and too young for that: "It was a very advanced age for resuming pleading as a barrister, yet perhaps not sufficient to secure a comfortable existence in the simple work of a practice (*travail du cabinet*), which is ordinarily fruitful only for older legal consultants."[26] His commitment to public service, the pressure of family responsibility, the lack of an agreeable alternative, and a lingering confidence in the revolutionary Bonaparte prevailed over his genuinely wounded republican values.

With a lesser degree of angst, the same was true of Boulay de la Meurthe. During the Council's debate on the imperial option, Boulay supported Berlier's attempt to at least postpone the transition. His spare memoir is regrettably vague about the dissenting opinion that he finally submitted to Bonaparte (although like Berlier he mentions with pride that he retained a copy of that opinion in his personal papers): "it was motivated by the political situation of the country and the state of the parties." In addition, he offered the advice that if hereditary power was adopted, Bonaparte "should have the right to derogate from the order of succession that will be established within his family, and to choose his immediate successor." Once the Empire was in place, Boulay like Berlier rallied without reservation, and readily rationalized his commitment: "that this political system can be reconciled with the principles proclaimed in 1789, and that [Boulay] regarded Napoleon as the man most capable of consolidating and terminating the Revolution."[27]

A "DEBATE" IN THE TRIBUNATE

With its public sessions and unfettered speeches, the Tribunate was the Consulate's most independent institution. If a government proposal provoked opposition in the Council of State or the Senate, it usually remained within the four walls of its chamber, but a dissident address in the Tribunate might incite a ripple of public interest in the informal communications networks that no government censorship could suppress. The Consulate had devalued oratory, deeming it an invitation to demagoguery, but oratorical prowess remained central to the job description for the one hundred tribunes. True, in 1802 the most contentious tribunes had been purged by the Senate at Bonaparte's behest during the prescribed renewal of one-fifth of the Tribunate's members, but it remained the least predictable forum in the French state.

To Bonaparte, the distinction between private and public meant everything. Accustomed to obedience in the chain of command and to military notions of honor, he tolerated dissent expressed privately but could not abide public criticism. After 1802, however, even if tribunes still raised objections to particular sections of proposed laws, the government reasonably assumed that on broad political issues the Tribunate would be as tractable as the Senate or the Council of State, perhaps more so since many tribunes were eager for advancement. Unleashing the oratory of the Tribunate therefore seemed the most useful way to lay the imperial option formally before the public. While hardly anyone would hear the speeches, they could read them in the *Moniteur* or other journals.

Tribune Jean-François Curée, a non-regicide member of the Convention and president of the Tribunate back in 1801, was tapped for the honor, and on 28 April he moved that "Napoleon Bonaparte, currently first consul, be declared emperor of the French and that the imperial dignity be declared hereditary in his family." Although the Tribunate had no power to enact this proposal, weeks of intrigue at last came to a head. Curée's colleagues crowded around the rostrum to support the motion, as the president drew up a list of speakers. In a sea of solemn rhetoric, "men of the Revolution" would publicly herald the transition from an elective republic of sorts to an hereditary empire—monarchy in a new key.

Beneath references to history, political theory, and effective forms of authority, gratefulness toward Napoleon dominated the discourse. The speakers invested this individual of extraordinary achievement with all the hopes they had attached before 1800 to abstractions like the nation, the principles of 1789, or the republic. In that respect, the Napoleonic Empire seems a logical culmination of Brumaire, when this psychological transposition, this escape from freedom, began.

An unscripted and discordant note, however, marred this marathon of adulation, as one tribune rose to oppose Curée's motion. Ultimately his speech had no effect on the outcome; if anything, it was invoked by Napoleonic loyalists to illustrate the increasingly hollow notion that French public life remained free. But in the short term the speech by Lazare Carnot, arguably the most renowned member of the Tribunate, exploded around his colleagues.

Unlike Berlier's stand in the Council of State, news of Carnot's address spread quickly, although police informers maintained that it had little impact. "I received letters of congratulation from all over," Carnot later claimed. "I was personally astonished at the prodigious success of this speech in a city accustomed for so long to bending without resistance to all the wishes of the master."[28]

A central figure in the two regimes that preceded the Consulate, Carnot was the leading military strategist on the Committee of Public Safety in 1793–94 and a member of the Directory on the losing side of the Fructidor coup in 1797. Historians in the republican tradition have always celebrated Carnot as "the organizer of victory" in the Year II, and Bonaparte too respected the former military engineer. After Brumaire, the first consul repatriated Carnot from exile and appointed him war minister until he soured on Carnot and accepted the resignation that he effectively provoked. After a brief return to private life, Carnot learned that the Senate had named him to a vacancy in the Tribunate in March 1802. Carnot stubbornly maintained his independence in that body and offered an escalating resistance to Napoleon's ambitions. To begin with, he opposed the Legion of Honor. Then he ruined the Tribunate's unanimous endorsement of the life consulate by recording a "no" vote in its official register along with the comment, "I realize that I have signed my condemnation." His outraged colleagues prevailed on him to retract that gratuitous addendum, and in fact he did not suffer retaliation, but his "no" vote stood.[29] Yet Carnot's participation in the "tyranny" of the Committee of Public Safety and his own miserable experience at the hands of his fellow directors in 1797 had left a troubling aura that now weakened his moral authority as a lonely defender of elective government.

Carnot's speech in 1804 conveyed no great articulation of republican ideology but simply a series of honest, critical observations. "I am very far from wishing to attenuate the praise given to the first consul," he began. As a direct beneficiary of 18 Brumaire, Carnot acknowledged the need for a temporary concentration of authority at that time to rescue the republic from "the edge of an abyss." But the very success of Brumaire now offered the opportunity "to establish liberty on solid foundations." The United States, he pointed out, was an example of a stable and prospering republic. In today's favorable circumstances, he added in his most striking phrase, "it is less difficult to form a republic without anarchy than a monarchy without despotism."

Carnot saluted accomplishments of Bonaparte's such as the Civil Code in advancing liberty, but asked: "would it be the proper recompense for him to

offer him the sacrifice of that same liberty?" Bonaparte has a unique opportunity "to resolve the great problem of public liberty," but has in effect turned
his back on it. The whole monarchical model offended Carnot: "nothing has
yet been invented to temper supreme power other than what has been called
intermediary corps or privileged bodies. Is it therefore of a new nobility that
one wishes to speak?" Having declared that "I will vote against the reestablishment of monarchy," however, Carnot concluded that if it was adopted by
the French people he would give the Empire his adherence: "I have always
made it my credo to submit to existing laws."[30]

The tribunes waiting to speak after Carnot scrambled to undo the damage and rebut this affront to the new consensus. Several attacked the mes-
senger as well as his message. Carnot, they declared, was hardly the man to
criticize his colleagues' political acumen.

With perhaps excessive subtlety, the learned financial specialist Arnould
asked: "What, then, is that unfortunate destiny that has dogged our colleague
in all phases of his political life? He who [in the Directory] could barely be
persuaded of the conspiratorial liaisons of Pichegru on 18 Fructidor V, liaisons
that revived proscriptions and placed France in peril had it not been saved by
the hero of 18 Brumaire. And today our colleague delays the expression of a
wish that the Nation clamors for and that is dictated by the terror of the past
[nice touch!] and fears for the future." Carrion-Nisas, playwright and former
classmate of Bonaparte's at the military academy, attacked frontally: Carnot's
first experience of democratic leadership on the Committee of Public Safety
placed him among the *proscripteurs*, exclaimed the tribune, while during his
second leadership stint, as a member of the Directory, Carnot was himself
proscribed, to be rescued only by the Consulate. Or as the lawyer Albisson
concluded (completely missing Carnot's sense of himself and the judgment
of posterity): "I cannot contain my astonishment at having heard the apologia for an elective and temporary magistracy coming from a mouth that ought
to have been sufficiently abashed by the mere recollection of the Year II or the
Year V."

Having disposed of Carnot, the tribunes justified the monarcho-imperial
option against his aspersions. Arnould invoked Jean Bodin on the superiority of hereditary over elective monarchy, and argued that the guarantee of liberty endured in the legislature's power over taxation. Carrion-Nisas replied
bombastically to Carnot's warnings against despotism: "What! Do we not
have law and a social compact? Eh! Who is speaking here of putting a man
above the laws?" Unlike a king, the emperor will not be the owner of the

country. "He is the chief of the French, by their wish; his domain is moral and no legal servitude can arise from such a system." Carnot had complained that a return to monarchy would not be consensual because the press was not free to debate it; Carrion-Nisas countered with Bonaparte's standard excuse for muzzling the press: "everyone knows how that liberty is fatal, how it promptly degenerates into license."

Costas, formerly a scientist on Bonaparte's Egyptian expedition, rejected Carnot's appeal to the example of the United States. In its geographic isolation, no great power threatened invasion or fomented internal upheaval in America. "The Americans have no need at all to defend themselves against the constantly reviving attempts of a family expelled from the throne. . . ." In France, only a fixed order of succession will put an end to the Bourbon's pretensions, he argued, as it has to those of the Stuarts in England. Carnot confounds the electoral system with liberty, Costas continued. On the contrary, an hereditary power can be a bulwark of public liberty. "The elective type of chief of state is useful only to the small number of those who can aspire to being elected [!]" In the same dubious vein Tribune Carret declared: "We are thwarting the avaricious and always bloody intrigues of elective regimes; we are precluding even the possibility of factions and party chiefs springing up."

But we have yet to extract the major theme in the tribunes' apologia for the elevation of Bonaparte to hereditary emperor. This was the argument from original revolutionary intent (to borrow a phrase from American constitutional history), an argument that of course cropped up in the abortive deliberations of the Council of State as well. Thus Regnaud's draft proposal to the Council declared

> That the Revolution had not been started by the nation, in 1789, against the heredity of the supreme magistracy, and that if it subsequently turned against the family in whom the representatives of the people had confirmed that heredity it is because that family armed itself against the Revolution and its principles. That the nation will confirm its desire to remove that [Bourbon] family by calling forth a new family and placing it at its head. That the heredity of the supreme magistracy in one family is not a concession to the interest of that family but an institution in the interest of the people. . . . That the heredity of the supreme magistracy conforms to the nation's moeurs, is suitable to its population, and appropriate to the extent of its territory.

In sum, Regnaud concluded, "heredity ought to be established in conformity with the principles developed at the beginning of the Revolution."[31]

This reference to original revolutionary intent became a litany in the Tribunate's discourse. Tribune Jard-Panvillier—one of the "perpetuals" of the revolutionary assemblies—explained. When the nation enjoyed its maximal freedom in 1789–90, before things began to go wrong, it chose to have a unified and hereditary executive power. By their conduct the Bourbons forfeited their right to that role and forced the nation into a democratic government, which in turn produced "scourges and anarchy." But under Bonaparte's "government of One," France recovered its unity and tranquility as well as glory abroad. Bourbon-English plots, however, still threatened to cause turmoil comparable to that caused by elections in the past. An hereditary emperor would definitively end that threat, return France to the path envisaged in 1789, and "preserve the advantages of the Revolution by the choice of a dynasty equally interested in maintaining them."

Costas (rejecting Carnot's claim that only public functionaries were advocating the imperial title) maintained that the whole nation had expressed this kind of preference at the start of the Revolution, and that the likely plebiscite to come would represent public opinion more faithfully than "the deliberations of those tumultuous assemblies, where one voted under the knife of parties." Albisson too emphasized the original design of 1789: "The Revolution attached heredity to the executive power. . . . That was one of the fundamental principles with which the Revolution began, and with which it was destined to be consummated." The goal of 18 Brumaire, "to terminate the Revolution by fixing it to the principles with which it began," is therefore about to be realized at last. Bringing the tribunes' speeches to a close, Savoye-Rollin conceded that absolute monarchy was the most absurd and degrading form of government, but ended on this fanciful note: "I adhere to Curée's motion, whose aim is to unite hereditary power to a representative government."[32]

This is actually a preposterous claim. Indeed, the whole argument from original revolutionary intent distorted the reality of 1789. The foundational principles of the National Assembly were perfectly expressed in its official slogan of 1789: the Nation, the Law, and the King—in that order. In its first revolutionary act of 17 June 1789, by which it unilaterally transformed the three chambers of the Estates General into a National Assembly, the Third Estate asserted the doctrine of popular sovereignty as a theoretical justification for all that would follow. It then immediately instituted popular sovereignty by embedding it in the notion of representative government and the mechanism of elections: only the Assembly's elected deputies could speak for the people, as Sieyès had put it. Moreover, the Assembly vested the legislature (itself and elected legislatures in the future) with the power to initiate and enact the nation's laws. True, the Assembly integrated the existing Bourbon monarchy as the executive branch of government, but it limited the king's role in law-making to only a suspensive or delaying veto. The original model of revolutionary sovereignty made the elected legislature the supreme branch of government, standing as it were between the king and the people.

In contrast to traditional monarchs, Bonaparte retained a nominal recognition of popular sovereignty, claiming that his own power derived from the people in some vague consensual sense, and concretely through the mechanisms of the plebiscite (1802 and 1804). But—in accord with a chastened Sieyès and most other brumairians—Bonaparte eliminated any veritable form of representative government through elections. True, the new regime boasted a separation of powers, but bodies such as the Senate, the Tribunate, and the Legislative Corps were strictly cooptive with no accountability to the public. So, when Savoye-Rollin proclaimed: "I adhere to Curée's motion, whose aim is to unite hereditary power to a representative government," he may have been sincere, but he was assuredly mouthing an illusion.[33]

THE ARMY AND THE COMING OF THE EMPIRE

When the Brumaire plotters overthrew the Directory, they placed military units in the Paris region under General Bonaparte's command. Actively involved in the raucous showdown at Saint-Cloud, and deployed conspicuously in the capital, the troops were the supporting cast in a parliamentary coup; the army did not impose its will on a helpless civilian government. Now, in the ultimate defining act for the Napoleonic regime—the passage from Consulate to Empire—the army's role was at once less evident yet arguably even more significant.

In the spring of 1804, the officer corps and the troops they commanded set up an insistent clamor for the designation of Napoleon Bonaparte as emperor. Had Napoleon encountered serious resistance to his scheme, the threat of the army's manifest displeasure could have been invoked to sweep aside that resistance. In the event, Napoleon did not have to play that card. But one look at the petitions that poured into Paris from the military makes the proclamation of the Empire seem an irresistible proposition. The question remains, however: was this a genuine expression of military opinion or was it "the manufacture of consent"?

Collective petitions had long been stigmatized as factional provocations when used by local political clubs; the directorial constitution nominally prohibited them altogether, though to little avail. Now, commanders in army camps and garrisons across the country dusted off that potent medium of popular expression. It is difficult to reconstruct with exactitude how this campaign of pen and ink was orchestrated, but a few markers survive in the archives.

Just after Grand Judge Regnier issued his preliminary report on the Cadoudal-Pichegru plot to assassinate Bonaparte, War Minister Alexandre Berthier (Bonaparte's inseparable aide) swung into action. Berthier ordered commanding officers to read the Grand Judge's report to their assembled troops, and many understood that the appropriate response would be a mass petition expressing outrage at the plot and devotion to Bonaparte. Commanders of two large military encampments established for a cross-Channel invasion were especially zealous. General Soult, overall chief of the two camps, wrote to the first consul a few days later: "The divisions based in the camps of Montreuil and Saint-Omer . . . deeply desired that I place before your eyes the addresses in which they express to you their indignation . . . and renew before you the hommage of their sentiments of love, veneration, and devotion." The petitions contained over 21,000 signatures.[34]

Since Bonaparte had not yet openly revealed his imperial plans, this effort to mobilize military opinion initially led nowhere in particular. Before long, however, the campaign of military petitions was harnessed to Curée's motion in the Tribunate for vesting Napoleon with the hereditary imperial title. As the 69th line regiment put it: "The heredity and unity of the executive power appear to us as the only satisfactory means to assure France its tranquility and well-being."

The drumbeat of military petitioning for an imperial crown arose in part spontaneously, but in the main from the top down through the chain of command. Officers were made to understand by their superiors that they must board this convoy and bring their subordinates along. In several military divisions, the 2nd and 5th in eastern France, for example, divisional generals circulated model petitions for the convenience of local commanders.[35] Other petitions were more personalized and occasionally reflected a flash of passion about the revolutionary experience, either positive or critical. But all demanded that Napoleon must be invested with the title of emperor, hereditary in his family.

Berthier used a meeting of the general staff, commanders in the Paris region, and visiting commanders from other divisions to put the crème de la crème of the officer corps on record in one intimidating petition. This constituted an unprecedented intervention in the affairs of state at the highest levels of the army. Although it shares the language of base flattery common to other civilian and military petitioners, one should pause over this document because it crystallizes a distinct Bonapartist position, quite different from the speeches in the Tribunate and essentially independent of any connection with the revolutionary experience. The array of military leaders who signed Berthier's petition called for

> an immutable order, a solemn law which will crown all your benefits, by establishing well-being in France and the Government in your family. . . . You owe it to the France that has chosen you for its chief, and that regards you as its second founder, indeed you owe it to yourself to assure for your handiwork the same immortality as for your name. Shall the fruit of so much effort and so many triumphs be surrendered to the caprices of blind chance? . . . Let this glorious heritage remain in perpetuity in your family!
>
> Henceforth the French armies will march to victory only under the banners of a Buonaparte. The law that must cement that precious guarantee of public security will be forever inviolable and sacred. It will be the seal of an immortal alliance that you contract with the French nation. . . .
>
> The moment has come when the Nation, proud of its chief, must invest him with an éclat that will reflect back upon itself. It is time that it confer on him a title more proportionate to his exploits, to the extent of the French empire, to the rank which he holds in Europe. . . . The title of Emperor that Charlemagne carried, does it not belong by right to the man who recalls it to our eyes as a legislator and warrior?[36]

Berthier's petition effectively leaves behind the dialogue over the revolutionary legacy and looks forward to a generically new order, an imperial Bonapartist order with special meaning for the army.

Certain other addresses from army units, individual officers, and groups of pensioned veterans were more conventional in arguing that Bonaparte was the one sure bulwark against a royalist restoration. As sixteen pensioned officers residing in Vannes (Morbihan) put it simply, the title of emperor "must be hereditary in your family in order to destroy the hopes formed by the counterrevolutionaries." Such petitions projected a "revolutionary legacy" vision of the Empire increasingly out of step with actual developments in Paris, but a sentiment that Napoleon could always invoke to generate support. In hindsight, such petitions convey a poignant optimism. "Which is the family that can offer us a greater guarantee for the maintenance of public liberty and equality?" asked the Toulouse garrison. "To whom can we better confide the deposit of our constitutional charter . . . [to preserve] all the grand things you have done for the well-being of the Republic?" Or as the garrison in Tarbes declared hopefully: "The French people, having become your subjects, will not for all that lose their rights to liberty and to equality, which you yourself have cemented."[37]

Some petitions, on the other hand, notably those circulated by General Dupont in the Montreuil encampment, aggressively distanced themselves from the Revolution in commending Bonaparte as the irreplaceable benefactor: "Abandoned to a total subversion, France endured in ten years of revolution every evil that can desolate a nation. . . . It is time that strong institutions guarantee us a durable prosperity. Accept the imperial crown!" Or as the 82nd infantry regiment observed: "We have been spoken to endlessly of liberty . . . that delicious chimera."[38]

Thus the military petitions demanding in one voice the elevation of Bonaparte to an hereditary imperial title actually represented three distinct visions. The "official" petition circulated by Berthier among the general officers and their aides, with its emphasis on military glory, evoked a post-revolutionary future founded on the unique talents and achievements of Napoleon Bonaparte. A second view welcomed the Empire as an extension of the republican Bonaparte to thwart the counter-revolution definitively and guarantee the future of liberty and equality. A third variant, as in the petitions circulated by General Dupont, anticipated the Empire as a final burial of the Revolution's legacy of anarchic disruption. We can see at once the great advantage of this ambiguity in creating a broad base of acceptance for the Empire. As in Brumaire, people still saw in Bonaparte what they hoped to see, but now the degree of wishful thinking is more apparent. In the end, Berthier's petition stands as the most accurate portent of what the future would hold.

THE SENATE RESPONDS

Napoleon's soaring ambition thus set in motion a wave of responses. While members of the Council of State argued heatedly over the imperial option behind closed doors, the tribunes drowned Carnot's remarkable public dissent in a chorus of enthusiasm, especially by linking Napoleon's imperial status with the Revolution's original intent to incorporate hereditary monarchy. Army units across the country meanwhile generated a mass of petitions so intimidating that they made the transition to Empire seem irresistible. This in turn influenced the response of the Senate, which alone could formally sanction the change.

The Senate had itself initiated the movement toward hereditary government in an address to the first consul on 27 March 1804 that vaguely stressed the desirability of making his achievement permanent. By early May, the Senate was more than ready to endorse the imperial transition, with the added urgency of precluding any military démarche that might preempt civil authority altogether. In its official address, the Senate would add to its many justifications of an imperial dynasty the startling contention that "it alone can curb the dangerous rivalries in a country covered with numerous armies commanded by great captains."[39]

The Senate was well primed to play its supporting role. In a colossal act of bribery following the life consulate, Bonaparte had created special dignities called "senatories" to cement the loyalty of the most favored senators while planting hope among others for such rewards in the future. The thirty-one senatories coincided with the circumscriptions of the nation's courts of appeal, each comprising three or four departments. The designated senator was to keep watch over his region, with the obligation to tour it once a year. In exchange he received a generous endowment of property in the senatory from *biens nationaux* yielding an annual income of at least 20,000 livres, with higher revenues in the choicer ones. Bonaparte had also ingratiated himself with the Senate by enhancing its public status as against the Council of State. In an audience for the diplomatic corps in September 1802, he unveiled a new order of precedence (*préséance*). Previously, the Council of State had grouped itself to the left and right of the first consul in front of the senators; now the senators entered first and stood to his right while the Council of State followed and stood to his left.[40]

According to Thibaudeau, after the life consulate, "the assault on every vestige of popular government continued to be pressed. Former [royal] intendants and local parlements were cited as excellent examples. . . . Not a single discredited institution of the old regime was not extolled." Even Bonaparte seemed annoyed that "there is an idea afloat of creating bodies of great proprietors appointed for life, possibly making these posts hereditary." Yet permanence and recognized status were qualities that Bonaparte valued. In a discussion with the Council of State on the creation of new departmental electoral colleges of propertied local *notables*—bodies that would generate lists of nominees for cooption by the Senate into public offices—Bonaparte insisted that they should have lifetime tenure. "The Electoral Colleges will form a link between the higher powers and the people. . . . If the members of the Electoral Colleges are constantly liable to reelection they will lose their influence and cease to be respected." He also saw another advantage to lifetime tenure: "Today a large proportion would be the men of the revolution; as time goes on there will be fewer and fewer each year. It is high time to come to a permanent settlement."[41]

Roederer, however, was not satisfied by such halfway measures, and was lobbying relentlessly not only for an hereditary dynasty but for a concomitant hereditary body of Napoleonic servitors. Bonaparte had wearied of Roederer's pedantic zeal and had moved him into the Senate in 1802 to get him out from underfoot in the Council of State, where he had initially seemed indispensable. Yet Roederer remained a tireless advocate for his theories of government. His voluminous, prolix papers, published by his son in the 1850s, contain several memos from this campaign. "Around imperial heredity there must be a grand dignity that should be at the same time a great hereditary magistracy," he argued. "Without that precaution, the supreme prerogative will lack support and guarantee." As a magistrate on the Parlement of Metz before the Revolution, Roederer was perhaps nostalgic for such tenured "intermediary corps," which Montesquieu had famously extolled as bulwarks of liberty against despotism—exactly the kind of hereditary bodies abolished by the National Assembly in 1789 and derided by Carnot in his speech.

But Roederer shrewdly understood the precarious condition of the Napoleonic regime—that Bonaparte was, as his royalist opponents always insisted, a usurper. Hence the Senate must have the strongest motivation "to see to the conservation of imperial heredity. . . . Just as the proprietor is the sole faithful guarantor of property, the hereditary magistrate is the sole assured guarantor of the supreme heredity." He conceded, however, that the ground must be laid for an hereditary Senate by making the utility of its role more evident, especially as a body charged with adjudicating the constitutionality of laws.[42]

In an undated letter from the Year XII to Joseph Bonaparte, Roederer pressed these ideas on his friend. "All is not completed with heredity and imperiality. It is necessary to establish new families around a new dynasty." Think twenty-five years ahead, he urged, when most of young Napoleon's original supporters will be gone and he will be surrounded by potential enemies. The interests of the next generation must be anticipated. No matter how generous the emoluments and perquisites for those now in favor—and Roederer did not believe them adequate; even generals and senators, he claimed, can barely manage the outlays for presenting themselves and their wives appropriately in society—their children might find themselves without patrimony or profession, but "with the memories and habits of a lavish lifestyle." As potential supporters par excellence of the new government in the future, the sons of today's senators need access and wealth. We must of course "honor economic activity" (for Roederer held a family interest in the Saint-Gobain glassworks, and was a serious publicist for entrepreneurial capitalism), but more to the point, "create hereditary seats in the Senate, which will thereby become a corps homogeneous with [imperial] power."[43]

In the notes Roederer used to prepare for the Senate's deliberation on the hereditary Empire, this idea persisted among the talking points he listed:

- appeal to unconstitutionality
- judgment on a resolution by the Corps Législatif
- a jury for crimes of state
- policing of the book trade
- guarantee against arbitrary arrests
- guarantee for the Senate: senatorial heredity[44]

The first two points addressed potential objections to be refuted (that the change was unconstitutional or that the Corps Législatif had to be consulted). The others laid down elements for a senatorial quid pro quo. While eager to bless this momentous transition, the Senate hoped to extract certain concessions for itself and guarantees for public liberty. The Senate's official response, delivered by François de Neufchâteau, framed this event with the "revolutionary legacy" vision of the Empire that we have encountered along the way in other forums. But beyond proclaiming this notion, could the Senate put some flesh on the bones?

François de Neufchâteau had impressive credentials as a liberal and revolutionary public servant: poet, playwright, and man of letters during the old regime; departmental administrator elected to the Legislative Assembly of 1791; a deputy to the Convention who declined to take his seat and was arrested during the Terror; a member of the Directory after Fructidor. His most important service came as minister of interior from June 1798 to June 1799, where he promoted statistical surveys, modern agronomy, industrial development, and public education—what one scholar has described as an Enlightenment project for a commercial republic.[45] François welcomed Brumaire, entered the Senate in its first cohort, steered clear of any dissident actions, and when the time came advanced the transition to Empire. For his zeal in this cause, Napoleon remained grateful. When the new constitution gave the emperor power to name the Senate's president, his first choice was François de Neufchâteau. Two years later when his second term expired, Napoleon sent him a personal note of thanks, without the use of titles or flowery salutations but with a simple candor, "for your zeal in service to the *patrie* and for your devotion to my person. Do not doubt my eagerness to give you always the proof of my affection."[46]

François's address described the essence of the imperial transition accurately enough: "This glorious repose we will owe to an hereditary Government of one man, elevated above all others, invested with a great power, surrounded with éclat." But he projected utter confidence that this new government would "defend public liberty, maintain equality, and dip its banners before the expression of the sovereign will of the people." Imperial power would be vested in a family "whose destiny is inseparable from that of the Revolution," and who will therefore protect the purchasers of national properties that the counterrevolution would like to wrest from them; guarantee the safety of all Frenchmen "who have remained faithful to the sovereignty of the People"; and defend even those who, misled during the Revolution's political torments, have since sought indulgence. Finally, the new regime ought to render futile any plots in behalf of the Bourbons, those upholders of "a throne uniquely composed of feudal trophies."

The final peroration of this official Senate response turned into a liberal epiphany, a wish list of core liberal values: "Liberty and equality must be sacred; the social compact cannot be violated; the sovereignty of the people will never be ignored . . . with the independence of the great [institutional] authorities assured; the free and enlightened vote of taxes; the security of properties; the liberty of individuals, of the press, of elections; and the inviolability of constitutional laws."[47]

Napoleon, who publicly vaunted his dedication to "the triumph of equality and public liberty," readily agreed to proposals by the Senate that confirmed its symbolic role as guardian of liberal values. Under the organic law for the Empire the Senate would create two standing committees. One, misleadingly called *la commission sénatoriale de la liberté de la presse* (but flagged more accurately in Roederer's notes), was to assure that no abuses occurred in the government's policing of the book trade. This committee proved a dead letter from the start, in part because the regime's efforts at regulating, manipulating, and censoring the written word focused on newspaper and periodicals, from which domain the senatorial committee was expressly excluded. The second committee, *la commission sénatoriale de la liberté inviduelle*, on the other hand, merits considerable attention. In effect it became the repository and last vestige of the Senate's self-image as a liberal institution, and as such will be discussed in another chapter.

For the present, these provisions of the organic law establishing the Empire sufficed as a quid pro quo and balm of good conscience for senators who were "men of the Revolution" like François, although they did not suffice for Lambrechts, Garat, Lanjuinais, Sieyès, Volney, or Grégoire (the lone senator to speak out repeatedly against the transition), who are believed to have cast the Senate's three recorded "no" votes and handful of abstentions.[48]

In the rush to closure, however, the Senate also launched a trial balloon in an entirely different spirit, the spirit of Roederer's campaign for an hereditary oligarchy to surround the new dynasty. Might not the Senate be made an hereditary body alongside the Bonaparte family? Gingerly venturing to ride Napoleon's coattails to hereditary status for itself, the Senate provoked a firm and contemptuous rebuff from Napoleon. Which is not to say that the emperor entirely rejected Roederer's logic. On the contrary, he would later implement it on his own terms. Once ensconced on the imperial throne, Napoleon recognized that an emperor required a nobility to validate and refract his own eminence; that permanence and heredity had their place in a new social infrastructure. In 1808, Napoleon would create an hereditary imperial nobility from across the spectrum of his collaborators, including leading generals and veteran servitors from the Council of State and the Senate. But he would not sanction an hereditary *body* like the House of Lords.[49]

An imperial nobility would be entirely consistent with Berthier's vision of the Bonapartist future, but for the moment it was François de Neufchâteau's "revolutionary legacy" version that framed the upcoming plebiscite on the hereditary succession, the last act of the sovereign people in France until 1815.

The official results of the plebiscite matched almost exactly the previous vote in 1802, with 3,572,000 votes cast (of which a mere 8,272 were "no"). But if we look behind the raw total, we find some interesting nuances in the all-important turnout numbers. For this was not a robotic replay of the previous vote.

In the first place, "France" was more extensive than in 1802, since the annexation of Italian territory had created several new departments that increased the total voting population. Secondly, concerted efforts had raised the turnout in a handful of departments significantly—notably the Dyle in Belgium (from 21,000 to 74,000 in round numbers); the Seine (from 70,000 to 121,000); and the Seine Inférieure (from 46,000 to 64,000). But against those rare higher totals, thirty-nine departments in almost all sections of France proper—Brittany, the East, the Center, the Southwest, Languedoc— saw substantially *lower* turnouts than in 1802, with at least 10,000 fewer votes and in most cases over 20,000 fewer, remarkable falloffs of 25 to 40 or even 50 percent from the impressive levels of 1802.[50]

The explanation cannot be determined with any certainty: perhaps the resumption of war had a souring effect, or resentment by sentimental royalists against the murder of the duc d'Enghien, or chagrin among republicans at the demise of the republic; perhaps the falloff came from a spreading cynicism or indifference. We can conclude only that the support of popular opinion on which Bonaparte claimed to rely for his legitimacy, canvassed in his preferred form of a plebiscite, was eroding at the margins instead of growing with the transition to Empire.

V

The Second Most Important Man in Napoleonic France

*T*HE NAPOLEONIC ruling elite presents a singularly bland image. Unlike the brilliant orators, fervent idealists, and shameless demagogues of the previous decade, few of Napoleon's collaborators ever made much of an impression on their contemporaries or on posterity. Alongside a handful of dashing, bumptious generals, only Talleyrand and Fouché, among the civilian servitors of Napoleon, have commanded attention in their own right.

The aristocratic bishop of Autun had thrown himself into the Revolution's early phase as a member of the Estates General/National Assembly, despite his enviable position in the old regime. After sitting out the Terror abroad, Talleyrand served the Directory for a time as foreign minister, where he extended a helping hand to young General Bonaparte. Once in power, Napoleon chose Talleyrand as his minister of foreign affairs and relied on his experience in numerous diplomatic engagements. They parted company in 1807, however, when the emperor could no longer abide Talleyrand's resistance to his expansionist ambitions and punitive treaties.

Jospeh Fouché, an ex-Oratorian and deputy to the Convention, lasted longer in Napoleon's service. A notorious terrorist during his mission to Lyon in 1793, Fouché escaped a reckoning for his sanguinary acts by helping to engineer Robespierre's fall and then losing himself in the thermidorian reaction. Under Barras's patronage, Fouché reemerged as the Directory's last police minister, and continued in that post under Napoleon. While keeping a low public profile, he made himself seem indispensable to Bonaparte by his calm aura of omniscience and the ubiquity of his informants. Napoleon never trusted Fouché entirely, however, and in 1810 finally pensioned him off to the Senate.

Despite his misgivings about each, Talleyrand and Fouché proved extremely useful to Napoleon as he put his stamp on the public life and international position of France. But alongside a mastery of foreign relations and political police work, respectively, their historical interest derives as well from their intrigues against Napoleon in 1814 and 1815 in the cause of a Bourbon restoration.

Lacking the sharply etched character of those two colleagues, sharing neither their confinement to a particular sphere of activity nor their ultimate desertion of Napoleon, there is one other figure on a par with Talleyrand and Fouché as a key civilian servitor of Napoleon, arguably his most significant collaborator from the beginning of the Consulate until the last day of the Empire in 1814. But who, outside the ranks of Napoleonic scholars, has even heard of Jean-Jacques-Régis Cambacérès?

A DECADE OF REVOLUTION

With the draft of a new constitution satisfactory to Bonaparte in hand, the legislative commission of Brumaire—the fifty self-selected remnants of the former legislative houses—had one final and supremely important task to perform. For they had reserved to themselves the power to choose the new heads of their government, the first, second, and third consuls. In the future, this duty was to be performed by a yet-to-be-chosen Senate, but the commission had decided that the first occupants of those offices should be named in the constitution itself. When the citizens of France voted in their forthcoming referendum, they would be approving not simply a constitution but the designation of their new leader.

An oft-told and irresistible account has come down to us about this event. Slips of paper were distributed to the members of the commission, filled in, and collected. But with perfect timing Bonaparte gathered up the ballots and said that it would be more fitting for Sieyès, the founding father of the new regime, to name the consuls in behalf of his colleagues. Such a stroke would ensure that Sieyès himself did not somehow emerge at the last moment at the head of the new government—an utterly unlikely possibility by then in any case—or that disgruntled parliamentarians might slip in the name of Daunou as third consul. Fatalistic enough to bow before this maneuver, Sieyès declared that General Bonaparte should be first consul, and then named as second and third consuls the two men known to be Bonaparte's choices. With that, the general tossed the unopened ballots into the fireplace, and the names of citizen Cambacérès and citizen Lebrun were duly inserted into the constitution alongside his own.[1]

Neither the second nor third consuls had any substantive power at all. Their functions were largely symbolic, their presence signifying only that in principle the French Republic still honored a notion of collective leadership as against bald one-man rule. In actuality, the constitution made the first consul supreme. True, he was to consult them on matters other than appointments (entirely his domain), but he did not need their approval of his decisions. An awkwardly phrased Article 42 stated: " . . . they have a consultative voice: they are to sign the registers of governmental acts in order to signify their presence; and if they wish they may enter their opinions, after which the decision of the first consul suffices." (Never, it hardly needs to be added, did they make use of that right to register public disagreement with Bonaparte's views.)[2] Despite their lofty titles, the second and third consuls were simply prominent, highly paid aides for the head of the government, entirely subordinate to his will.

The experience of the two men varied enough to create a supposition that each might reassure different elements of the body politic about the Consulate. Aged sixty-one at the time of Brumaire, Third Consul Lebrun came from a family of the judicial nobility and had achieved significant rank in royal service by the 1770s as secretary to Louis XV's chief minister Maupeou. Although he sat in the National Assembly of 1789 and later in the directorial legislature, the brumairians considered Lebrun a man of the old regime whose presence might appeal to moderate royalists. Cambacérès, forty-six at the time of Brumaire, also belonged to the nobility of the robe in Languedoc, where he had served as magistrate on an important royal court. Disappointed at falling short of election to the Estates General, he was later elected as head of his department's new criminal tribunal and then to the Convention in 1792. His reputation as a stalwart of the moderate revolution would presumably reassure republicans about the Consulate's future. Beyond that presumed difference, Lebrun's expertise lay in financial affairs while Cambacérès was known for his skills in legal and judicial matters, and in both those domains General Bonaparte presumably required a good deal of guidance.

Notwithstanding differences in age and experience, both consuls were men of the old regime who had readily adapted to the Revolution. Experienced public servants who had avoided any personal disaster during the revolutionary decade, both could be counted on for their malleability, an obvious prerequisite for collaboration with Napoleon. Given such fundamental similarities and their common lack of any constitutional authority independent of the first consul, one could reasonably conclude that little would distinguish the second from the third consul in the future. In reality, nothing could be further from the truth. Although the aging Lebrun remained a loyal servitor of Napoleon, munificently rewarded and among the notables of the regime until its end, their roles diverged quickly and decisively.

Cambacérès soon emerged as the second most important man in Napoleonic France. Perhaps that is not saying much, given the absolute grip on power that Bonaparte eventually established, but Napoleon's regime still bore the marks of Cambacérès's continuous presence: of his punctilious administrative skills, of his poise and distaste for intrigue, of his moderate inclinations, of his dedication to legal forms, of his prudent manner in exercising authority or counseling Napoleon that on occasion blunted the raw impact of the leader's willfulness.

WHEN the first consul regarded Cambacérès, he must have seen a man for all seasons of the Revolution, whose vicissitudes of fortune during that decade had left intact a respected figure in the the new national political elite. A typical deputy of the unaligned center of the National Convention, Cambacérès had, with nettlesome but minor qualifications, managed to survive with honor. Bonaparte chose a man whose recognized capacity for hard work and competence bespoke dedication without fanaticism, ambition without inordinate egotism, a sense of realism and adaptability.

The trial of Louis XVI, however, had proved to be an excruciating ordeal for the representative from Montpellier. Cambacérès initially joined those deputies vainly opposing the Convention's right to hold such a trial in the first place, for which he earned a denunciation back home in the local Jacobin club. During the trial he did not wish to condemn the ex-monarch to death, but did see the merits of that distasteful option or at any rate the need to appease its advocates. In the series of votes that followed, few if any members of the Convention agonized and waffled as much as Cambacérès. Indeed, to this day it is difficult to integrate his contradictory turns into a clear sense of whether or not he was actually a regicide. He did vote for the death penalty, but with the explicit qualification that the sentence be carried out only if the national territory was invaded. After a slim majority of his colleagues had voted unequivocally for execution, they balloted on a reprieve (*sursis*) and Cambacérès voted affirmatively. Yet on the question of holding a referendum (an "appeal to the people"), he voted against. That equivocal series of votes would haunt him for the rest of his life, as we shall see, but in the immediate aftermath of the trial his radical colleagues seemed sufficiently placated to regard him as an asset.[3]

Subsequently, Cambacérès, unlike about one hundred other moderate deputies, accepted the purge of the Girondins (who had denied him the ministry of justice back in 1792) and accommodated himself to the Montagnard radicals of 1793–94. Out of the spotlight in the Convention's obscure committee on legislation he began the herculean task of crafting the first draft of a civil code. His moment in the sun came after the fall of Robespierre, when the Convention turned to him as one of its ablest and most reliable members. For almost the entire thermidorian period they invested him with leadership positions on their committees and he clearly seemed destined to be named to the five-man Directory under the new constitution of 1795.

During that interim period, since the Convention still exercised functions that would normally fall to the executive, a routine decree suspending a recently promoted military officer was handed to Cambacérès for his co-signature. The young general, furious at this arbitrary treatment, went directly to Cambacérès's residence early one morning to plead his case and demand redress. Fortunately for both their sakes, Cambacérès did not take offense and throw the man out. The officer's intensity impressed the legislator, and he agreed to rescind the decree. Perhaps neither forgot this passing episode; certainly General Bonaparte did not.[4]

AS THE CONVENTION drew to a close, however, Cambacérès's fortunes took a sudden plunge. A tangential involvement with a notorious royalist plotter caused his colleagues to back away from him, and to reconsider the ambivalence of his votes during the king's trial. Since they wanted to populate the new Directory with regicides as a guarantee against any compromise with royalism, they excluded Cambacérès from consideration for a position that he manifestly merited and deeply desired. "A kind of cabal was formed with the purpose of keeping me out of the Directory," he claimed in a short unpublished memoir written during the Restoration. "Soon I was being presented as a deserter of the republican cause . . . that it would be imprudent to confer the reins of the State on someone who had not voted for the king's death."[5]

Ironically, Cambacérès could not really object to that interpretation since he had convinced himself that he was not in fact a regicide. Later, when Bonaparte took the more conventional view and twitted him for being a regicide, Cambacérès did not think it very amusing. More to the point, voices in the Restoration government of 1815 continued to see him as a regicide and as such they exiled him from France. To the end of his days he could not erase that stigma, try as he might. As the young aristocrat and imperial servitor Pasquier observed in his valuable memoirs: "The care he has taken to wash his hands of the death of Louis XVI sufficiently shows that it has been the torture of his life."[6]

In any case, instead of reaching the summit of political power in the republic, a chagrined Cambacérès continued on in the new legislature until 1797, when his term expired and he failed to win reelection in the royalist tide. This halt in his political career at least spared Cambacérès from the factional conflict that exploded when the new deputies of 1797 (a mix of ultra-conservatives and outright royalists) took their seats. The rancorous confrontation between centrist republicans and their opponents on the right eventually spilled beyond normal politics into an apparent willingness on each side to resort to force. The directorials acted first (with the backing of General Bonaparte in Italy, it will be recalled), by purging their parliamentary opponents in the coup of Fructidor Year V and deporting over fifty outspoken oppositionist politicians and journalists. In some quarters Cambacérès was suspected of sympathy for the losing side—he had after all been spurned by the directorials and was no doubt repulsed by yet another purge. Had he actually been in the legislature at the time, he might well have ended among the victims of the purge, as his friend Thibaudeau almost did. No doubt exaggerating, Cambacérès later claimed that "it was not without difficulty that I was able to escape from deportation on 18 Fructidor." Be that as it may, he was not directly involved in the great schism of Fructidor that shredded republican legality in order to save the republic.[7]

Meanwhile, Cambacérès turned for his livelihood to the practice of law.

While still a legislator in 1797, he had already opened an office specializing in financial, maritime, and international consultations. Thanks to his many connections in Paris and Montpellier, his honoraria quickly grew. While he recorded a modest 708 livres in fees for the first month of the Year VI (1797–98), in the last month of that year he earned 3,505 livres. Across the Year VI, a year of stable money, his practice brought in an impressive total of 22,669 livres.[8] Intent on amassing capital, Cambacérès not only lived within his means but took pains to save systematically. His accumulated assets rose during the Year VI from 5,608 to 21,142 livres, a pattern that would continue in the future at ever-increasing multiples, as we shall see.

Temporarily relegated to private life, Cambacérès was not forgotten in political circles. In the spring elections of the Year VI (1798), he found himself in the strange position of being supported by the Neo-Jacobins, who dominated the majority faction of the Paris electoral assembly after that body split apart. The Neo-Jacobins chose Cambacérès and a few other moderates such as Monge, Berlier, and Roger Ducos as a cover for more partisan and notorious Neo-Jacobin candidates. Cambacérès (who garnered 336 votes out of 396 cast) would have been pleased to return to parliamentary life, but was probably more bemused than infuriated when the Directory orchestrated a purge of *that* year's elections, having concluded that a mortal threat to the republic now came from the left. The coup of Floréal Year VI nullified the elections of some or all deputies in twenty-nine departments, including the entire slate chosen by the majoritarian Neo-Jacobin faction of the Paris electoral assembly.[9]

The Floréal purge devastated the Neo-Jacobins, but for Cambacérès this passing episode did not preclude a rebound in more auspicious circumstances. A year later a new Directory led by Sieyès tapped him to serve as minister of justice, and in that post he readily transferred his loyalty to the brumairians a few months later. Although he was not part of the inner circle of plotters, he signaled his support, and, as we have seen, proved useful to them in the early days of the coup.

THE SECOND CONSUL

So much, then, for Cambacérès's résumé. To Bonaparte, Cambacérès appeared as a stalwart but moderate revolutionary, despite his elusive political convictions and the two or three bumps in his public career. With his lawyerly temperament—a certain gravitas, a capacity for attention to the smallest detail—Cambacérès was widely respected for competence, hard work, and a mastery of legal and legislative arcanae. A realist rather than the kind of ideologue or "man of systems" that Napoleon despised, the cautious Cambacérès had accommodated himself to several unappealing political conjunctures. A negative view of that quality is easy enough to imagine. As Molé, a thoroughly offensive aristocratic servitor of Napoleon after 1806, put it in his memoirs: "Having no other passion than to take care of himself, Cambacérès waited for circumstances to bring him to the attention of the prevailing party. . . . There he sought out the men of action flushed with victory, who wished to give their success the sanction of law." Typical of Restoration polemics against Cambacérès, Molé's words contain a measure of truth but are too uninflected and one-sided.[10]

The words Cambacérès used in his twilight years to describe his behavior in the Revolution are more apt and could as easily describe his subsequent relationship to Napoleon: "One has to know how to move with one's century. . . . I had to cede to the general movement and give myself over to the torrent of innovation."[11] These lines mirror the more nuanced portrait of Cambacérès in the memoirs of Pasquier. This young ex-aristocrat of distinguished lineage entered Napoleon's service in 1806 in the Council of State, came to know Cambacérès, rose to become prefect of police in 1810, and made a brilliant career during the Restoration after abandoning Napoleon. Pasquier no doubt took Cambacérès's measure so perceptively because he himself was a prize-winning opportunist and worshiper of power.

> A stranger to any system of philosophy, endowed with one of the most positive minds that ever existed, he had allowed himself to be carried away by the first waves of the Revolution, rather than plunging into them. The advantages he could derive therefrom were counter-balanced by many dangers, which would doubtless have held him back, had it not been that the party of the Revolution was the strongest. His was a nature governed more by prudence than by courage. . . . [In the Convention] he soon made his mark by his remarkable aptitude for work, by his genuine acquaintance with all questions of jurisprudence. . . . [and by] his obsequiousness towards the revolutionary party.

With survival as a priority, and the assumption that influence comes most readily from power, Cambacérès waited patiently for recognition.[12]

So different from Bonaparte in personality, upbringing, and experience, Cambacérès proved to be an indispensable adviser and agent. Were he inclined to think in American terms, Bonaparte might have seen in Cambacérès the ideal vice president. Less obvious at first, but fortuitously suited to Napoleon's own evolution, Cambacérès, for all his immersion in the Revolution, remained (like Talleyrand) nostalgic for the grace, security, and order of the old regime. Again, Pasquier points us in the right direction: "His memory dwelt with pleasure on the times which preceded the Revolution. When in his private circle, he enjoyed recalling and extolling the advantages of the social organization of those happy and tranquil days."[13]

Moreover, Cambacérès proved to be exceptionally vain about the outward signs of recognition, a quality that expanded apace alongside the new perquisites and status symbols offered in abundance by the Napoleonic regime. Censuring this "pettiness of spirit," Pasquier described the sheer personal enjoyment that Cambacérès derived from social distinctions: "Never did titles, crosses, and ribands give anyone more pleasure than they did him. His whole delight lay in displaying them."[14] But this personal idiosyncrasy made Cambacérès just the man to internalize Napoleon's more cynical belief in the value of "baubles" in governing his people. Thus, when Napoleon decided to create a new imperial nobility in 1808, Cambacérès became president of his *Conseil du sceau* and willingly took on the tedious detail of titles, hierarchies, entails (*majorats*), and even the design of escutcheons.

WHEN he took the oath of office as second consul, Cambacérès entered terra incognita, an entirely unconceptualized situation. The Consulate's underlying agenda was clear enough—depoliticization, strong executive leadership, peace through military victory, and movement toward national reconciliation. But what would be his veritable role, since the constitution seemed to make his post a sinecure, a window-dressing of collegiality disguising one-man rule?

At the least the post of second consul brought access to Bonaparte. The general could of course discourage or ignore any advice coming from his second consul, but he did not. Access translated into the role of private adviser on a range of crucial matters. Besides seeking his recommendations on major appointments (senators, ministers, prefects, judges), Bonaparte over the years invited Cambacérès's candid opinion on the most sensitive issues such as the reintegration of émigrés, the Concordat, the treatment of the duc d'Enghien, the life consulship, the transition to an hereditary empire, the creation of a new nobility, the invasion of Spain, the divorce and Austrian marriage, and the problem of Russia. Often Cambacérès counseled actions more prudent than Napoleon's rash inclinations; by his own account, he consistently urged a less belligerent foreign policy and sang the virtues of peace. Obviously his influence in that domain was negligible. But on more limited matters he seemed to exercise a salutary calming influence. Here is how a reliable eyewitness, Cambacérès's boyhood friend Chaptal, the minister of interior from November 1800 to July 1804, described it:

> The only two people who succeeded in mitigating Bonaparte's angers were Cambacérès and Josephine. The former never attempted to confront or contradict that impetuous character directly. That would have only pushed him to greater violence. Rather, he gave his fury a chance to develop fully, he gave him time to dictate the most iniquitous decrees; he prudently waited for the moment when that temper had spent itself without constraint to then offer some reflections. And if he did not always succeed in getting the measure in question revoked, he frequently managed to soften it. I have often admired the calm and skill of Cambacérès in such matters, and several times I have seen him ward off great misfortunes.[15]

Less to Cambacérès's credit, Bonaparte relied on him to help sidestep the inertial effects of existing laws when he wished to act decisively. With his detailed mastery of law on one side and his opportunistic bent on the other, Cambacérès played that game deftly. And if all else failed—if reason of state dictated a course of action simply incompatible with existing law—Cambacérès could advise Napoleon that he need not be constrained by technical legalities, although no minister or faceless bureaucrat could authorize such extralegal measures, only the first consul or emperor himself. In framing the question of how to combat severe brigandage in two interior military divisions, for example, Cambacérès acknowledged that an existing law authorizing the war minister to create military commissions (ad hoc military courts under martial law) did not apply in this case. He suggested, however, that Napoleon was free to order their establishment himself, regardless of that law. With typically supple (or cynical) reasoning he explained:

> The establishment of two military commissions obviously exceeds the ministerial power. The situation is not grave enough to require emergency

action (*procéder d'urgence*); the War Minister proposes to address a draft decree to Your Majesty which seems to me well crafted. The interest of the state being always the supreme law, it is sometimes necessary to move away from the ordinary route. But that power belongs only to Your Majesty alone. It was that way in the Year IX when, to pacify the departments of the Ardèche and the Lozère, military commissions were established, despite the fact that the legislation did not in any way authorize such a disposition.[16]

There were limits to how far Cambacérès would go. When the first consul ordered the kidnapping to France of the duc d'Enghien—the Bourbon prince residing in Baden whom Bonaparte believed (mistakenly) to be involved in a royalist plot against the Consulate—Cambacérès strenuously counseled Bonaparte against executing the hapless prince. When Bonaparte spurned his advice and ordered a summary military trial, the second consul literally turned his back in revulsion. But in the main, the devastating comment of Molé is not too far from the mark: "No one could employ greater knowledge or skill to justify with legal forms the acts of sheer power, and give the appearance of legality to [Napoleon's] most violent rashness."[17]

With the rarest exceptions, once Napoleon made up his mind, all previous reservations usually evaporated and Cambacérès could be counted on to support his course of action. From that fount of trust on Bonaparte's side and of unqualified submission on Cambacérès's part, and from his demonstrable competence in matters large and small, other roles followed. Cambacérès regularly chaired the Council of State when Bonaparte was otherwise engaged or uninterested. Overseeing major policy debates and supervising complex drafting projects became his most sustained and tangible contribution to the Napoleonic regime. (That he would contribute substantively to the Council's great efforts at legal codification goes without saying, although he was not a member of the original drafting committee for the Civil Code.) In addition, he early became Bonaparte's point man for managing the pliant but prickly Senate. But it was Bonaparte's unique dual power as head of state and active commander-in-chief of the army that engendered Cambacérès's most distinctive role.[18]

WARMING NAPOLEON'S CHAIR

From 1800 to 1814, Bonaparte spent nearly a third of his time far from the Tuileries, Malmaison, or Saint-Cloud, mostly on military campaigns. The brumairians expected him to secure a comprehensive peace through military victory and at first Bonaparte did not disappoint them. His victory at Marengo (June 1800) combined with General Moreau's triumphs in Germany finally culminated in March 1802 in the Peace of Amiens with an isolated Britain. That treaty brought Bonaparte passionate acclaim from his collaborators and from the French people, but it proved only a truce, not a genuine peace. War resumed on an ever greater geographic and human scale, as Napoleon embarked on more frequent, longer, and more distant campaigns. Thus, between 1804 and 1810, Napoleon led his armies in the field for about thirty-eight months, including a stretch from September 1806 to July 1807 for campaigns against Prussia and Russia, and from April to October 1809 for yet another war with Austria.[19]

Guarding Napoleon's seat (or, after 1804, his throne) therefore became Cambacérès's preeminent duty. Bonaparte's first absence in the spring of 1800 for the Italian campaign lasted two months, and occurred well before the regime had settled in, so to speak. In that interlude Cambacérès exercised a degree of initiative that would not be permitted in the future. While prefects and councilors of state had been selected before Bonaparte's departure, Cambacérès on his own authority saw to the appointment of various sub-prefects, judges, mayors, and departmental counselors. Work also began on the clearance (*radiation*) of émigrés who applied for repatriation. While a commission of thirty members had been appointed to carry out the actual vetting, its personnel ("thirty illustrious unknowns," as one historian put it) required direction from Cambacérès, Bonaparte's designee to supervise the whole process. Beyond such matters, Bonaparte's very absence could produce negative side effects back home, which became matters of urgent concern. The uncertainty entailed in a distant military campaign, for example, might encourage speculation in shares of the public debt on the Bourse or in the price of subsistence supplies.[20]

The second consul's responsibilities were all the greater since several ministers were proving ineffective or untrustworthy. The loyalty of Fouché, seemingly indispensable as police minister, was always suspect; War Minister Carnot, away at the front himself for much of that time, left something of a vacuum in Paris; Minister of Justice Abrial, at best a cipher, would be pastured out to the Senate in 1802; and Minister of the Interior Lucien Bonaparte (to be relieved of his post even sooner, in November 1800) was negligent in his own domains and meddlesome in everyone else's.

As the first consul's grip on the reins of power tightened, Cambacérès never enjoyed the same latitude of action during Bonaparte's subsequent campaigns, but he continued until the end of the Empire to be Napoleon's surrogate back in Paris and his principal source of information during those intervals. After 1800 Bonaparte in effect took the government with him when he left Paris in the person of Hugues Maret's secretariat. Henceforth he himself would be signing all decrees, no matter how far from Paris he was or how long the delays.[21] Still, while his ministers reported to Napoleon directly, he instructed Cambacérès to coordinate their activities when necessary, and to convene weekly ministerial meetings for that purpose. In addition, Cambacérès would preside over the Council of State, lead the Senate, monitor the legislature when it was in session, and supervise any *conseils privés* deemed necessary. When the establishment of the Empire eliminated the post of second consul, one of Napoleon's very first acts was to name Cambacérès as archchancellor of the Empire, under which title he carried on exactly as before.

His principal skill lay in distilling the essentials of any situation and clarifying the issues awaiting Bonaparte's decision. This information he conveyed in daily letters sent out by courier, and despite time lags that sometimes became agonizing, the steady flow of correspondence back and forth kept the wheels of government turning, however ponderously. In these letters, Cambacérès also proffered the kind of advice that Napoleon always sought from him on personnel and policy issues. But instead of doing so orally and in private he was now making these comments part of the documentary record, to the benefit of historians.

Amazingly, these letters from Cambacérès to Napoleon vanished completely after 1815 for almost one hundred fifty years. Historians had long since reconciled themselves to the permanent loss of this invaluable source when the original drafts of 1,397 letters surfaced in the hands of a private collector, who eventually turned them over to the French National Archives. After authentication, these letters written between 1802 and 1814 (with a gap for 1812) were published in 1973 in a superb edition by Jean Tulard, a leading Napoleonic scholar.[22]

The letters show that warming Napoleon's seat during his prolonged absences drew on every bit of Cambacérès's finesse and insight into his patron's temperament. With a scrupulous, self-effacing competence, he was expected to handle any unforeseen contingency, yet was also enjoined to defer any decision, if at all possible, until Napoleon had been consulted. It was a constant challenge for Cambacérès to operate effectively within these prescribed limits, to avoid any irreparable blunders, and to maintain Napoleon's trust yet defend his own sense of status and dignity. How anyone could be suited for such a bizarre job description remains a matter of wonderment, but Cambacérès filled it with poise and a high measure of success. His aversion to intrigue surely contributed to this success, and a fawning epistolary style no doubt reassured his chief even as Cambacérès, in a sometimes whiny fashion, defended himself against Napoleon's periodic reproaches.

THE CHALLENGE in steering between subordination and deference on the one hand and effective stewardship on the other can be seen in a minor incident that erupted in the spring of 1807, when Cambacérès became embroiled with Monsieur de Luçay, Napoleon's prefect of the palace. With jurisdiction over the state theaters of Paris, de Luçay had just dismissed Bonnet as director of the Paris Opéra after a mishap had occurred in that theater. Cambacérès objected to the dismissal as being beyond de Luçay's authority, since Bonnet's original appointment had been signed by Napoleon. He insisted that de Luçay's *arrêté* be suspended for the time being, and the two men became locked in a contest of wills. As Cambacérès first described the situation to Napoleon—encamped in eastern Germany as he prepared to resume battle with Russia—he recapitulated his sense of serving as the Emperor's surrogate:

> I regard it as unnecessary to point out to Your Majesty the insolence of M. de Luçay's conduct in my regard. The excessive impropriety that it presents will not escape Your Majesty. You invested me, Sire, with your confidence and with a great latitude of power [not exactly!]. Your Ministers take no important decision without informing me: I transmit their reports to you along with my opinion, and it is strange that M. de Luçay wishes to treat with me as equal to equal, and submits a decision that has nothing urgent about it, and which he ought not have permitted himself to carry out until he had received orders from Your Majesty to do so. However, I am not in the habit of tolerating someone who violates the rules and commits excesses. If Your Majesty was in Paris, M. de Luçay would doubt-

less have reported to you on what he believed he had to do, so that Your
Majesty would have been able to pronounce at the same time on the
claims of M. Bonnet. I have [therefore] forwarded to the Minister of Interior the *arrêté* of M. de Luçay and his letter, directing him to draw up a
report. As soon as that report is presented to me, I will call in the Minister of Police, and after consulting him, will take the decision that seems
most fitting under the present circumstances and will have the honor of
reporting it to Your Majesty.

I have reason to hope, Sire, that this resolution will obtain your approval.
Your Majesty certainly does not desire authority to weaken, and you have
advised me never to be feeble.[23] As long as M. de Luçay only committed
imprudent acts in his administration, I have not had to concern myself
with it at all. But I cannot remain indifferent when he has allowed himself
to deprive a man [Bonnet] provisionally of a position that he holds from
Your Majesty. . . .[24]

In subsequent letters Cambacérès revealed his strong opinions about the
principals in this little drama. "M. de Luçay is a good fellow (*bonhomme*),
who is not too smart and who lets himself be led by someone named Lecraye,
his secretary, a man with a bad reputation who gives him very poor advice."
As to Bonnet (an ex-*conventionnel* and Girondin no doubt known to Cambacérès personally from the 1790s): "What is said about M. Bonnet is false;
he is an honest man, devoted to Your Majesty's service, whom M. de Luçay
does not like because the sieur Lecraye wishes to become Director [of the
Opéra], which on no account must happen."[25]

Yet the forceful and considered line that Cambacérès had taken did not
meet with Napoleon's unqualified approval. While apparently backing Cambacérès on the substance of the matter for the time being, he felt that the
archchancellor himself had exceeded his authority in some subtle fashion.
Cambacérès replied to this admonition with a combination of contrition and
self-justification that further clarifies how he tried to operate within his constricted limits:

Your Majesty in his letter of the 7th has informed me that I must take no
resolution until I have received from you a special authorization. Henceforth I will conform to that order.

The error that I committed arises from my reading of the decree of 21
March less as containing a new attribution than as regulating the exercise

of a power already delegated in the general order of service. The latter authorizes me to decide, in urgent situations, after having heard the Ministers, but it does not prescribe anything about the form of the decision. . . . From now on I ought only to resolve, instead of deciding, and I must remain within the limits of the powers that Your Majesty has traced, provided that I am careful to pronounce only on urgent matters, upon the impetus of a Minister and while taking care not to make my signature public. Your Majesty's letter informs me of his intentions in a precise manner, and I will follow them to the letter. I would be grieved if Your Majesty could believe that I had permitted myself to extend the attributions that he has deigned to confer on me. Such a course will never enter my thoughts: it would be contrary to my duties and contrary to my conduct past and present.[26]

INSISTENT on retaining all authority in his own hands even when away from Paris, Napoleon also obsessed about controlling every morsel of information that reached the public about his military campaigns. When leading his armies, however, this masterly manipulator of public opinion had to rely on Cambacérès as his agent on the scene to control the flow of information, monitor the newspapers, combat false rumors, and arrange for the optimal distribution of his *bulletins*, which converted costly victories on distant battlefields into reassuring images of glory. Both before and after the fact of any military victory, Cambacérès helped conduct the ongoing battle for public opinion on the home front as a low-keyed minister of propaganda.

In private, to be sure, he confided to Napoleon his concern over the inordinate risks that the emperor took. Cambacérès knew better than to appeal to Napoleon on the grounds of his personal safety, since the general was genuinely indifferent to danger, but chided him in the name of the French people. I try to ignore dark rumors, he wrote to the emperor in Austria in May 1809, "but I still endure a kind of terror and, even if you must reproach me for this, I will permit myself to say to Your Majesty, in the name of all his subjects, that henceforth he ought not expose himself [to such danger] as he has done up to this point."[27]

While deploring empty rumors about his demise, Napoleon insisted that no one in Paris jump the gun with premature messages about far-off victories, since he wished to fashion his subtly mendacious narrative of these events himself. Thus, in March 1807, Cambacérès reassured him: "Your Majesty informs me by his letter of 5 March that he was troubled to see the notes placed in the *Moniteur* on 20 and 21 February. Circumstances seemed to us to require the placement of those items. Henceforth, I will permit only the publication of the Bulletin."[28] But the emperor continued to complain about this matter, to which Cambacérès responded first by contrition ("I have experienced a painful and sorrowful feeling" at having mishandled this) and then by offering a detailed account in justification of his action. In conclusion he addressed a point of special concern to the emperor: "Your Majesty has reiterated what he has said previously about the exaggeration of our losses. I have taken pains on all occasions to impart the direction to public opinion that it requires on this important issue. . . . I have spoken with animation in a salon of new converts who do not express themselves as I would desire on the events of the campaign. . . ."[29]

MANAGING THE LEGISLATURE

Bonaparte assigned Cambacérès to monitor the legislature, the more so when he could not exert his influence on the legislators personally. After colluding with the Senate to suppress the Tribunate in 1807—that element of the Brumaire settlement most explicitly keyed to liberal values—the emperor reorganized the surviving Corps Législatif. Until then, its three hundred deputies had been entirely passive: they listened to presentations about proposed laws from spokesmen for the Council of State (which had drafted the laws) and for the Tribunate (which had debated the proposals and cast non-binding votes); then they voted by secret ballot without debate. Now the Corps was authorized to name three committees (finances, legislation, interior), parallel to sections of the Council of State, to review bills sent up by the government (as the executive branch was invariably called). Such preliminary discussion would give the Corps a new proactive role, and was intended to promote greater harmony in the legislative process, since the committees could propose modifications to the Council of State before a bill was sent to the full house for an up or down vote.

Napoleon considered the legislature an encumbrance to be minimized and avoided as much as possible. Over the years he submitted fewer and fewer laws for its consideration, as he governed increasingly by executive decrees and shunted the approval of conscription levies to the pliant Senate. But he could not sidestep the legislature when it came to annual budgets or the great work of codification in civil and criminal law. Whatever Cambacérès personally may have felt about this vestige of representative government, he adapted to Napoleon's grudging stance. "The committees of the Corps Législatif have been meeting," he reported in October 1808 to the emperor, who was in Erfurt negotiating with Tsar Alexander. "It is necessary to give them something to do. We have a few minor laws for the [committee on] Finances and two sections of the Criminal Code for the [Committee on] Legislation."[30]

Napoleon could not abide significant negative votes even if the Corps hardly ever rejected a proposed law outright. When he sensed that a proposal faced serious opposition, Cambacérès had to decide whether to withdraw it before any voting took place. Usually negotiation between the government and the legislative committees worked smoothly under the new system. During the session of 1808, the Corps's finance committee suggested certain minor modifications to a proposed law on finances, which the Council of State adopted before resubmitting the law, and the committee's observation on laws regulating monetary exchange led the Council of State to withdraw one of those laws altogether. Sometimes, however, Cambacérès balked at criticism in these legislative committees and recommended sterner tactics. When a proposed law on national properties met resistance in the Corps Législatif's finance committee (as it had in the Council of State itself), Cambacérès dug in his heels: "The observations were so numerous and tended so directly to undermine the system of the law, that the Council of State was of the opinion not to present the law during the course of the present session, which is already well advanced. It is believed in any case that it would be easy to attain the same end by an imperial decree, which would be preferable to the course of confronting the Corps Législatif with this matter. There, Sire, is what was resolved in the Council of State yesterday, awaiting your pleasure."[31]

The five great legal codes drafted in the Council of State—the Civil Code, Code of Civil Procedure, Penal Code, Code of Criminal Procedure, and Commercial Code—formed the most complex and contentious matters placed before the legislature. Fierce debates in the Tribunate and even the rejection of several sections of the Civil Code had marked the first presentation of these projects, as we have seen. With the Tribunate now abolished, the process became less daunting for the government, but still, as Cambacérès reported in 1808, "The Code of Criminal Procedure is not universally savored by the Corps Législatif. I would imagine that the Penal Code is even less so if presented in its present form."[32] Determined to proceed nonetheless, Cambacérès sought the help of Napoleon's handpicked president of the Corps— a key ally in managing that body.

When Napoleon became emperor, he decided to provide the Corps with a president named by himself instead of an inconsequential rotating presidency. As Cambacérès remarked à propos of the president's tenure: "The Corps Législatif is now governed monarchically; it would fall into anarchy if one left it without a leader for a month."[33] Napoleon chose the president each year from a list of five nominees presented by the house in an order of preference which he was free to ignore.

Louis Fontanes—an ex-noble, classical poet, playwright, and man of letters in the old regime—had turned to political journalism during the Revolution and found himself on the deportation list of Fructidor Year V for his royalist-leaning opinions. Repatriated after a brief exile in England, where a strong friendship with Chateaubriand began, he rallied to Bonaparte unlike his new friend. Well connected through the social circle of the first consul's sister Elisa, he was named by the Senate as a deputy to the Corps Législatif in 1802, and stood out enough in that body of faceless men to win nomination for its presidency and Napoleon's designation in 1804. His lush, obsequious rhetoric in service of the regime kept him in the post for five successive terms, after which he was promoted to the Senate and named first grand master of the Napoleonic University. By 1808 the Corps understood the rules of the game, as Cambacérès reported: "After the message that you have addressed to the Corps Législatif, Sire, M. de Fontanes was presented, with an almost unanimous vote, as its first candidate for the presidency."[34]

Cambacérès now closeted himself with Fontanes to avoid any embarrassments for the government. "Having been warned that the first section of the code of criminal procedure was encountering opposition, I thought it useful to invite the president to make known to his colleagues all the reasons for not rejecting a project that must at least be given a trial." Fontanes did so and the Corps adopted one section of the code that day by a vote of 178 to 85, while a second section passed a few days later with 72 negative votes. "The president's presence was necessary," Cambacérès reported, "for the salutary influence that he exercised on his colleagues . . . in regard to the sections of the criminal code, which would have veritably been rejected if the president had not brought over several voters by his counsel." Knowing that the emperor would still react angrily to so many dissenting votes, Cambacérès reminded him how issues such as trial by jury made this a legitimately contentious issue, one which had divided, indeed immobilized, the Council of State itself for several years.[35]

Fontanes had warned Cambacérès "that there are also some difficulties with the budget law" stemming from a last-minute addenda to the project. But a few days later, the archchancellor had good news to report: "The budget law passed yesterday, most honorably, since out of 272 votes cast there were 262 for the adoption of the project. . . . The deputies from the departments where viticulture dominates were resistant to the new organization of the taxes on wines; it was necessary to convert them, and we succeeded thanks to the effect of the good spirit that reigns in the Corps Législatif." To Napoleon, this was the way things were supposed to work.[36]

THE PRIVATE SIDE OF A PUBLIC LIFE

The Cambacérès family had deep roots in the elite of old-regime Languedoc. Four generations held the post of *conseiller* (magistrate) in the prestigious Cour des Comptes of Montpellier, Languedoc's second city, while other relatives ensconced themselves in the middle ranks of the church. Through the influence of his uncle, a prominent regional notable, the second consul's father Jean-Antoine Cambacérès (1715–1801) won a choice royal appointment in the 1750s as mayor of Montpellier.

The domestic fortunes of the family, however, were less enviable than its public position. Jean-Antoine's wife bore eleven children, but only two survived, the future consul (b. 1753) and Etienne-Hubert (b. 1755). When Cambacérès was sixteen, his mother died and his father formed a household with Jeanne Dittry, whom he eventually married and who bore him a son and a daughter. While not estranged from his father and stepmother, Cambacérès was not especially close to them as he continued his education and followed family tradition in 1774 by entering the company of magistrates in the Cour des Comptes. By that time, his quarrelsome father had little to offer him: embroiled in various public controversies, Jean-Antoine dissipated his financial resources and ended his days in debt. Cambacérès could count on nothing from his father's tangled and deteriorating finances—indeed, in 1802 he would be obliged to settle the debts in his father's estate for 60,000 livres.[37]

Both Jean-Jacques-Régis and Etienne-Hubert remained celibate, the latter having entered the priesthood. When he became second consul in 1800, Cambacérès thus enjoyed neither the encumbrance nor the rewards of a large immediate family. He had no wife, in-laws, children, or children's spouses and in-laws to deal with. His collateral and step-relatives, on the other hand, formed a web of important relationships around him; the two sons of his half brother Hubert—a front-line general in the revolutionary and imperial army—indeed became Cambacérès's official heirs. The eldest, a particular favorite of the archchancellor, inherited his Napoleonic title, two-thirds of his enormous estate, and the task of defending his uncle's posthumous reputation.

The second consul did a great deal for his younger sibling, Etienne-Hubert, who experienced the revolutionary decade as a harried refractory priest. Cambacérès had no problem with his brother's clerical vocation for, as he stated in his last will and testament, "I have lived my life in the faith of the Catholic apostolic church." This he reaffirmed by leaving a valuable property in Languedoc to a monastery in exchange for its pledge (typical of old-regime practice) "to have a grand mass said each year on the anniversary of my death for the repose of my soul."[38]

When Bonaparte signaled his desire to negotiate an agreement with the papacy, his closest advisers split into opposing camps, with Cambacérès prominent among the initiative's supporters. On the political plane this reflected his sense of realism—that *la France profonde* rejected the secularizing legacy of the Revolution and desired the restoration of its accustomed religious practices. His own low-keyed religious traditionalism, including regular attendance at Sunday mass after 1802, evidently meshed comfortably with his lifelong commitment to Freemasonry—whose filiations and importance to him are documented in remarkable detail by a recent biographer.[39]

When the Concordat of 1802 restored the fortunes of the refractory clergy, Cambacérès prevailed on Bonaparte to appoint his brother as archbishop of Rouen, just as the first consul was naming his own uncle, Joseph Fesch, as archbishop of Lyon. Three years later, a cardinal's hat and an appointment by Napoleon to the Senate elevated Etienne-Hubert even higher, right alongside Cardinal Fesch. In sum, Etienne-Hubert received the most bountiful patronage imaginable from the influence of his eminent brother.

While the cardinal repaid this consideration with an unquestioned devotion to the emperor, he was not especially sensitive in his relations with local officials. In April 1805, Napoleon complained to Cambacérès about an embarrassing conflict between the cardinal-archbishop of Rouen and the prefect in his diocesan seat, Beugnot. Archbishop Cambacérès insisted on the prerogative of local vestries (*fabriques*) to control interments (and the fees resulting therefrom), while the prefect defended the rights of entrepreneurs who had previously won contracts to provide that service. With each side making legitimate claims, the emperor expected that the dispute would be settled in a spirit of compromise—a quality the archbishop conspicuously lacked, just as his father before him reputedly lacked it as mayor of Montpellier.

This imbroglio took Cambacérès by surprise since he had believed that the two principals enjoyed a cordial relationship. He of course offered to mediate, although he expressed sympathy for the canonical interests defended by his brother, and believed that "it would also be good if those who hold civil authority were, at least in appearance, a little more religious." On the other hand, he knew his brother's prickly temperament and would gain an even sharper sense of it as relations between archbishop and prefect grew more "envenomed." Each submitted angry briefs to the emperor, but the archbishop surpassed his adversary by tendering his resignation until such time as "Your Majesty appointed a prefect in the department who justified his confidence." Failing as a mediator, Cambacérès glumly admitted: "I appreciate that the expressions used by the Cardinal are most inappropriate and I disapprove of such blustering (*jactance*), for which I ask Your Majesty's indulgence." Nepotistic patronage certainly carried its burdens.[40]

Etienne-Hubert was not the only relative to embarrass the archchancellor. Reading through Cambacérès's generally monotone correspondence to Napoleon, one is jolted by a letter of October 1804, addressed to the emperor in Boulogne where he was inspecting a military encampment:

It is with regret that I am obliged to occupy Your Majesty with a personal matter. The widow of my father, a very dangerous woman by her character and her conduct, about whom I have strong reason to complain on every count, has just arrived in Paris. This despite the fact that I had informed her that this trip, without any purpose for her, is gravely inconvenient for me and for her son [General Hubert Cambacérès], who is employed in the army at Boulogne.

I pay her a pension, although the law requires me to do nothing for her; and last year I paid her debts. She is coming here only to harass me and make scenes. I even have reason to believe that she is being urged on by enemies of the State; it is men of that type that have loaned her the money for her trip to Paris. And she has been received and lodged by one Mersan, a fructidorized ex-deputy, who could know her only through such intermediaries. Without dwelling any further on my fears, I limit myself, Sire, to invoking your authority to deliver me from this bloodsucker. I supplicate Your Imperial Majesty to have the Minister of Police order that Mme Veuve Cambacérès leave Paris and not approach within forty miles of my residence. I will pay the expenses of her trip if necessary. . . .[41]

The normally unflappable archchancellor seems almost terrified by what this mercurial woman might do to his reputation. But the same exalted position that made him vulnerable to public scandal also gave him the influence to shield himself from her tentacles. In short order Napoleon authorized Fouché to expel her from Paris as requested by his archchancellor.

GROWING RICH

Cambacérès arrived in Paris as a deputy to the National Convention in September 1792 with limited financial resources. His own property in 1792 consisted of a rural *bien national* near Montpellier purchased for 50,000 livres in 1791 that was not yet producing income, and some modest annuities (*rentes*) that yielded less than 1,000 livres a year. Both the *rentes* and the property were presumably financed from the compensation he received when the National Assembly abolished venal judgeships, including the Cour des Comptes, in 1790.[42]

Unlike many of his fellow deputies, he depended on his monthly parliamentary indemnity of 540 livres as his principal source of support in a time of galloping inflation. But Cambacérès brought to Paris an ingrained habit of living within his means and of putting money aside no matter how straitened his circumstances. As a reflection of this frugality, and of his obsession with money, he listed in his financial diaries (*livres de raison*) for 1792–94 virtually every expenditure no matter how trivial, alongside his monthly costs for food at 150 livres, rent of 72 livres, and wages for domestics of 25 livres. With his expenses averaging 350–400 livres a month, his cash balance increased modestly even in these cramped conditions. Since he kept these *livres de raison* across the years, it is easy follow his gradual financial ascent and then his spectacular enrichment under Napoleon.

In the Year VII (1798–99), after he left the legislature and consolidated his private law practice, his annual income grew from the 7,500 of his years in the Convention to 27,550 livres. Cambacérès earned over 24,000 livres that year from the practice of law, collected 1,450 livres from his national property in Languedoc, and drew 2,100 livres from *rentes*. Meanwhile, his living standard improved modestly as he paid rent of 1,200 livres for the year, purchased furniture (2,550), and employed more domestic help (1,300). Moreover, he could now offer assistance to his relatives: 1,860 livres for his father, 1,100 for his brother the priest, 1,100 for his half brother the general, and 1,220 for an uncle. Even so, his expenses totaled only 14,300 livres, meaning that he had saved almost half his income. Accordingly, his assets on hand grew from 14,600 livres at the beginning of the year to 29,500 by the end.[43]

Appointment as second consul brought a quantum jump in Cambacérès's income and lifestyle but no change in his habit of living within his means, saving, and investing carefully. With an income during the nine months of his first year as consul totaling over 203,000 livres, Cambacérès's lavish outlays included food at 17,926 livres; wine, 11,382; wages for domestics, 10,329; silverware, 14,402; stabling, 9,202; linen, 7,559; clothing, 5,853; and wood, 5,302. Still, his expenditures totaled only 102,700 livres, meaning that again he had saved almost half his annual income.[44]

Three years into the Consulate, the revenue side of his ledger rose dramatically. His official salary as second consul reached 271,000 francs (as the livre was now known), with a bonus (*supplément*) of 100,000 francs that year, plus an extra maintenance allowance of 77,000 francs—altogether 448,000 francs, apart from any private investment income. In the early years of the Empire his salary as archchancellor reached 50,000 per month, but after 1808 it was set at 32,777 francs per month, because he now drew substantial income from new Napoleonic endowments, first in the duchy of Parma in Italy (the emperor had named him duke of Parma), and later from German properties in Westphalia, Saxony, and Danzig—which the archchancellor prudently listed as "uncertain revenues" by 1813.[45]

Cambacérès had various ways of itemizing his revenues and assets, but the clearest picture comes from his *livres de raison* for the late Empire, where he recorded his private income separately from his official salary and emoluments. Although the latter did not equal the astronomical rewards going to Napoleon's favored marshals, they still dwarfed the income from his personal investments. But that private income stream was growing apace, and Cambacérès wisely gave pride of place in his accounting to those more durable revenues (see table).

Cambacérès invested shrewdly during the Napoleonic years, capitalizing on his connections and special opportunities without resorting to anything that smelled of corruption, such as involvement in the lucrative business of military supply contracts. His portfolio had the classic solidity and modest

Cambacérès's Income, 1810 and 1813

I. INCOME FROM LAND AND PERSONAL INVESTMENTS (including sums due)

	1810	1813
Land	52,800	110,952
Rentes (Annuities)	53,000	59,800
Interests in enterprises	17,800	27,000
Public Funds	26,800	5,400
(Subtotal)	150,400	203,152

II. OTHER REVENUES

	1810	1813
Archchancellor	330,000	330,000
Institut	900	750
Duchy of Parma	130,000	231,000
Saxony, Westphalia	—	100,000
(Subtotal)	460,900	661,750
Total	611,300	864,902

SOURCE: A.N. 286 AP 1: Livres de Raison, 1810, 1813.

breadth of a wealthy old regime *notable*. Land naturally constituted the core of his fortune. He had begun by purchasing a *bien national* in his native department of the Hérault in 1791, but thereafter shifted his purchases to the North. By 1813, he owned twelve substantial properties worth over 3 million francs, mostly in Normandy and the Paris region, including five holdings in the Seine-et-Marne department. In 1810, for example, he purchased the forest of Neuville (Aube) from Casimir Périer for 440,000 francs and then leased it back to him at 19,000 francs per annum. His most recent acquisition, Pléssis-Belleville (Oise), a 363-hectare property purchased in March 1812, cost him 900,000 francs and yielded over 40,000 francs annually in the first negotiated leasehold. Urban real estate did not figure significantly in his investments, but after residing for eight years rent-free in a state-owned building, the archchancellor purchased a luxurious mansion in the faubourg Saint-Germain in 1808 at a cost of 390,000 francs with a comparably large outlay for renovation, offset by a gift of 300,000 francs that Cambacérès solicited from the emperor for that purpose.[46]

Cambacérès's portfolio included annuities drawn on the consolidated national debt, and shares of the Banque de France, the Caisse de Services de Paris, and two canal companies. Between 1801 and 1811, he made three purchases totaling 200,000 francs in shares of the nation's blue-chip mining company, the Mines d'Anzin, a true insider's opportunity that yielded a lucrative return averaging 17 percent over the years. Capital also went out as a loan to Monsieur Gilles, who had married his half sister. As principal tax collector (*receveur général*) of the Seine-et-Oise department, Gilles required a substantial surety bond (*cautionnement*) that Cambacérès helped cover with 215,000 francs, bringing him a return averaging around 10,000 francs in annual interest when he bothered to collect it. After his exile in 1816 he diversified his holdings with investments outside of France, guided by baron Thibon, a director of the Banque de France whose daughter had married one of Cambacérès's nephews.[47]

With his increasingly generous emoluments from Napoleon, his habit of saving, and his meticulous investments, Cambacérès estimated that his accumulated assets totaled 5,370,000 francs by the end of 1813. About 1.3 million consisted of liquid assets—partly in household furnishings but a good part in specie, gold, and diamonds ("unproductive assets," as one might say), which he kept available in a strongbox for obvious reasons. In the ledger listing his living expenses for 1813, there is an enigmatic notation of 200,000 francs "for a particular use" (*pour un emploi particulier*), perhaps earmarked to build up his cash-on-hand reserves. Notwithstanding the subsequent vicissitudes of Cambacérès's political fortunes and the loss of his Napoleonic emoluments, the final probate of his estate two years after his death in 1824 valued it at the regal sum of 7,291,000 francs. With his expenses dropping substantially after 1814, his estate had actually grown by almost 2 million francs since the end of the Empire.[48]

A NOTORIOUS LIFESTYLE

When Bourrienne, Napoleon's schoolmate at Brienne and his personal secretary in 1799–1802, published his memoirs in 1829, Cambacérès's nephew and heir found them offensive on the subject of his late uncle. He took particular umbrage at claims that Cambacérès had effected an excessively luxurious lifestyle marked by "gastronomic prodigality." The nephew countered that such "insipid pleasantries, invented by envy and spread by baseness" at the behest of the royalist police, had been intended to drive Cambacérès from the political scene in 1814 by a campaign of ridicule. Since his uncle's public career had been above reproach, "one was reduced to slandering the private man."[49]

Cambacérès himself maintained after 1814 that his public role and private life were both shaped by Napoleon's wishes. "My time was divided between the examination or expedition of affairs, and the fatigues of a grand representation, which task the Emperor had imposed on me. To that end he added to the salary that was ascribed to me first a supplement, then some sizable endowments."[50] But if Napoleon expected his second consul and archchancellor to maintain an elegant lifestyle and tender lavish dinners, Cambacérès certainly did so willingly, given his penchant for gastronomic indulgence and his desire to cut a figure in society.

While he was undoubtedly an avid gastronome and epicure, the scale and formality of his entertaining clearly reflect the imperatives of his official position. Twenty-three percent of his living expenses during the Napoleonic years on average, and actually up to a third in most years, went to food, wine, and related costs, which he designated as *dépenses de bouche* in his accounts. (They totaled 74,000 francs in Year X, reached 96,000 francs in the first year of the Empire, and topped out at 109,000 francs in 1811.)[51] Every Tuesday and Saturday, Cambacérès hosted a formal dinner party for as many as fifty guests. The protocol, including a punctual start at 6:00 P.M., was strict, the menu elaborate and voluminous, the eating serious, the socializing afterward formulaic, decorous, and stiff. Gaiety or sociability was not the byword for these affairs, but the sumptuous food gave him a reputation for possessing the finest table in Paris. (Talleyrand would have disputed that claim, and Talleyrand's ex-chef Carême assuredly did. The archchancellor, he claimed, meddled inordinately with the planning of meals by his chef and sometimes obliged him to use foodstuffs from previous dinners.)[52]

After his guests departed, Cambacérès might attend the opera or light theater at the Variétés, but he was happiest when strolling outdoors with a small entourage of close friends. Only in this company did he feel wholly at ease. His private court, as it were, included several friends from his days in Montpellier—bachelors, aesthetes, and Freemasons all. With Cambacérès decked out in the finery and decorations that he loved to sport, with one companion gauntly thin and another extremely stout, these post-prandial strolls formed a decidedly odd procession that became a familiar sight in Paris.

Such are the bare facts of the matter, but it is easy to appreciate that the lifestyle of this prominent figure in the Napoleonic firmament became an object of gossip during the Empire, and worse after its fall. His gastronomic excess (manifest in his rotundity); his legendary vanity for titles and insignias of status; his aggressively celibate ambiance with its aura of homosexuality—all this added spice to the royalist propaganda machine of 1814–15 as it vilified and ridiculed the Napoleonic regime.

Lewis Goldsmith's *Histoire sécrète du cabinet de Buonaparte*, first published in London in 1810 and republished in 1814, became a seminal text for the "black legend" of Napoleon. This well-informed and artfully mendacious volume, by a man who had worked in France as a translator but later fled to England, offered a feast of vicious portraits and anecdotes about Napoleon and his servitors. In skewering the archchancellor's character, Goldsmith casually mixed the public and the private man.

Goldsmith began in a low key with Cambacérès's gourmandise: "He maintains the best table in Paris. Every week he gives an obligatory dinner that is always sumptuous; and at least once a month, his chef invents a new dish to further stimulate his sensuality. His maitre d'hôtel is as much of a *glutton* as he is [italics his]." A more malicious claim followed: "Cambacérès has a *tender* propensity toward a taste that is not *altogether* natural. That revolting perversity has exposed him to endless puns." Need one say more? As to Cambacérès's notorious vanity, Goldsmith made his point with a glancing reference to 1793, when Cambacérès "played the *sans-culotte*. But today, when the scene has changed so much, this miserable person never leaves his home without being decorated with all the medals of his Orders, of which he has five or six. A short time after the *farce* that *disguised* him as a *Prince*, he told his secretary Monvel: 'When I am out in public, you must always address me as *Votre Altesse Sérénissime*; but when we are alone there would be no point in that, and *Monseigneur* will do very nicely.'" Looming over all this, Goldsmith emphasized Cambacérès's votes as a regicide in the Convention, implying that his hands dripped innocent blood when he took his seat next to Napoleon.[53]

It is hard to evaluate the impact of innuendoes about purported homosexuality. However odd or even ludicrous the post-prandial processions of Cambacérès and his male entourage may have appeared, the archchancellor otherwise maintained absolute discretion in his conduct. The leap from insistent bachelorhood to alleged homosexuality remained pure (if logical) speculation. Unlike Napoleon's intimate correspondent Fiévée, who as prefect in the Nièvre in 1811 established a household in open partnership with his male lover, no direct proof has surfaced about Cambacérès's homosexuality.[54]

Yet the presumption had dogged the archchancellor long before 1814, since Napoleon occasionally twitted him about his relationships with the opposite sex. Finally the emperor insisted that he at least associate himself in public with a woman. Since Cambacérès enjoyed attending theater at the Variétés, he obeyed by taking up with an attractive young actress. But according to one chronicler of gossip, this tactic did not help much, since Cambacérès made a spectacle of himself in his feigned attentions to the woman: "One made fun of the amours of the grave archchancellor."[55] All of this no doubt rankled him. In dinner table conversation after the fall of the Empire in 1814, Cambacérès recounted one of Napoleon's digs at him about his attitude toward women and then commented to his companions: "That was, Messieurs, an allusion to those infamies, which I do not think necessary to justify myself against today, although the royalist police are cruel to me with the hideous caricatures they permit."[56]

SUCH "atrocious calumny" circulated abundantly in 1814–15, but French royalist caricature about Cambacérès did not depend on that theme alone. Among the anti-Napoleonic drawings that flooded the marketplace after the Restoration, as many as fifty featured Cambacérès alongside the emperor.[57] By giving parity in size and prominence to the two figures, these images confirm the supposition that Cambacérès was indeed the second most influential man in Napoleonic France. All such pictures depict the archchancellor's girth—which no caricaturist could fail to seize as the subject's leading physical trait—but not all are especially scabrous or unusually brutal toward him. One that does flaunt his gourmandise with mordant wit is entitled *Ambition and Gourmandise Contemplate Their Victims* (Figure 1). It depicts Napoleon surveying smoldering buildings at his feet labeled Madrid, Moscow, and Vienna, while Cambacérès stands next to him holding cutlery and fowl, with various half-eaten dishes and empty bottles at *his* feet. Another image tellingly evokes his purported homosexuality. Entitled *The End of the World* (Figure 2), it conveys two visions of the extinction of humanity: for Napoleon it is death, as he brandishes weapons and treads on bloodied bodies; for Cambacérès it is the unwillingness to procreate, signified by the rotund archchancellor turning his back on three attractive young women clad in white.[58]

FIGURE 1. *Ambition and Gourmandise Contemplate Their Victims*—by any standard a telling caricature of Napoleon and his most important collaborator. ⚜

LA FIN DU MONDE.

FIGURE 2. (Above) *The End of the World.* In this most explicit evocation of Cambacérès as a homosexual, he turns his back on feminine beauty and by implication refuses to procreate. ❧

FIGURES 3 & 4. (Opposite) Anti-Napoleonic caricatures frequently attacked the Napoleonic conscription system as a kind of killing machine. Since the Senate approved troop levies after 1803, and since Cambacérès was Napoleon's principal liaison with the Senate, it is not unreasonable that the archchancellor is depicted in these images of 1814 as feeding Napoleon his troop levies. ❧

Le Minotaure Corse

FIGURE 5. (Above) This image from 1814 seems to suggest that Cambacérès would be accompanying his master into exile, which was far from true.

SOURCE: These caricatures are all from the Collection De Vinck of the Bibliothèque Nationale de France.

FIGURE 6. Visually, this image from 1814 is a rather benign depiction of Napoleon and Cambacérès. Indeed, it seems flattering to Cambacérès's stature by having him form a kind of dyad with Napoleon. The inscription on the pedestal, however, is far from benign. Cambacérès is taxed with homosexuality ("It is the mark of an offensive nature never to procreate") while Napoleon's motto connotes violent aggression ("To invade and expel").

Taken together, the numerous images seem to be making one particular point: in the person of Cambacérès they link the Empire to the Revolution, the better to condemn both. In any case these caricatures depict Cambacérès as Napoleon's indispensable associate—whether in feeding the detested conscription machine (Figures 3 and 4), or even in seeing Napoleon off to an exile that Cambacérès was not actually intended to share (Figure 5). Indeed, one caricature fuses the two men together in absolute parity as a dyad (Figure 6). This particular image would likely have brought a frisson of satisfaction to the fallen archchancellor, or at least have caused him to reflect on his long and intimate collaboration with Napoleon.

CAMBACÉRÈS'S original commitment to Bonaparte after Brumaire had been entirely pragmatic; it served his well-established political desire for a stable consolidation of 1789 as well as his personal or career interests, and what better combination could one hope for? But Cambacérès's unswerving loyalty, subordination in public and candor in private, and willingness to condone nearly every act by Napoleon resonate with psychodynamic implications that are hard to ignore—although his biographers invariably manage to do so. Cambacérès did not find in Bonaparte a father figure in the conventional sense (their age difference precluded that), but Bonaparte did serve as a father substitute who provided the consideration and security that Jean-Jacques-Régis had never received from his own father during a childhood and youth filled with loss (several siblings and a mother), insecurity, and likely neglect. Finding a generous and protective patron in Napoleon, Cambacérès like a good son was in turn devoted, respectful, and protective of Napoleon. And for good measure he stepped in to play the benefactor to his younger brother the priest and his half brother the general.

In his psychological profile there are residues of inordinate guilt over his ambiguously regicidal votes, which haunted him after 1793 and help to explain his singular outburst of rage at Bonaparte over the execution of the duc d'Enghien. Perhaps too his notorious preoccupation with food and obsession with money are markers of anxiety dating from his childhood. But on the whole Cambacérès appears as a man content with himself, consistently effective in his work and adaptive in his manifold relationships, especially in his ability to placate a volatile and willful patron without losing his dignity. At the same time, their relationship reflects favorably on Bonaparte. Despite the general's need to control everything and his misplaced trust in a few unsavory servitors, Bonaparte excelled at finding capable civilian subordinates and within limits encouraged them to use their talents productively.[59]

It is almost reassuring that Cambacérès never found reason or sufficient hypocrisy to repudiate his collaboration with Napoleon, even though he accepted the finality of the Restoration in 1814 with relative equanimity. Napoleon's return from Elba, however, posed a difficult conundrum. Out of prudence and fatigue Cambacérès used his age and infirmities as an excuse to minimize his commitment, but Napoleon insisted on his participation: "It was necessary either to serve the Emperor or to array oneself among his enemies. The latter course could not suit me," he later recalled. Since the Bourbons had excluded him from any recognition because of his presumed regicidal votes in Louis XVI's trial, Cambacérès had sworn no oath to them and was therefore conscience free to rejoin Napoleon. "It was thus with an extreme repugnance that I took up the essentially nil functions of archchancellor," and in pro forma fashion headed the ministry of justice, while leaving the real work to Boulay de la Meurthe by prearrangement.[60]

Even this relatively minimal involvement cost him dearly, for he ended up on the Bourbons' proscription list after Waterloo and was forced into exile in Brussels from 1816 to 1818. Not surprisingly, his tone grew melancholy in his declining years, and in 1821 he left these oddly somber words of advice to his heirs: "I exhort my two nephews to live and die in the Catholic faith, to be loyal to their *patrie* and to their Sovereign, and never to involve themselves in any revolution, if they wish to conserve their fortunes and their lives."[61]

VI

In the Service of
the Emperor

*B*UILDING ON HIS success as military leader, legislator, and
pacifier of France, Napoleon did not vault onto the imperial
throne but moved toward dictatorship gradually. Each assertion of new power came gilded with a veneer of legality and a
rhetoric of commitment to the principles of 1789. In this fashion Napoleon did not simply gain the upper hand over his
partners of Brumaire but retained their loyalty and services
going forward. Far from shunting aside those former revolutionaries, he put them to use in ways that satisfied their most
emphatic needs: political security, material self-interest, social
status, and (not to be underestimated) the opportunity for
high-level public service. His favored servitors could consider
themselves the founding members of a post-revolutionary governmental meritocracy.

FINDING THE RIGHT PEOPLE

The memoirs of Napoleon's private secretary Fain offer many
astute observations about his master and none more useful than
the following (echoed as well by his predecessor Méneval): "He
had a horror of change, feared new faces, and held single-mind-
edly to conserving all the men who were formed under his

shadow."[1] Even men whom he did not really trust—like the ineffable Fouché—he would keep at hand rather than exclude.

Very few of his chosen servitors lost Napoleon's confidence completely. Occasionally he did rid himself of a prominent subordinate who had displeased or irritated him (Daunou, Carnot, Roederer, and the erratic General Junot come to mind), but only to move them into more innocuous posts instead of cashiering them altogether. True, from time to time a key figure in his government suffered a veritable "disgrace" for misconduct or foolishness and was dismissed under a cloud. But the list that follows is remarkably short and the worst fate anyone suffered was exile.

> For all his fervor in behalf of his brother before, during, and after Brumaire, Lucien Bonaparte proved too mercurial, independent, and contentious for Napoleon. First he lost his job as minister of the interior in November 1800 after only eight months in office. Following a peripatetic career as envoy, tribune, and senator, Lucien was forced into permanent exile in Rome, and he eventually ended up in England by a quirk of circumstances. Among other offenses, Lucien had insisted on entering an unsuitable marriage after the death of his first wife when the Bonaparte siblings were expected to make princely matches.

> Bonaparte's private secretary after Brumaire and a comrade since their days in military school together, Louis-Antoine Bourrienne lost his sensitive post in 1802 following a financial scandal that stemmed from Bourrienne's interest in a shady military supply contract. After effectively exiling him from France as minister to Hamburg, Napoleon replaced Bourrienne with the self-effacing Méneval, who had no personal ties to the first consul and therefore wielded none of the influence Bourrienne was presumed to have.[2]

> François Barbé-Marbois, a pompous right-wing deputy deported in Fructidor 1797 and repatriated after Brumaire, was appointed to the Council of State thanks to his friendship with Third Consul Lebrun. In 1801, Bonaparte chose him as minister of the treasury where, among other things, he negotiated the sale of the Louisiana Territory. But in January 1806, Napoleon brusquely ousted Barbé-Marbois for gross ineptitude in managing the nation's finances. Napoleon later relented, however, and appointed him in 1807 as president of a new financial court (the Cour des Comptes), and in 1813 to the Senate.

> Thanks to the esteem Napoleon felt for Portalis (an architect of the Civil Code and his first minister of religion until his death in 1808), the emperor appointed his son to the Council of State and later named him director of the

book trade, making him the government's chief censor. But Portalis *fils* infuriated the emperor when he allowed circulation of a pamphlet by the pope in 1810 attacking one of Napoleon's nominees for archbishop. Napoleon excoriated Portalis *fils* in the Council of State "as the first individual in my regime who has betrayed me," exiled him from Paris, and barred him from any public office until the emperor relented in 1813.[3]

Finally, Napoleon ridiculed and dismissed Frochot, the longtime prefect of Paris, for his credulous behavior during the Malet conspiracy of 1812 (see next chapter). The usually reliable Frochot had accepted the false news of Napoleon's death in Russia and had prepared rooms in the city hall for Malet's self-proclaimed and entirely factitious provisional government, while ignoring the presumptive claims of Napoleon's infant son.[4]

These rare exceptions, interesting as they might be, in no way invalidate Fain's insight that Napoleon clung steadfastly to "all the men who were formed under his shadow." To be sure, his penchant was reinforced by the longevity of his civilian collaborators, very few of whom died in office (the exceptions included Tronchet, Portalis *père*, Fourcroy, Crétet, and Treilhard). More fundamentally, it reflected Napoleon's generally sound judgment about the capacity of individuals and their potential usefulness. As the Empire evolved, bringing palpable changes in atmosphere, a core of supporters present from the outset remained at Napoleon's side. No single individual became indispensable, with the possible exception of Cambacérès, but collectively they came close to being so. Almost all "men of the Revolution," they were certainly not the emperor's friends or intimates—to the extent that he had such comrades they wore military uniforms, like Duroc or Berthier—but simply close collaborators at work day in and day out for the government of France.

These men formed the civilian backbone around which the regime's vaunted order and stability took shape. In addition to Cambacérès, Secretary of State Maret, three or four ministers, and a few senators, this core of collaborators could be found in the Council of State, which remained a fulcrum of government even if its institutional importance diminished over time. Members of the Council of State, like senators, received salaries of 25,000 francs, inferior only to a very small number of functionaries and to the handsomely paid ministers who averaged around 200,000 francs. At any given time the Council of State had between thirty and thirty-five active members, but eighteen counselors held that position for over ten years, and six for the entirety of the Napoleonic regime (Berlier, Boulay de la Meurthe, Defermon, Duchâtel, Réal, and Regnaud)—men of experience, talent, and integrity, as well as the loyalty to Napoleon that went without saying.[5]

Bonaparte divided the Council of State into five sections (legislation, interior, finance, military, naval), where drafting and discussion of most projects began before reaching one of the Council's plenary sessions. For each section he named a president, a singular mark of confidence that carried a supplementary stipend and a great deal of responsibility.[6] Two of his initial choices proved unsatisfactory. General Brune, the first president of the military section, made Bonaparte uncomfortable at such close proximity—perhaps for being too wedded to republican attitudes, or because he had been too successful a rival in the past. Bonaparte preferred to use Brune away from Paris for various diplomatic missions and military commands, and soon turned to J.-G. Lacuée, a former general and military intellectual with extensive legislative experience during the revolutionary decade. Eventually he appointed the dedicated and capable Lacuée as director general of conscription and finally named him minister of war administration.[7]

The first consul also dispensed with the services of Pierre-Louis Roederer after three years. This former magistrate in the Parlement of Metz had been an active member of the National Assembly, intervening 259 times in its debates, but his subsequent administrative career as chief executive officer of the Paris department came to an abrupt end with the fall of the monarchy. After lying low during the Terror, Roederer reemerged as a journalist and political economist during the Directory. A core member of Sieyès's Brumaire coterie, he shifted his loyalties enthusiastically to Bonaparte. At the first consul's request, he turned down his nomination to the Senate in order to accept the presidency of the Council's interior section. Energetic and visionary but also quarrelsome, sanctimonious, and tactless, Roederer eventually irritated the first consul beyond endurance. In 1802 he was pastured out to the Senate, and subsequently served his friend Joseph Bonaparte in the Kingdom of Naples, despite Napoleon's warnings about Roederer to his brother.[8]

NAPOLEON'S IRON MEN

In the end, three members of the Council of State besides Lacuée endured as the most valued of Napoleon's collaborators: Boulay de la Meurthe, the first president of its legislative section; Regnaud, Roederer's successor as head of the interior section; and Defermon, head of the finance section. Esteemed by Napoleon and completely loyal to him, they were by most accounts effective officials of the highest order. As such, they would have argued, they were serving France as much as Napoleon. As we take a closer look at these iron men of Napoleon's regime, we may ponder that question.

Boulay's role in establishing the Consulate has already been discussed— his vigorous but moderate republicanism in the 1790s, disenchantment with the Directory regime, active role in the *journée* of 19 Brumaire at Saint-Cloud, and pivotal swing away from Sieyès toward Bonaparte in the constitutional drafting that followed. At the inception of the Consulate, Boulay wanted nothing more than a medical leave and a seat in the Tribunate. But Bonaparte would not hear of this. While Boulay declined his offer to take over the ministry of police—a startling claim in light of Fouché's seeming inevitability—he could not refuse a bid to join the Council of State and head its all-important legislative section.[9] In this capacity Boulay helped shape the initial spate of foundational Napoleonic legislation, and then coordinated revisions of the original draft of the Civil Code submitted by a four-man drafting committee (composed of Tronchet, Portalis, Bigot, and Maleville). Having finally achieved consensus after extensive and painstaking debates, Boulay personally presented the first titles of the Civil Code to the legislature along with Berlier and Portalis. Like Bonaparte, he was upset when the Tribunate, "without justification," hammered and rejected them. Apparently he did not object to the first consul's tactics for squelching this opposition by withdrawing the project altogether until a renewal of the Tribunate promoted a more favorable response.[10]

In Brumaire's program of national pacification, the *biens nationaux* (property seized by the state from the church and the émigrés) loomed as an extremely divisive issue, even though the new constitution proclaimed the transfer of this property to be irreversible. As émigrés began to return en masse to France, the government created an agency called the "Contentieux des Domaines" to settle disputes over the sale, disposition, and claims surrounding this property. The Brumaire legislator and counselor of state Regnier headed this agency, but when Bonaparte elevated him to minister of justice in September 1802, the first consul tapped Boulay de la Meurthe to take over. Ceding the presidency of the legislative section to Bigot, Boulay cut back on his activity in the Council of State to devote sufficient time to this demanding agency, where he proved a tireless facilitator and mediator. In effect, Boulay established an informal jurisprudence in the thousands of individual decrees that he hammered out and sent on to the Council of State for approval. By 1810, the demand for the agency's services had dried up and it closed down. Since the current head of the legislative section, the ex-*conventionnel* Treilhard, happened to die at that time, the emperor returned Boulay to his original post.[11]

The legislative section had less work to perform in 1810 than under the Consulate, but its president continued to scrutinize the work of various ministries, and by this time Boulay seemed irreplaceable to Napoleon. After the electoral college of the Meurthe nominated him for a second time as a candidate for a Senate seat in 1811, the emperor indicated that he was too valuable to pass into the Senate. "You and Defermon, you will die with me in harness," he told him. Indeed, the emperor suggested that Boulay should reside in the Tuileries to be closer at hand.[12]

Jacques Defermon (metaphorically yoked to Napoleon alongside Boulay) was a successful attorney (*procureur*) in Rennes before 1789. A prominent deputy in the Estates General/National Assembly, where he intervened 270 times, he subsequently won election to the Convention. Although he presided over several sessions devoted to Louis XVI's trial, Defermon voted against execution. Later he was expelled from the Convention for his support of the Girondins, but managed to elude arrest during the Terror. Carried over into the directorial legislature in 1795, he specialized in financial matters, and in 1797 the legislature appointed him as one of the independent commissioners of the treasury. A respected anti-terrorist revolutionary poised between politics and technocratic expertise, Defermon was an obvious choice for Bonaparte's new Council of State and quickly rose to head its finance section, where he remained until the fall of the Empire. Bonaparte also named him to head the agency supervising the liquidation of the national debt, and in 1810 put him in charge of the "*domaine extraordinaire*," a vast slush fund of resources seized in occupied territories on which the emperor could draw for his own purposes. Defermon usually presented fiscal legislation and rosy annual reports to the Legislative Corps, where he extolled the regime's balanced budgets, revenue surpluses, and the growing share of wartime expenses drawn from abroad without burdening French taxpayers.[13]

Michel-Louis Regnaud (known as Regnaud de St. Jean d'Angély, after his hometown near La Rochelle) figured even more conspicuously in Napoleon's government. A self-made lawyer and royal official in the old regime, Regnaud like Defermon was an active but conciliatory deputy in the National Assembly, a gifted orator, and the sixth most frequent speaker in that body despite his tender age of twenty-eight.[14] After the Assembly dissolved in 1791, Regnaud turned to journalism and as a moderate constitutional royalist opposed the growing movement to dethrone Louis XVI. Twice, in fact, he led his neighborhood company of Parisian national guards in efforts to protect the royal family from popular wrath, in June 1792 and again on the fateful day of 10 August. Forced into hiding after the fall of the monarchy, Regnaud thus shared the fate of Boulay and Defermon during the Terror, although much earlier than his two colleagues.[15] For Regnaud as for so many brumairians, the fall of Robespierre brought a reprieve from danger. But Regnaud did not return to the legislature during the Directory. Instead, he kept a low profile as director of military hospitals for the Army of Italy, where he began his long association with Bonaparte in Milan as editor of the general's house organ, *La France Vue de l'Armée d'Italie.*

Assuredly a "man of the Revolution," Regnaud in his private life cultivated the atmosphere of enlightened society before the Revolution with its salons, Freemasonry, and cultural pursuits. Notwithstanding his moderate stance as a revolutionary, for example, Regnaud was known for his anti-clericalism. Molé, who worked under Regnaud in the interior section without enthusiasm, claimed that Regnaud especially warmed to subjects like public education, where "he could indulge his aversion for priests and religion, about whom he spoke with the cynicism of the eighteenth century." An amateur intellectual of sorts, he was elected to the most recent incarnation of the Académie Française in 1803 and the Académie de Législation in 1805. With a young and attractive *salonière* for a wife, he maintained a wide circle of artistic and literary friends and a cultured, pleasure-loving lifestyle that generated a faint whiff of sexual scandal. Napoleon purportedly expressed his regrets to Molé "that Regnaud is so fond of money and the pleasures that it procures. What a Minister of Interior he could have made! And never have I been able to find a satisfactory one!" But Regnaud's prodigious capacity for work, as even Molé admitted, made him an invaluable collaborator for the emperor just the same, although (he claimed) Regnaud's working day and night did not cause him to forego "any of his vulgar penchants."[16]

Regnaud served Napoleon ably and endlessly. He was indeed, as he signed himself in correspondence to the emperor, his "most humble, most obedient servitor and faithful subject."[17] But he was also articulate, concise, efficient, and indefatigable, qualities that made him an excellent head of the interior section in 1802–14, with nearly as much influence as any minister of the interior. Even the mordant propagandist Goldsmith, who mercilessly ridiculed

Cambacérès and most other prominent Napoleonic servitors, had kind words for Regnaud, perhaps having known him during his years as an official translator in Paris before he bolted to London. Monsieur Regnaud, he allowed, "has a great deal of merit. I know of no man in France to whom he can be compared. He is very erudite, a fine speaker and virtually a revolutionary statesman. He is without question Buonaparte's best minister. M. Regnaud is obliging to his friends and very helpful to all the people of his acquaintance. I have never heard him spoken of badly."[18]

For the entirety of the Napoleonic era Regnaud labored away in the interior section of the Council of State. In effect he scrutinized the interior ministry in its great project of administrative centralization, which sought to integrate France's ninety-odd departments and forty thousand towns and villages into a national civic order. In the year 1809, for example, Regnaud reported that the section had drafted 4,869 decrees (every single one approved by the Council of State) giving final authorization to proposals that had worked their way up from the grass roots for the necessary approval in Paris. The section's responsibilities included the review of departmental budgets submitted by the prefects, and as Regnaud commented, this work was best carried out by one person conversant with the experience of previous years and possessing a sound set of "general perspectives." Never one to shirk responsibility, Regnaud took on this work himself. In addition, the section reviewed communal budgets in 320 *états* previously consolidated at the ministry—"a long and minute work" dealing with such issues as communal debts and communal assessments for the upkeep of churches and local roads.

The interior section also made final recommendations for the approval or rejection of proposed charitable bequests to hospitals and the like; signed off on public construction projects; adjudicated boundary disputes among communes, cantons, or arrondissements; approved or annulled mining concessions—a contentious, high-stakes domain in which Regnaud was aided by the former chemist Fourcroy; approved or rejected hundreds of transactions involving leases, concessions, or exchanges of communal property—purely local matters over which the French state had long claimed stewardship. With the usual budgetary strictures capping the expenditures of his section, Regnaud had to employ supplementary clerical workers in his own home, "which has necessitated setting up an office with all the expense that entails." To cover those outlays, he was promised an annual *gratification* of 30,000 francs that was sometimes paid and sometimes in arrears.[19]

Beyond these relentless, routine yet vital matters, the section worked on special projects that arose, such as the status of French Jews, or the preparatory work for drafting a Rural Code. The latter (never consummated) was intended as the sixth and final installment of Napoleonic legal codification, following the regime's Civil Code, Code of Civil Procedure, Penal Code, Code of Criminal Procedure, and Commercial Code. Regnaud began collating and assessing the bewildering variety of regional customs on all aspects of agriculture and husbandry as a preliminary step to drafting uniform national standards and permissible exceptions to those standards.[20]

With his worldly manner, oratorical skill, and reputation for concise analysis, Regnaud did not simply function behind the scenes as a bureaucrat. During the Empire, Napoleon chose Regnaud more often than anyone else to advocate proposed laws before the legislature, and often used him as his representative in the regime's public rituals such as the annual "state of the Empire" report to the legislature, or the government's formal address at the close of a legislative season. Thus, in 1810, Regnaud grandiloquently passed in review the legislature's unanimous adoption of a budget "without additional costs for the nation"; its approval of the new Penal Code; and its enactment of a law on judicial organization providing judges with "a degree of consideration and authority proportionate to the grandeur of the monarch." He also recapitulated important happenings in such areas as foreign relations "in which you have participated only through your admiration[!]"[21]

Regnaud's titles and compensation grew apace. By the end of the Empire, in addition to presiding over the interior section of the Council of State at 30,000 francs, he had attained a lucrative sinecure in the imperial court as secretary of state for the imperial family at 72,000 francs, in which capacity he occasionally received sensitive assignments such as preparing the act for the civil marriage of Jérôme Bonaparte.[22] Napoleon also named Regnaud procurator general of the Imperial High Court (a constitutional mechanism for high state trials which never actually convened) at 36,000 francs. And like Defermon he held the title of minister of state without portfolio at 48,000 francs, in addition to membership on the Grand Council of the Legion of Honor at 4,800 francs.[23]

RESPONSIBILITIES AND REWARDS

In a singularly important feature of Napoleonic governance, members of the Council of State often received supplementary appointments as heads of important agencies or other institutions. Such dual responsibilities, which at least doubled one's salary, not only provided handsome recompense for a score of favored counselors but gave them an opportunity for public service that straddled the conventional boundary between lawmaking and administrative functions. The roster of dual appointments for members of the Council of State in 1806 included (in alphabetical order):

Berlier: president of the Conseil des Prises, the commission dealing with maritime seizures and salvage claims, whose importance grew as the maritime war with Britain intensified

Boulay: director of the Contentieux des Domaines, the agency adjudicating disputes arising from the transfer of *biens nationaux* in the 1790s

Collin: director general of the Douanes, the customs bureau

Crétet: director of the Ponts et Chaussés, France's renowned bureau of bridges and highways. When Crétet became interior minister in 1807, he was succeeded by counselor *Montalivet*, who in turn became interior minister when Crétet fell ill in 1809

Daru: general intendant of the emperor's civil list

Defermon: director general of the Liquidation Générale de la Dette Publique, the agency that managed the public debt

Duchâtel: director general of the Enregistrement, the national land registry bureaus created by the Revolution

Fourcroy: coordinator of public education

Français de Nantes: director of the Droits Réunis, the agency overseeing collection of the tax on alcoholic beverages and similar excise taxes on consumer goods

Frochot: prefect of the Seine department

Lacuée: governor of the Ecole Polytechnique, the elite institution training future engineers and officers

Lavalette: director general of the postal service

Merlin de Douai: procurator general of the Tribunal de Cassation, the nation's highest appeals court

Mollien: director general of the Caisse d'amortissement, designed to keep the public debt stable and to facilitate other aspects of public finance. After his appointment as minister of the treasury in 1806, Mollien was succeeded by Counselor *Bérenger*

Muraire: first president of the Tribunal de Cassation

Réal: seconded to Fouché in matters of *police générale,* joined later by counselors *Miot* and *Pelet de la Lozère,* each of the three responsible for a geographical region known as "an arrondissement of the general police"

Ségur: head of protocol in the imperial palace after 1804[24]

From the outset, Bonaparte had insisted on such dual appointments despite opposition from brother Lucien, his first minister of the interior. At a key planning meeting on the structure of the Council of State, the first consul explained that he wished to offset excessive burdens on the interior minister (not to mention his potentially inordinate power) by distributing certain responsibilities to selected counselors of state under the first consul's direct nomination. More fundamentally, Bonaparte believed that "legislation must arise from memories of implementation." Members of the Council of State who will be drafting laws would profit from knowing how things actually worked, he argued. "These needs can only become known through the work of implementation. It is therefore useful that a counselor of state be involved with the management of affairs." Lucien still disagreed and won support from Crétet, who mused that "it is perhaps preferable to regard a counselor of state as a head rather than an arm." Ever fast on his feet, Bonaparte replied that "nature has conjoined the head and the arm in the same individual." And there the debate seems to have ended.[25]

THE COMPELLING APPEAL of such dual appointments is evoked by the case of Antoine Thibaudeau, who yearned for one himself but failed by a hair's breadth to attain it, and relived his frustration years later in his revealing memoirs. Thibaudeau's political trajectory had an elusive quality, but he was assuredly a "man of the Revolution," as he kept repeating. A young regicide in the Convention who steered clear of the Terror, he ended up as a prominent figure in the thermidorian reaction. Despite his professed and probably sincere commitment to the republic, Thibaudeau allied himself with the right during the epic political battle of 1797 and barely escaped deportation in Fructidor. No doubt his network of friends on the other side of the fence saved him. Thibaudeau rallied to Brumaire, and joined the Council of State after serving briefly as prefect of the Gironde.

His first set of memoirs, covering the years of the Consulate, reported in unmatched detail on politically sensitive debates in the Council of State. They also recorded the private conversations in which Bonaparte used Thibaudeau as a sounding board to justify innovations such as the Legion of Honor or the life consulship that raised the hackles of certain former revolutionaries.[26] In April 1803, however, Thibaudeau's situation changed dramatically when Bonaparte appointed him as prefect in the Bouches-du-Rhône. The volatility of that southern department during the revolutionary decade made it a difficult assignment for anyone, and Charles Delacroix, the experienced republican first assigned there, had apparently failed to master the situation. One might assume that an appointment to a prime prefecture reflected the first consul's confidence in Thibaudeau, and on one level it surely did. But this transfer to Marseilles was a great blow to someone who manifestly preferred to remain in Paris and enjoy the opportunities that were coming to other members of the Council of State.

Thibaudeau's "exile" from Paris generated the kind of private correspondence between highly placed individuals that is extremely rare in the documentary record of the Napoleonic era, and when he compiled his second set of memoirs covering the period from 1799 to 1815, he used that correspondence as a principal source. In these memoirs Thibaudeau claimed that Bonaparte had promised him appointment as a "director general" in tandem with his service on the Council of State; at one point, he claimed, the first consul hinted that he would head the national domains bureau, whose director Regnier was about to be promoted to minister of justice. After he actually appointed Boulay de la Meurthe instead, the first consul became evasive and finally stunned Thibaudeau by dispatching him south to the Marseilles prefecture. For the time being Bonaparte allowed him to retain his salary as a counselor of state (like Frochot, prefect of the Seine), and Thibaudeau drew a year's installment in advance, since Bonaparte wanted him to make an appropriate "representation" in Marseilles.[27]

Thibaudeau lobbied intermittently over the next few years for a return to the Council of State along with a coveted "director generalship" in Paris. In July 1807 his friend Regnaud assured him of his good faith and support:

> You can be sure of my keen desire to be of help, to the extent of my slight influence, in bringing you back together with us [in Paris]. True friends

of the Emperor, courageous partisans of moderate ideas, defenders of all that is good in the Revolution—we are few in number. We need to hold together with one another, and the loyalty of your character suits mine. . . .

Yet Thibaudeau was perhaps stretching Regnaud's sentiments further than intended when he commented in his memoirs: "Thus men such as Regnaud, the most moderate men of the Revolution and the ones most attached to the Emperor, sensed themselves isolated and overwhelmed by the new men with whom the Emperor was surrounding himself. His project is little by little to substitute the imperial school for the revolutionary school." To Thibaudeau, the very reason Regnaud gave for personally wanting him back in Paris was "precisely the reason for which the Emperor does not desire it."[28]

To his chagrin, meanwhile, Thibaudeau looked on as Napoleon propelled Mathieu-Louis Molé onto the fast track from which he himself had been shunted—thus reinforcing the belief that his own fate fit into a larger pattern: former revolutionaries were fading in the Napoleonic firmament. Molé was indeed anything but a "man of the Revolution." Born in 1781 into a notable family of the Parisian judicial aristocracy, Molé spent several boyhood years as an émigré but returned to France in 1796. As early as 1801, Bonaparte invited him to become an *auditeur* in the Council of State, but Molé declined in the belief that he was too young. More to the point, he had not really put the family tradition of royalism behind him. A friend of Chateaubriand and Fontanes, he busied himself with a treatise in political thought, and by 1806 his reservations had evaporated. With supreme self-confidence Molé now solicited that appointment directly from the emperor. Napoleon not only agreed but invited Molé for a personal interview where mutual flattery filled the air.[29]

Molé was just the kind of person the emperor was starting to court—someone without ties to the Revolution whose loyalties would focus entirely on his person and who would in turn bring along the cachet of a distinguished traditional family. Molé became a trailblazer for such types. Despite his modest talents and haughty personality, he rose with spectacular rapidity. After he served briefly as an *auditeur* and then as a master of requests in the Council of State, Napoleon appointed him prefect of the Côte d'Or in 1807, brought him back from Dijon to the Council of State as a full member in 1809, and named him director of the venerable Ponts et Chaussés that same year before he had reached the age of thirty. Molé had gained just the kind of "director generalship" that eluded Thibaudeau, owing such favor to his name and his monarchical values, Thibaudeau believed, and illustrating that "imperial favor was increasingly deserting the men of the Revolution."[30]

THE NAPOLEONIC NOBILITY

The emperor was certainly recruiting new kinds of servitors among the descendants of the old aristocracy, but he remained steadfastly loyal to his original supporters as well. Both tendencies were inscribed in the imperial nobility that he launched in 1808.

Proponents of this innovation depicted it as a codification of meritocracy, perfectly consistent with modern equality. In a prologue, as it were, Lacépède had justified before the Senate in 1804 the titles proposed for the three dozen or so dignitaries of the new imperial court: while these "grand dignities add to the splendor of the throne," they also "offer the most brilliant accolade to the greatest services."[31] When Cambacérès presented the *senatus-consulte* of 1808 establishing the titles of duke, count, baron, and chevalier of the Empire, he emphatically portrayed them as the reward for exceptional service: "The preeminence that such an institution establishes, the ranks that it sets out, the memories that it transmits are the sustenance of honor. . . . Such titles will henceforth serve only to mark for public recognition those already noted for their services, for their devotion to the prince and the fatherland." Such titles, he added, were the best means "to extirpate the last roots of a tree that the hand of time has toppled"—meaning the traces of the old non-meritocratic, privileged nobility. Nor did this close off opportunity and recompense in the future: "Careers still remain open to virtues and useful talents; the advantages that [the new titles] accord to proven merit are in no way injurious to merit as yet undemonstrated."[32]

In fact, the term "nobility" was not formally employed to describe the titles and *lettres patentes* granted in 1808 as a mark of recognition for service. Nonetheless, while a title was personal in the first instance, it could become hereditary provided that the recipient guaranteed it by a *majorat* or entail, whose amount varied according to the title; in the Napoleonic social order, no titles were transmissible without a guaranteed level of wealth to sustain their dignity. Moreover, the transmission to an heir could occur only if the proposed *majorat* was approved after close scrutiny by the Conseil des Sceau des Titres chaired by Cambacérès. The *majorats* (an obvious derogation from the inheritance laws of the Revolution and even the Napoleonic Civil Code) and the accompanying certification of a coat of arms testified unmistakably that Napoleon was indeed creating a new nobility.[33]

In 1808 Napoleon bestowed 740 titles. After this first promotion of his veteran collaborators, the emperor granted hundreds of new titles each year, with a peak of 1,085 in 1810. By 1814, 3,263 citizens of the Empire had received titles. The lion's share of 59 percent went to military men, and 22 percent to high functionaries such as prefects, counselors of state, or bishops, while men of achievement in the arts or in business had scant representation. Napoleon's attempt to woo families from the old regime nobility, which began in earnest in 1810, bore some success, as 22 percent of all the new titles went to such old names. But as the historian Jean Tulard argues in his thorough study of the Napoleonic nobility, this new emphasis did not bear quite the fruit that Napoleon had wished. Many old families refused to rally no matter what the inducements, while among those that did bend their knee, many did so for opportunistic reasons combined perhaps with a sense of duty that entailed no serious loyalty to the new dynasty.[34]

At the pinnacle of the new nobility stood a small number of princes and dukes (only thirty-four altogether at the end of the Empire) drawn from a handful of early imperial dignitaries such as Cambacérès, Lebrun, and Talleyrand, long-serving ministers like Fouché, Gaudin, and Regnier, and twenty marshals. Between these grandees and the lesser categories of barons and chevaliers of the Empire came the counts. This prestigious title went not only to a host of favored generals and virtually all senators but to the long-term members of the Council of State, some twenty-five in number by 1808. Earlier, all members who had served in the Council for five years had been granted the honorific title of "counselors for life," and those quintessential collaborators were now anointed as counts of the Empire en bloc. Thus, one-time republicans such as Berlier, Boulay, Français de Nantes, Merlin de Douai, Réal, Treilhard, and Thibaudeau were now addressed as "comte," with the possibility of arranging for the hereditary transmission of their titles to their eldest sons.

This was an odd state of affairs for men who had abolished all noble titles in the National Assembly or who, like Boulay de la Meurthe, treated former nobles with suspicion later in the decade. Some former revolutionaries had earlier tried to stop Bonaparte's more innocuous proposal for a Legion of Honor in 1802, as reminiscent of old regime privilege. Following one of the most open debates of the Consulate, the Legion of Honor won approval, but only after a wave of opposition at every stage. The Council of State endorsed it after a vigorous debate by a vote of 14 to 10, while only fifty-six tribunes voted in favor, with thirty-eight opposed. Finally, the Legislative Corps adopted it by the embarrassingly close vote of 166 to 110.

Berlier had joined this opposition and in his memoirs he reflected wryly on his experience: "What a singular destiny was mine! In 1802 I had combated the establishment of the Legion of Honor; and when it became law I was called to become part of it with the rank of commander. [Then in 1808] I found myself enrolled in a new nobility by virtue of the functions that I exercised [in the Council of State] for more than five years!" Everything changed around me, he continued uneasily, "and, caught up in the general movement, I yielded to it, but without renouncing either the liberal ideas that remained compatible with the new institutions or my [previous] amicable relations. . . ."[35]

As if the title of count were not discomfiting enough, Berlier faced the question of establishing the *majorat* or entail required for transmitting the title to his son. He did not have the resources to establish a *majorat* that would "favor one of my children to the prejudice of the others," he recalled, and would have been disinclined to do so out of principle even if he had been wealthy enough. For the former deputy to the Convention, the groundbreaking equal inheritance law of 1793 was an article of faith, notwithstanding the restoration of a limited testamentary discretion to fathers in the Napoleonic Civil Code. But Napoleon understood the problem faced by the likes of Berlier or Boulay, and he solved it "by personally providing to [certain] title holders the capital necessary to establish their *majorats* from the immense reservoir of his *domaine extraordinaire*." From the far corners of the Empire Berlier received an endowment (*dotation*) that comprised assets in Swedish Pomerania producing an estimated 10,000 francs annually; mines, foundries, *rentes*, and rural properties in the Illyrian provinces yielding 4,000 francs a year; and four shares in the Canal du Midi paying 2,000 francs.[36]

Of course, as Berlier's last will and testament confirms, only the shares from the Canal du Midi remained after the collapse of the Empire. But even decades later the remnants of Napoleon's endowment gave Berlier pause in arranging an equitable inheritance for his beloved children and grandchildren. After leaving small legacies to distant relatives, the children of old friends, and faithful domestics, the long-lived Berlier addressed his principal heirs about the bulk of his estate:

Given the equal affection that I carry toward my children and grandchildren, it remains for me to provide for the distribution of the remainder of my possessions according to the customary law that designates equally for that division my son Gustave, my daughter Aimée, married to Dr. Masson, my grandson Lucien, and my granddaughter Amelie Baudot[37]—all present in my thoughts, and none of whom, I hope, will misconstrue the motive that dictates the stipulation that follows.

The awkward provision in question involved the four shares in the Canal du Midi that he possessed—"which come from an imperial endowment that, after me, must pass to my son by virtue of the statutes governing that matter"—along with another share of the company he had subsequently purchased from an in-law who needed to raise cash. "In this situation, it seems to me suitable to set aside from any division the share in question, but under conditions that will satisfy the dictates of equality." That arrangement concerned only the fifth, discretionary share, for Berlier could do nothing about the four shares remaining from his imperial *dotation* that he was obliged to pass on to his son.[38]

The self-esteem of former republicans like Berlier and Boulay caused them to be skittish about the financial rewards that Napoleon was ready to shower on his favored collaborators. When Napoleon accorded Berlier a special bonus (*gratification extraordinaire*) deriving from maritime seizures in Hamburg, he accepted it in good conscience as an appropriate recompense for the president of the Conseil des Prises, and not as a kind of imperial largesse. Referring to the assets granted by Napoleon for his *majorat* as well as that *gratification*, Berlier maintained that "I did not in any fashion solicit or bring about those favors and benefits. . . . They did not result from any request on my part, nor were they the compensation for any base complacency (*vile complaisance*). I was never in any way a courtier . . . [but simply] was assiduous in fulfilling my duties."[39]

Boulay de la Meurthe claimed to have similar scruples. To begin with, he refrained from purchasing any *biens nationaux* during his tenure in the national domains bureau, although this was the preferred means of investing one's capital, as exemplified by Cambacérès. When the bureau closed down in 1810 and Boulay lost his second income, Napoleon wanted to indemnify him. Using Maret as an intermediary, he offered Boulay a mansion or the funds to purchase one himself, but Boulay refused in order, he said, to maintain his independence. Napoleon took offense at this attitude and their relationship chilled briefly, but the emperor soon relented. On the other hand, Boulay accepted endowments from Napoleon for a *majorat*, and promotion to one of the highest positions in the Legion of Honor.[40] But in language almost identical to Berlier's (a copy of whose memoirs Boulay possessed), Boulay "made it a point never to ask any favor from the Emperor, not even to claim what seemed to be due him"—doubtless referring to the fact that as president of the legislative section in 1810 he should have been made a minister of state without portfolio like Defermon and Regnaud, an oversight that purportedly astonished Napoleon when he became aware of it during the Hundred Days.[41]

TOWARD THE NEXT GENERATION: THE CORPS OF *AUDITEURS*

Back in 1804, Roederer had urged Napoleon to make the Senate an hereditary body in order to establish a future phalanx of loyalists rooted in the families of his original collaborators. In establishing a new hierarchy of titled nobles that initially favored those present at the creation of the Napoleonic regime, the emperor seemed at last to be acting on that advice. But in fact he did not really share Roederer's belief that such "men of the Revolution" promised the highest order of loyalty compared to the newcomers who would inevitably join their ranks in the future. With a misplaced confidence, Napoleon in 1809–10 began to pursue new supporters among the aristocratic families of the old regime. While he elevated numerous men of such background directly into his new nobility (22 percent of the total by 1814), his highest priority was to nurture a younger generation of high-ranking servitors. Though he remained comfortable with the veterans of Brumaire and the Consulate, he relished the prospect of personally molding young men in the "school of the Empire," men presumably free of nostalgia for either the old regime or the Revolution.

The corps of *auditeurs* in the Council of State, numbering up to four hundred men, would be his principal instrument.

> The purpose of the institution (Napoleon told the Council of State in 1809) is to bring under the Emperor's wing men of the elite who are sincerely devoted to him, who have sworn an oath between his hands, whom he will observe closely enough to appreciate their zeal and their talents.

They will be formed, so to speak, in his school, and he will be able to employ them wherever the needs of his service will make them useful. From this will emerge veritable magistrates and administrators. . . . His Majesty's intention is [also] that the *auditeurs* be received at court, so that if they are on the one hand trained in work, they will on the other hand develop urbanity, the good taste and usages of society, which are necessary in the places where they might be assigned.[42]

As an initial hurdle for consideration, candidates had to meet two formal qualifications. First, they had to prove that they had satisfied the conscription laws. Like prospective state-certified attorneys (*avoués*), who faced the same requirement, the vast majority did so without actually having served in the army. Either they were not called, having drawn a low number in the lottery for their local contingent that placed them outside its quota, or (under relatively strict and costly regulations) their family had hired a replacement if they had drawn a high number. Secondly, aspirants for the post of *auditeur* had to demonstrate that they commanded a minimum income of 6,000 francs annually. A third condition, starting in 1812, would require a higher degree in law or science.[43]

For a sample cohort of one hundred twenty candidates from 1809, the dossiers included comments on the status of the candidates' families (some from "revolutionary" families, more from old-line families); the full extent of the family's property; and recommendations by highly placed persons— including ministers, generals, senators, and such familiar names as Defermon, Regnaud, Duchâtel, and Muraire. Often the local prefect and mayor lent their support as witnesses for the notarized documents being submitted. Some candidates had to cobble together the capital for a 6,000F annual income, but most of the aspirants, typically in their mid-twenties, already possessed substantial wealth. Families normally met the income qualification by settling property on a younger child earlier than usual, but some older children had already become family heirs. In either case most of these families stood among the six hundred highest taxpayers in their department, lists of whom had been compiled early in the Consulate. Real property—a marker of both wealth and status—was the sine qua non for entry to this corps, but family reputation counted as well.[44]

The corps of *auditeurs* was intended as the seedbed for a second-generation civilian meritocracy in the Empire, and candidates were screened by veterans like Boulay before winning appointment.[45] Most spent their probationary period seconded to a section of the Council of State or a government ministry; some also served as couriers over the vast distances between Paris and the emperor's camp when he was out on campaign. The case of Monsieur Dudon, who lost a dispatch case containing ministerial reports when his trunk was stolen between Leipzig and Wittenberg in December 1806, must have produced nightmares among his peers. Dudon had been a courier to Maret on several previous occasions and was well regarded until this disaster, which he compounded by returning to Paris instead of writing ahead to Maret and awaiting instructions. Cambacérès reprimanded him severely and demanded a written account, while he looked into the circumstances of the incident. Dudon, he reported, was "a person who led us to have high hopes, and who carries a distinguished name from the old magistracy [of Bordeaux]." In the end, the archchancellor recommended leniency to Napoleon since Dudon's disastrous misadventure was the result of "thoughtlessness or stupidity rather than cowardice." After passing muster in their apprenticeship, *auditeurs* might reach the next rung as sub-prefects, ministerial functionaries, or aides in the satellite kingdoms. From there they could aspire to appointment as *maîtres de réquêtes* (associates) in the Council of State—a position that Dudon managed to win against the odds in 1810—and finally as prefects.[46]

AT WORK WITH NAPOLEON

Napoleon spurred his subordinates to hard work by the example of his own zeal for governmental affairs. From the highest functionary to the lowliest *auditeur*, none would have denied the emperor's lively interest in everything from cultural policy to the minutiae of fiscal administration. Depoliticization may have eviscerated representative government, but it did not preclude honest and efficient administration. Working through his handpicked ministers and counselors of state, Napoleon energized a relatively small central bureaucracy that guided the network of prefects and mayors in the provinces.

But Napoleon's immersion in the business of civil government gradually changed character after the transition to Empire. The learning process that marked his years as first consul ran its course and his openness to disagreement diminished. After the early spate of foundational legislation, and as the great work of legal codification neared completion, the legislature had little to do, and the primacy of the legislative section of the Council of State began to ebb.

The emperor's interest in the machinery of government, on the other hand, never flagged. As Mollien remarked, "he believed he could maneuver statistics like his battalions."[47] His private secretary Fain summarized Napoleon's schedule in the months before he departed for the Russian campaign of 1812: Monday & Saturday, a *conseil d'administration*; Tuesday & Friday, the Council of State; Wednesday, a council of ministers; Thursday, review of public works. Sunday was devoted to court life, or what Napoleon called the "representation" of imperial dignity; here people who had labored with him during the week now came as courtiers.[48]

Apart from the head of state, no organ of government had any power to initiate policy in Napoleonic France. While the Senate became the principal body for ratifying Napoleon's political will after 1804, it remained an entirely passive instrument in his hands: only when the emperor drafted and submitted a specific measure (*senatus-consulte*) could the Senate deliberate on a matter of policy, its approval a foregone conclusion. Similarly, in the words of Fain, the Council of State "was not a power . . . it counseled only when the emperor told it: advise me."[49] Only Napoleon's initiative brought any policy issue before the Council of State, and only his approval gave any of its policy decisions effective writ. Napoleon could approve a proposal from the Council, direct that it be modified, or shelve it.

Within those limits, the Council of State worked continuously on policy and administrative matters. With Napoleon in attendance or not, it debated issues he broached, formulated and revised proposed decrees, and hammered out the regime's five great legal codes. When a draft law or section of a code won Napoleon's approval, he designated the members who would present it to the legislature for its sanction. In a more mundane register the Council scrutinized ministerial *arrêtés*, administrative rules, and all local initiatives; investigated and judged allegations against public officials; and adjudicated conflicts arising among public officials or between public officials and private citizens. The Council thereby served as a check on the various ministers, particularly the minister of interior who, for example, could not permanently dismiss a derelict mayor without the Council's approval.

The first consul recruited men with varying political pasts but with experience and expertise in judicial, legislative, financial, or administrative matters. Molé aptly described some of these appointees as "living dictionaries" for their ability to provide historical perspective on issues under discussion. Despite Molé's low opinion of the ex-revolutionaries who dominated the Council, he regarded them as effective instruments in Napoleon's hands, like the generals in his armies. "In putting them in their places, in asking them to do only what they could and what they knew, he doubled their aptitude and their success."[50]

While rivalries and personal animosities could not possibly be absent around the table, Thibaudeau (as we saw) evoked the harmony and even camaraderie that prevailed during the Consulate in the legislative section and by implication in the Council as a whole. This is not inconsistent with Molé's observation when he began attending the Council as an *auditeur* in 1806 that it had two parties—one generally wedded to residual revolutionary values, the other more comfortable with departures from them. But, as he observed, Napoleon reconciled potential antagonists around *his* opinions, leaving each to believe that they'd best support him lest the other side prevail. This is perhaps an excessively cynical view of the matter. In the years of the Consulate, at least, the forced depoliticization created a climate where men of talent and experience but of differing opinions could work together, listen to each other, debate in good faith, and marshal their eloquence and expertise to reach consensus with the first consul over the thorniest issues, such as the problems faced by purchasers of *biens nationaux*.[51]

Debates in the Council of State during the Consulate, according to Thibaudeau and other observers, were wide-ranging, uninhibited, and robust. Since Bonaparte needed to learn about many things foreign to his experience, he encouraged discussion even when it began to flag. Sessions often went on for hours when the first consul presided, as opposed to Cambacérès, who preferred concise summaries of different positions, brief debates, and a quick resolution. Bonaparte welcomed contradiction, but once he made up his mind he took pleasure in imposing his opinion by the force of argument. For as Mollien later observed, Napoleon displayed the same will to dominate in policy debate as he did on the battlefield—yet another form of combat to be won.[52]

When Thibaudeau returned to Paris in 1809 on a four-month leave from his Marseilles prefecture, however, he found a decidedly different atmosphere in the Council of State. The emperor attended sessions less frequently than in the past, and when he did preside, he no longer seemed to welcome diverse opinions. Napoleon sometimes displayed impatience, silenced people who irritated him, and cut short the discussions. Members holding dissenting opinions now offered them cautiously instead of vigorously. "Read the draft proposal aloud," Napoleon would say to Regnaud or Defermon; then he would given his own views on the matter at hand and conclude by asking: "Does someone wish to speak about the wording?"—meaning the details of language rather than the substantive provisions. Rarely did he bother putting anything to a straw vote. Mollien, though thoroughly in thrall to Napoleon, confirms that the emperor often acted like a bully in these years, although Napoleon never attached any importance to his outbursts against a particular member. If he administered a stinging rebuke to a counselor on one day, he had forgotten it by the next. The emperor meant no personal injury with his cutting remarks nor did they serve the interests of a party, concluded Mollien: "they served only the chief's passion for seeing and knowing everything, always ordering new efforts by demonstrating that one had never done quite enough."[53]

During his tenure at the Council of State in the early years of the Empire, Molé witnessed two episodes in which the emperor memorably manipulated and bullied the members. In the discussions of public education that eventually led to the founding of the Napoleonic University—the misnamed system of centralized state supervision over secondary and higher education—the emperor knew that Fourcroy, ostensibly the point man in that area, had not grasped his intentions and was unlikely to share them when he did. He therefore came down hard on his loyal servitor, while playing with the heads of the anti-clerical contingent by lauding the Jesuit order as model educators. In the end Napoleon summarily repudiated Fourcroy's labors and set the planning in a new direction, just as he had once rejected the project crafted at his instigation by Mathieu Dumas for the Legion of Honor.[54]

In Molé's second example, Napoleon did not share the qualms of certain former revolutionaries in the Council about restoring the indirect taxes on consumption that the National Assembly had abolished. Other governments, he knew, had always found such consumer taxes highly productive of revenue despite their extreme unpopularity. Molé noted how Napoleon maneuvered around dissenting members like Defermon, Regnaud, and Treilhard, and eventually brought them on board, even if they were "more resigned than converted." Their interventions to minimize the incidence of these taxes or to restrain aggressive methods of collection ultimately had only minor impact on the outcome. Molé saw it as a kind of scripted game: the ex-revolutionaries would register their objections; the emperor would listen and respond aggressively; his viewpoint would prevail in the end; and the dissenters could emerge with a minimally clear conscience.[55] Napoleon's "living dictionaries" still provided historical context and technical information on such subjects, but the debate was now a matter of educating the members in the emperor's opportunistic notions of taxation.

WHETHER in Paris or out on campaign, Napoleon constantly scrutinized the work of his ministers and did not hesitate to overrule them. With Napoleon, or when he was away from the capital, Cambacérès in the chair, the ministers assembled once a week. These "councils of ministers" were an economical way of consulting key people and of dealing with matters that overlapped jurisdictions. Here Napoleon could enlighten himself by tapping various kinds of expertise as he did in the Council of State. But as time went on, the converse again became more common. Indulging in frequent monologues, he was educating his subordinates in his views the better to understand his intentions in the future.[56]

Napoleon usually approved the proposals submitted by his ministers, but they could never be sure. The most mundane matter might provoke a sharp question and a delay or an outright rejection. The records of the emperor's decisions on ministerial proposals during and just after his triumphant campaign against Russia in 1807 offer a good example of how he operated. The minister of war administration was of course most likely to be overruled by the emperor, who regularly modified his proposals for the assignment or promotion of military personnel. But Napoleon was equally aggressive with the flow of proposals from the minister of the interior. A project for distributing partial scholarships for vacant places in state *lycées*, for example, aroused his objections because it did not sufficiently address the claims of serving officers who could not afford to pay demipensions for their sons. When the minister presented a list of candidates for appointment by the emperor of a mayor in the 7th arrondissement of Paris, Napoleon shrewdly asked for information on whether the fathers and grandfathers of the candidates had been born in Paris, and whether their branch families were also established in the capital.[57]

For the minister of religion, Napoleon approved by-laws for the vestries and the seminaries in the diocese of Digne. But regarding a statue he had requested to honor the late bishop of Vannes, Napoleon objected to its proposed placement inside the church where the cleric was buried. Instead, he insisted on differentiating this memorial from conventional religious statuary honors; he wanted the statue in the open, out front and on a pedestal.

Then it was the Grand Judge's turn to be overridden. The minister had ordered the investigation and arrest of individuals who had created a disturbance in Nancy during the funeral of a former constitutional or pre-Concordat bishop, but Napoleon decided "that no further action should be taken in regard to this affair."[58]

WHEN NAPOLEON returned from his campaign against Russia in 1807 and the diplomatic triumph at Tilsit, he told Mollien that having acted the general for so long, "he was anxious to take up again the functions of *prime minister*. To carry out what he called his *grand reviews*, he arranged a series of ministerial councils lasting five or six hours a day" on top of his other activities.[59] Then in January 1808 the emperor held a marathon of "*conseils d'administration*"—a virtuoso feature of Napoleonic administrative performance.

Each *conseil d'administration* focused on a specific area, usually interior, finance, or war, and less frequently naval affairs, justice, or foreign affairs. Especially after he returned from a military campaign, Napoleon would convoke the appropriate ministers, division chiefs, and even bureau chiefs in a ministry, as well as heads of specialized agencies and the president of the relevant section of the Council of State. By the count of historian Charles Durand, he presided over at least 167 *conseils d'administration* on the interior; 88 on finances; and 74 on war. Sometimes he chose a particular theme for sustained attention: in 1810 he decided to scrutinize the accounts of a major agency every Thursday, and in 1810–11 he devoted 73 sessions to the administration of commerce and manufactures.[60] Minister of the Treasury Mollien attended innumerable sessions since he was responsible for the actual payment of expenses no matter what their origin. The treasury's records of payment could be used to check the accounts of officials authorizing expenditures.

In January 1808 Napoleon set up a schedule for *conseils d'administration* that would last the better part of two months: every Monday, war; every Thursday, interior; every Sunday, finances. Under each rubric he laid out agendas for successive sessions. The five sessions devoted to war administration were a tour de force in which the emperor displayed his breadth of knowledge and mastery of detail on all aspects of the armed forces, including troops, equipment, supplies, clothing, rations, and horses. But he was equally dazzling in the two other domains. Under the rubric of interior (with Min-

ister Crétet and the appropriate subordinates as well as Regnaud in attendance), he took up the following matters in four sessions:[61]

1. Budgets, credits, and expenditures for the past year as well as proposals for 1808;
local expenses; abuses in the prefectures; prisons and other local public establish-
ments

2. The grain trade and provisioning of markets; meat supplies; public instruction,
including the University apparatus and the *lycées*

3. Commerce and manufacturing, including foreign trade; public buildings

4. Public works; roads and bridges

Under the rubric of finance (with Minister Gaudin and his subordinates
as well as Defermon in attendance), he planned five sessions:

1. The ministry's budget; land tax revenues; the national registry bureau (*Enregistrement*); the *biens nationaux*

2. Customs; the mint; the salt and tobacco monopolies; the Banque de France

3. Indirect taxes (Droits Réunis); forest administration

4. The public debt; the national lottery; the postal service

5. The drafting of next year's general budget for presentation to the legislature

The minutes of these *conseils d'administration* are spare in the extreme and
do not indicate their duration; but Mollien claimed that one in January 1806
lasted nine hours, while Fain stated that they sometimes ran from 9:00 A.M.
to 7:00 or 8:00 P.M. Napoleon seemed to take pride in outlasting his ministers, who often emerged visibly exhausted, only to return to their offices and
find letters from the emperor requiring immediate response.[62]

At these administrative councils Napoleon scrutinized status reports, questioned statistics, and often demanded more detailed presentations for a future
session. At times he invited discussion, which might lead him to request
modifications in the way some function was being managed; he occasionally
deferred a project because it had "not been thought through sufficiently." As
in his councils of ministers, the emperor sometimes digressed into general
issues, either to educate his subordinates out of their narrow ways of thinking, or simply for the love of talking.[63]

In the *conseils d'administration* and councils of ministers, Mollien recalled,
Napoleon displayed an "insatiable penchant for detail, and a restless spirit

always avid for new concerns. He did not limit himself to governing but continually *administered*, not like a prime minister but even more minutely than each of his other ministers." The emperor wanted to see for himself "how all the gears of this administration, this immense machine that was his own creation, actually worked, to assure himself of the accuracy and regularity of their connections." Was this painstaking concern with administrative detail a derogation from Napoleon's veritable rank and function? his minister of the treasury asked. He agreed with the emperor that it was not: "He lost nothing of his superiority in the long course of these examinations. He could not reign like other princes, he said; his position imposed extraordinary duties upon him."[64]

AN INNER CIRCLE: THE *CONSEILS PRIVÉS*

Unlike the Council of State (a permanent consultative body mandated by the constitution), or the *conseils d'administration* (informal mechanisms which suited Napoleon's convenience), *conseils privés* of two kinds were constitutionally mandated yet ad hoc. *Conseils privés* dealing with acts of clemency by the head of state (*grâces*) will be touched on in the next chapter. In the other and more frequent usage, the constitution of 1802 mandated a *conseil privé* each time the first consul (later the emperor) intended to submit a proposal for approval by the Senate. Napoleon convened sixty-five *conseils privés* to draft such *senatus-consultes*. Twenty dealt with constitutional issues, mostly minor, such as electoral eligibility and regulations for the legislature; eighteen authorized conscription levies; nine concerned the annexation of foreign territory; and seven suspended constitutional guarantees under martial law in troubled departments. The three most notable *senatus-consultes* drafted by a *conseil privé* established the hereditary Empire in 1804; created hereditary titles in 1808; and paved the way for Napoleon's divorce from Josephine in 1810.[65]

According to the constitution, each *conseil privé* would consist of the three consuls (later the emperor and his archchancellor Cambacérès), two ministers, two senators, two counselors of state, and two grand officers of the Legion of Honor (who generally overlapped with the other categories)—all of course named by Napoleon. About three-quarters of the senatorial designations fell to eight senators, including Napoleon's favorites, Lacépède (fifty-eight times, but usually in his capacity as chancellor of the Legion of Honor) and Laplace (thirty times). For the Council of State, he turned repeatedly to Regnaud (fifty times), and also to Defermon, Lacuée, Treilhard before his death in 1810, and Boulay de la Meurthe after. Grand Judge Regnier and successive ministers of the interior most commonly filled the ministerial slots. While he also spread the honor of a summons to a *conseil privé* to over forty other individuals, Napoleon depended on a small and stable body of advisors of proven loyalty and presumed competence. With the *conseils privés* we come full circle back to Napoleon's closest collaborators from the Council of State and Senate, most present from the creation of the regime.[66]

The extremely sketchy minutes sometimes indicate that each member gave his opinion, and occasionally note that objections were raised to the provisions of a draft, but they do not provide the content of any debate. It is unlikely that a *conseil privé* ever thwarted Napoleon's intentions outright, but at times the participants did modify the fine points of a *senatus-consulte* or delay it for redrafting, so these conclaves cannot be dismissed as entirely pro forma.[67] In practical terms, they stand as testimony to the continuing quest for the precision in governmental acts that Napoleon and his faithful secretary of state Maret could not alone provide. These councils also reiterate the former revolutionaries' standing symbolic gesture in the Napoleonic regime against one-man rule.

THE ULTIMATE EXAMPLE of this ritual of collaboration came with the Dupont affair. A favored and winning general until his ill-fated campaign in Andalusia, Dupont saw his isolated and poorly supplied army surrounded by Spanish forces in 1808 and driven to despair by hunger and thirst. With no obvious relief in sight, Dupont surrendered at Baylen on 22 July. Napoleon reacted furiously when he heard the news and denounced the surrender as both stupid and cowardly. Worse yet, the Spanish did not honor the terms of the capitulation; while they repatriated General Dupont and his staff to France, the rank and file languished in prison hulks off Cadiz. In the emperor's view, this ignominious and treasonable surrender had disgraced the French army and merited summary execution. Upon their return to French soil, Dupont and five subordinates were arrested and slated for trial before the Imperial High Court, an institution provided for in the constitution of 1804 but yet to be convened.

Regnaud, the procurator general of the phantom court, meticulously prepared the government's case. When he was finally ready, however, Cambacérès advised the emperor against convening the High Court. For a start, there was the embarrassing detail that the original constitutional provision called for the participation of three tribunes, but the Tribunate no longer existed.[68] More fundamentally, a decree laying out the details about this court had never been approved by the Senate. Assuming that the measure could now be completed, were Dupont to be tried before the High Court, "we would expose ourselves to judging under that law an offense committed before that law's very existence—a system of retroactivity that is neither in Your Majesty's personal principles nor in those of a sound social organization. On the other hand a Grand Officer of the Empire like Dupont cannot be tried for such an offense before the ordinary courts." The archancellor further cautioned that an open trial before the High Court would reopen old wounds and generate adverse publicity. Better, he advised, to convene a special *conseil privée*. In the end Napoleon agreed that Regnaud should instead present the case in secret to a council of inquiry named by the emperor and chaired by Cambacérès.[69]

The council of inquiry, which finally convened in February 1812, was a showcase, a who's who, of Napoleon's trusted servitors, civil and military. Its group portrait (had there been one) would be an excellent representation of Napoleon's collaborators in the high Empire. Sitting before Cambacérès and Regnaud as the latter laid out the case were Berthier (Napoleon's chief of staff), Talleyrand, Clarke (minister of war), Lacuée (minister of war administration), Marshals Moncey and Bessières, Senator Lacépède (grand chancellor of the Legion of Honor), General Dejean (grand treasurer of the Legion of Honor); Laplace (chancellor of the Senate), Muraire (president of the Cour de Cassation), and from the Council of State: Defermon, Boulay, Andréossy, and Gautheaume (presidents of the sections along with Regnaud).[70]

At the conclusion of the hearing, which included the appearance of each defendant and lasted nine days, the council of inquiry rejected any notion that Dupont's surrender was a treasonable offense subject to the death penalty, and recommended a kind of disgrace for Dupont involving loss of rank and all perquisites, including his title of count, and banishment from a radius of twenty miles from the emperor's residence; for three other officers it recommended indefinite suspension or dismissal. Napoleon asked each member to submit in writing his own view of the case and recommendation for punishment. Boulay de la Meurthe, a civilian who had seen combat as a volunteer in 1792, performed just as one would expect. His judgment involved a careful parsing of the circumstances of the surrender as well as the applicable laws.

These led him to a stern view of the dishonor that Dupont had caused, but to a recommendation for leniency in punishing him and his subordinates.[71]

In the end, Napoleon spurned such advice. He not only cashiered Dupont and stripped him of all ranks and titles, as recommended, but bundled him off to a state prison for an indefinite detention. On the other hand Dupont was not shot, and could therefore enjoy a moment of sweet revenge in April 1814 when the returning Louis XVIII chose the former general as his first war minister.

Contrast this episode to the way Napoleon had handled the duc d'Enghien in 1804 after authorizing the kidnapping of the Bourbon prince from his residence in Baden, and bringing him to Paris under the unsubstantiated accusation that he was plotting to overthrow the Consulate. Acting hastily and emotionally, without consulting a range of advisers or holding any formal deliberations, Bonaparte personally ordered the summary court-martial of the hapless prince, who was shot under General Savary's supervision twenty-four hours later.[72] The "trial" of General Dupont exemplifies the regime's usual methods and the important relationship that prevailed between Napoleon and his collaborators: the scrupulous procedures and careful deliberations that these men could provide, and the possible tempering effect of this on Napoleon's volatile inclinations. The emperor of course settled things as he would, but did so with a better sense of what his decisions entailed.

VII

Living with the Erosion of Liberty

*I*N SUCCESSIVE rationalizations for Brumaire, for the Consulate, and for the transition to Empire, Napoleon's collaborators always insisted that conserving the basic gains of the Revolution stood as their highest priority. There was reasonable plausibility in their claim that the Napoleonic regime would guarantee such changes as civil equality, the abolition of feudalism, the transfer of the *biens nationaux*, or legislative sanction of taxes and budgets. But the enumeration of revolutionary gains invariably included "public liberty," and here we encounter a severe credibility problem. At best the inclusion of liberty in the Napoleonic catechism was wishful thinking, at worst a bizarre form of self-delusion or cynicism. Going about their business in the Council of State, the Senate, the prefectures, or the administrative bureaus, Napoleon's collaborators were at least passively complicit in a drastic erosion of the individual liberties instituted by the National Assembly in 1789. The tense discussion in the Council of State on the deportation overseas of "ex-terrorists" in December 1800 epitomizes the quandary of the revolutionary veterans in Napoleon's inner circle. They did not like the decree one bit, but most could acknowledge its possible prophylactic benefits, on which the first consul vehemently insisted. We have seen the counselors squirming uncomfortably in their seats, mumbling mild objections, and, in the end, doing nothing to prevent the deportations.

Such dramatic moments were in any case rare. The erosion of liberty occurred off center stage, in quotidian, unspectacular fashion, under the aegis of Fouché's police ministry. But everyone was aware of the regime's routine use of preventive detention and its control of the print media—two policies which caused occasional qualms even for Napoleon himself. It is therefore instructive to consider how these two issues played out; to determine what, if anything, Napoleon's liberal servitors could do to mitigate these affronts to the ideal of liberty.

PREVENTIVE DETENTION

"Injurious remarks" or "seditious statements" constituted a peculiar problem of public order for the Napoleonic regime. With the cult of personality created almost overnight by Brumaire, with so much power and prestige concentrated in Bonaparte's hands, French citizens knew better than to take that name in vain publicly. But when obstreperous individuals had their tongues loosened by drink, anything could happen, and it was not uncommon for tirades against the first consul to fill the air. Local authorities then found themselves dealing with the kind of mess that the blacksmith Jean Fortin of Beauvais created for himself when, in a drunken rage, he shouted: "Bonaparte, he's a wretch [*gueux*], a scoundrel [*fripon*], who deserves the guillotine." Upon learning of the incident, the Grand Judge (minister of justice) ordered Fortin transported to Paris for an interview. Since local testimonials spoke of a hardworking artisan and family man, prone to drunken outbursts but "decidedly incapable of any seditious acts," the minister eventually released him, no doubt in a chastened state of mind.[1]

From small-town mayors or justices of the peace to departmental prefects, government commissioners at the criminal tribunals, public prosecutors, and investigating magistrates, various officials had to deal with such cases in which personal freedom and threats to the integrity of the regime seemed to clash. Public imprecations against Bonaparte, even during drunken binges, could not be dismissed lightly. Yet substantial discretion existed in assessing the gravity or harmlessness of a given incident, and whether it ought to be treated with rigor or leniency. In particular, officials had to consider whether they risked enlarging the damage by pushing such cases into the open forums of criminal justice. Trial and punishment might well be a good local deterrent to potential troublemakers, but they could also bring embarrassing publicity, undercut the regime's aura of popularity, and even bring ridicule down around Napoleon.

In the Côte d'Or, for example, "injurious remarks" hurled in a drunken rage included the common taunt that the first consul's real name was not Bonaparte but Bonneatrappe. Yet the government's commissioner to the department's criminal tribunal had to admit that he was stumped. "I do not see any law that covers this case," wrote the commissioner to the Grand Judge. Moreover, he sensibly opined, "The remark in question is more fitting to be scorned than to give rise to a trial. But since you wish that he be punished, I beg you to indicate to me the law that can be applied to him." It would appear that the minister too was at a loss, since he eventually authorized the case to be dropped.[2] But that would be a misleading conclusion. For the accused had already been subjected to a period of discretionary, extralegal detention, which in itself constituted a form of punishment. This course had much to recommend it, as explained by the commissioner to the criminal tribunal in the Isère, where a similar case was pending. Two inebriated men in a café had "vomited imprecations against the First Consul, calling him a usurper, tyrant, and scoundrel." The accused could be indicted and sent to trial, observed the official, but this "procedure might arouse public curiosity, and possibly awaken malevolence and serve to stimulate wickedness. To avoid the publicity that this kind of trial would bring about, might I not limit myself simply to holding him in prison?" Or as a colleague in the Moselle put it a few years later in a comparable case: "The seditious proposals espoused by this man . . . might well call for a measure of *haute police* [i.e., extra-judicial detention] rather than a criminal trial."[3]

Preventive detention under the doctrine of *haute police* became the response of choice in such situations, and even in far graver cases of seditious behavior, where the law was murky and difficult for effective prosecution, or where the regime wished to avoid unwelcome publicity. Both Fouché (minister of police in 1800–02 and again in 1804–10) and Regnier (Grand Judge after 1802, as well as acting police minister in 1802–04) routinely ordered or countenanced preventive detention. Regnier, for example, resolved the troublesome case of Berthet in that fashion. "Fueled by wine," Berthet had declared that he far preferred Pichegru and Moreau (generals both under indictment for treason), who were just as well suited to rule as Bonaparte; he invited a companion to drink to the health of Generals Pichegru and Moreau, and upon his refusal, turned on him with obscene insults. Instead of allowing the case to go forward, Regnier directed that the accused simply remain in detention, and then ordered his release two months later. Fouché frequently resorted to the same procedure, as in another case where a man got into a drunken brawl with local gendarmes and compounded his offense by hurling epithets at the emperor and calling him "Bonneatrappe." The investigating magistrate in Painboeuf was inclined to let the matter go because of the drunkenness, but Fouché felt otherwise. "I have decided that he should remain in prison *par mesure de haute police* for two months, and that he be placed under special surveillance in his commune after his release."[4]

Allowing a drunken loudmouth to cool off in jail for a day or two might have been a benign measure, but an open-ended preventive detention lasting several months could be devastating. Thus Chuffrat, a plumber in Lille arrested for "injurious remarks" against the first consul, after languishing in jail for almost two months bitterly protested over the destruction of his livelihood and the humiliation of being "confounded with the dregs of society." After the Grand Judge finally ordered his release, the departmental commissioner cautioned Chuffrat "to display proper respect to this hero that the universe admires!" Piecq, a boatman from Condé, was not as fortunate. During a drunken binge he had called the emperor "Bonneatrappe," and allegedly denounced him "for killing off the French people, for seeking to ruin the whole world in order to satisfy his ambitions—but if he ever runs into him one day, the affair will soon be finished." As Piecq moldered in jail between January and March 1809 under the doctrine of *haute police*, his wife pled for his release, claiming that her husband was utterly distraught over what he had done. "Each day [spent in jail] he is pining away and seems now to be a dying person," she wrote. It turned out she did not exaggerate, for Piecq died in custody.[5]

Even in response to genuinely seditious activity the Napoleonic regime gravitated toward punishment by preventive detention, the equivalent of handling disorders within the family under patriarchal authority. Take "the anarchist intrigue of Lyon" (as Fouché called it), in which four men were seized in 1806 with printed placards to the French people emanating from a self-styled "Emergency Committee of Surveillance." Virulently anti-Napoleonic, recalling the sovereign people to its rights and obligations, urging a revival of revolutionary spirit (but shrewdly promising to respect the Concordat), the packets also included printed circulars appointing special commissioners to act locally in behalf of the committee, with blanks left for the names. Unlike an excited historian confronting such dramatic evidence decades later, the departmental prosecutor in the Loire took a calm view of this affair, assuming it to be the work of "a few miserable people" trying to stir up trouble at a time when the emperor was abroad, although he admitted the possibility that "this project might have a dangerous center somewhere." Naturally he passed the matter off to his superiors in Paris.[6]

Fouché and Regnier agreed that the government must investigate carefully but should not be overly concerned. "At this point one sees only several miserable and obscure individuals, absolutely lacking all means and destined to expiate their folly in Bicêtre [a prison/workhouse where vagabonds were held] rather than standing before an Imperial High Court," wrote the police minister. "It would be ridiculous and possibly dangerous to treat this affair in a manner that would make all of France as well as foreigners believe it to be a [veritable] conspiracy. . . . Let this offense be punished without lending it an importance that it would never appear to have on its own account."[7] Fouché's formulation can stand as the regime's definitive rationalization for preventive detention of political prisoners.

The practice of course had deep roots in the *lettres de cachet* used by the royal government as well as the administrative policing methods of old-regime urban police magistrates, and it increased exponentially during the Revolution with the law of suspects of 1793. But preventive detention was utterly contrary to the core liberalism of the National Assembly, which elevated legality over convenience and professed to despise arbitrary acts above all else. This spirit, it should be noted, extended to the issue of pardon. The austere, rationalized Penal Code of 1791 eliminated entirely the option of clemency or pardon by the head of state. No arbitrary personal consideration, no remnant of patrimonial justice, would intrude on the Revolution's notion of equal punishments for the same infraction. With the advent of the life consulship in 1802, however, Napoleon reclaimed the historic prerogative of pardon in article 86 of the new constitution adopted by the Senate. Standing alone, the very last article in the document, it seems at first an afterthought, but it should be taken as a marker toward the imminent return to monarchy. To be sure, the first consul or emperor was to exercise this power of *grâce* "in council." The institution of the *conseil privé* appears once more in this domain, requiring the intimate collaboration with Napoleon of eight handpicked senators, counselors of state, and other high functionaries.[8]

Preventive detention has deservedly gone down as a hallmark of the Napoleonic regime. Official documents customarily subdivided its targets into five categories. At the top of the list came "prisoners of state," or what we might simply call political prisoners. A partial list from 1811 of 128 such *prisonniers d'Etat* gives the following breakdown:[9]

- Accused of conspiracies in the revolutionary sense [including Malet]: 4
- Accused of conspiracies in the counterrevolutionary sense: 16
- Agents of espionage for England: 14
- [Resistant] Spaniards: 32
- Various offenses against the government: 20
- Vendéens and *chouans* [former royalist rebels]: 28
- Condemned [to death], their penalty having been commuted [e.g., Polignac]: 7
- Political intriguers: 7

"Seditious priests" constituted a second category. Then came "vicious men" (a misnomer since it included a few women), persons taken into custody for brigandage, murder, or lesser offenses for whom sufficient evidence was lacking to win a conviction in court. (The women in this category seem a particularly flamboyant lot, including Eloise Chaveriat, age twenty, "a prostitute who sought to corrupt her sister aged twelve"; Marie Creuze, age sixty, "given over to the most shameful libertinism; her scandalous conduct has caused her husband to die of chagrin"; and Françoise Bouton, age thirty-four, "guilty of the worst excess of drunkenness; her misconduct has caused the death of five of her children and almost burned down her house.") Preventive detention was also used against individuals tried for felonies and acquitted by the tribunals "despite presumptions of guilt, where the interest of society requires that their detention be continued as a measure of *haute police* because they are so dangerous"—the state's antidote, one might say, to the propensity of juries to acquit despite the prosecution's evidence. Finally, like preceding regimes, the Napoleonic state occasionally incarcerated incorrigible vagabonds and other *mauvais sujets* without trial.[10] In general, then, criminal justice in the Consulate and Empire was becoming more personalized and contingent, either more arbitrary or more pragmatically flexible, depending on one's point of view. In either case this left Napoleon's liberal servitors in an uncomfortable position.

THE SENATE AND INDIVIDUAL LIBERTY

During its rush to endorse Napoleon's elevation to emperor, the Senate inserted into the fine print of the new constitution a provision creating a "Senatorial Commission on Individual Liberty," part of a modest quid pro quo for its enthusiastic support. While not the actual sponsor of this initiative, Sieyès (Bonaparte's erstwhile partner in the Brumaire coup) was certainly its inspiration. Back in 1795 (at which time his ideas had been spurned), Sieyès argued the need for a "third force" to stand between the executive and the legislature and guarantee the integrity of the constitution. Sieyès also envisaged this institution as a defender of civil liberty. "The final cause of the entire social world must be individual liberty," he observed with characteristic finality, and his proposed "constitutional jury" would be the sentinel of that liberty.[11] After Brumaire, Sieyès won agreement for establishing his third force, but the defense of liberty did not figure among its enumerated functions at that time. Now in 1804 this role was finally incorporated into the Senate's vague mandate.

It made eminent sense. Since the very notion of an empire implied a concentration of power unknown in a lawful republic, the transition could well pose a threat to individual liberty. It must therefore have seemed fitting to create a visible counterweight at that moment against the state's increased potential for despotism. The more so since the Napoleonic regime from its inception resorted to extra-legal detention for a variety of reasons. There would be no shortage of work for the new commission. But what could it actually accomplish in behalf of individual liberty?

Comprising seven members chosen by the Senate and rotated partially every few months, the commission was authorized to review petitions by or in behalf of arrested citizens "who have not been brought before the courts within ten days since their arrest" as prescribed by ordinary criminal procedure. If the commission believed that this preventive detention "is not justified by the interest of the State," it would request the ministry of police or justice to release the citizen or arraign him in court. If after three such interventions the commission remained dissatisfied with the official response, it could place the matter before the full Senate, which theoretically had the power to indict the errant minister before a special high court—a drastic action that the commission never came close to taking.[12]

Each petition received by the commission was first given to an individual member for review. If he judged the affair to be within the commission's competence, he would write to the ministry or confer personally with one of its officials to seek information and clarification.[13] The commission quickly stipulated that certain types of cases lay outside its competence: pleas for clemency or pardon, which had to go directly to the emperor; cases actually before the courts or susceptible to ordinary appeals; claims against harassment by the police; or petitions from foreigners in trouble with the police or awaiting deportation. In such cases the commission rarely initiated any inquiries, and generally responded to the petitioner that the case was "outside the commission's attributions."[14] When the commission did pursue a case, the ministry often persuaded the senators that the authorities had acted appropriately, and the commission desisted. Claims by the ministry about "the interest of the state" or insistence that "detention must continue for reasons of public safety" usually sufficed, even without the occasional observation that His Majesty personally believed that the incarceration of the citizen in question must continue.[15]

At the outset the Senate populated the commission with parliamentary veterans of the revolutionary decade, including Abrial (Napoleon's first minister of justice), and three former deputies to the National Assembly: Boissy d'Anglas, Emmery, and Lenoir-Laroche—all subsequently redesignated for a second term as commissioners, at which time they were joined by their former colleague Lemercier. With Lenoir-Laroche and Boissy as the commission's first president and secretary, respectively, its dominant personalities were liberally oriented men of 1789 now part of the Napoleonic establishment. In its early days, these commissioners seemed taken with the importance and sheer novelty of their mission. With gravity and diligence they tested the waters, established guidelines, and shaped their procedures.

In October 1804 Lenoir reported to the Senate on the commission's activity since its inception. In its first four months it had received 116 petitions. "By its influence it has obtained 44 releases; 17 cases it has judged to be outside its attributions; 34 cases were adjourned indefinitely (*ajournées jusqu'à nouvel ordre*); and 21 remain pending for want of sufficient information [from the ministry]."[16] Lenoir went on to explain the commission's quest for a balance between liberty and order. Its mandate was to serve "as a sentinel established by the Constitution to keep watch that the liberty of citizens is guaranteed against any truly arbitrary acts; but it will never lose sight that a State can only maintain itself by order and by the firm action, fair and measured, of its government."[17] Altogether the senatorial commission on individual liberty docketed 585 cases between 1804 and 1814, some involving repeat petitions from the same individual. But the pace of its activity slackened with time. In the first four years it dealt with 344 cases, but in its last six years only 241. The commission typically met three times per month in the first few years, but after 1807 an average of once a month and even less frequently in its last four years. The commission's role diminished significantly when the government introduced a new procedure in 1810 for an annual review of preventive detention cases, to be discussed below.

THE SENATORIAL COMMISSION dealt with pleas from three types of citizens confined without recourse to trial. First, it received protests from individuals deemed by local authorities to be habitual criminals, who were kept in detention notwithstanding the lack of sufficient evidence to put them on trial for a particular crime, or the fact that they had already been tried and acquitted. Thus Louis Badaire, tried and acquitted for brigandage along with a group of co-defendants and ordered released by the criminal tribunal of the Loir-et-Cher, remained in custody on orders from the ministry of justice upon recommendation of the local prosecutor. The commission queried the minister twice, but he insisted that Badaire was too dangerous to release.[18] On a more mundane level, one Carré was held because he was deemed "an incorrigible *filou*, arrested sixteen times in the past for different offenses." In 1812, the commission received a group petition from "sixteen individuals who are still in detention. Most of them are habitual criminals and they must not be returned to society without great precautions being taken." After discussion with the commission, the minister "ordered a review with the object of granting freedom to those who could be released without danger."[19]

   The commission's second type of case involved anti-social behavior, individuals who were placed in custody ostensibly for their own good or for the sake of their families or communities. One subset of this category included "*fous et aliénés*," such as the marquis de Sade ("man of letters, detained for forty months at Charenton"), who makes an early appearance in the commission's files. The commission took no action on his case or on a petition from the poet Desorgues, also confined against his will in Charenton. Such prisoners, held on the equivalent of an old-regime *lettre de cachet*, also included vagabonds and "infirm beggars without means of support," as well as a few drunken, uncontrollable husbands, wives, and mothers, such as Romance ("his detention was provoked by fits of violence that have made him the terror of his family and his neighbors"), Péricault ("imprisoned on the demand of his very own family"), Mme Roget ("incarcerated by virtue of her misconduct and on the demand of her family"), or Veuve Blanc ("incarcerated by virtue of madness; the complaints of Dame Chaumand, her mother, are without foundation").[20]

The third type of case on the commission's docket and by far the most challenging concerned political prisoners of one kind or another, mainly amnestied Vendée rebels, former émigrés, and unbending refractory priests deemed by the government to be irreconcilable and extremely dangerous. (Only a scant two or three Jacobin militants turn up in its records, the deportations of Nivôse evidently having had their desired effect.) A typical example was Pioger, an amnestied Vendée rebel, rearrested in Paris, who spent thirty months in detention before being tried and acquitted by a military tribunal, but who continued to be held in prison under orders from the emperor himself. Or Desol de Grisolles, another amnestied Vendéean, rearrested and kept under lock and key despite his acquittal by a military tribunal, "His hatred against the government being the motive for his detention"— an imprisonment that lasted until 1813. Similar observations by the ministry sufficed to close the file of Planchon, "a priest known as a dangerous troublemaker who has openly preached revolt; he must remain under detention."[21] The spectacular trial of royalists in the Cadoudal-Pichegru plot against Bonaparte spawned several such cases among its minor characters. In reference to Monsieur d'Atré, for example, Fouché explained that "the wrongdoing (*grefs*) with which he is charged is sufficiently grave for the public safety and has determined His Majesty that, although acquitted, his detention should be prolonged."[22] It is easy to conclude, then, that the commission simply would not stand up to the routine practice of preventive detention, let alone the emperor's personal insistence on such measures in particular cases.

YET NONE of this should imply that the commission's efforts amounted to an empty gesture, that it lacked spurts of energy or the occasional clear success. One early case may stand as a model of how the commission could fulfill its purpose. Arnaud, a former road inspector, "protested against being detained in Bicêtre for over nine months by virtue of an order that contained no charge of any crime and no judgment by any court. He knows of no reason for his detention." When the commission requested an explanation, the Grand Judge replied that "this type of detention might well be considered as a humanitarian act rather than a police measure"—implying that the petitioner was destitute or unable to care for himself. Since Arnaud himself demanded his freedom, however, the commission considered this explanation unconvincing and argued that "there would be little drawback in freeing Arnaud." Shortly thereafter he was released, subject to surveillance.[23]

Then there is the Lasalle case, perhaps the most bizarre in the commission's annals. The unusual circumstances led Lenoir-Laroche (the commission president) to confer personally with Cambacérès, who reported back that "only the emperor himself could decide the fate of M. Lasalle." Lenoir then drafted an unprecedented letter directly to Napoleon, signed by all seven senators, which set out the facts of the case and the commission's position.

Lasalle was arrested on the grounds of the imperial palace in Saint-Cloud on 24 September 1806. He had gone out there, as Lenoir explained, "to solicit the justice and beneficence of Your Imperial Majesty in connection with the indemnities that he claimed were due him from General Savary [one of Napoleon's favorites] by virtue of a contract that he had executed with him." No doubt, the letter admitted, Lasalle went about this in an entirely inappropriate manner, and he was arrested on Napoleon's personal order. Shortly thereafter the emperor departed on military campaign in Prussia, leaving Lasalle in prison as a forgotten loose end. "For over three months this unfortunate person has repeatedly presented to the commission his complaints, which have grown more emphatic each time. His health has deteriorated in deplorable fashion and this *père de famille* is on the brink of complete ruin." The commission therefore urged clemency, and appealed to Napoleon for the unconditional release of Lasalle, "pleased with the opportunity to address Your Majesty directly with our sentiments of respect." To the senators' great delight, Napoleon responded by ordering Lasalle's release.[24]

More typically, of course, the commission dealt with the hard cases of preventive detention without trial for political offenses, where it rarely achieved much success. Yet the more determined the petitioner, the more interest the commission usually displayed, provided that the incarcerated citizen seemed more misguided than dangerous, or that he had been held long beyond any reasonable length of time. For almost three years the commission advocated the cause of Joland to the police ministry. Held without trial, Joland was "accused of conspiracy, notably for having hawked seditious addresses." In December 1807 the commission urged the minister of police to release him, "taking into consideration the condition of this unfortunate *père de famille*," and the certificates from his hometown of Valence "attesting to his morality and good conduct." Their intervention having failed, the senators took up the case again in June 1809, emphasizing this time the exorbitant prolongation of Joland's detention, but the minister responded that he must remain in prison until 1810. Joland was finally released that year, upon the recommendation of a *conseil privé*.[25]

Most political prisoners were beyond help from the commission but it could not hurt to have its sympathy. Thus Eve Demaillot, an unregenerate Jacobin pamphleteer, known as a blustering intriguer, was arrested and thrown into the harsh Saint-Pélagie prison in December 1803. But Demaillot suffered from crippling rheumatism. Convinced that "his health was being irreparably damaged," the commission helped secure his release under police surveillance, which it later had cause to regret. (Bloodied but unbowed, Demaillot found himself back in prison for his tenuous complicity in the Malet conspiracy of 1808—he admitted that he was aware of the plotting but insisted that he had taken no part in it—and this time he stayed there. In 1814 he capitalized on his miserable experience by publishing a sensational pamphlet about prison life under Napoleon.)[26]

The commission's most frustrating case had to be the abbé David, another unconvicted minor character in the Cadoudal-Pichegru royalist plot against Bonaparte. David evidently fixated on the senatorial commission as his best hope, and maintained a steady barrage of petitions that quickly won the senators' sympathy. Indeed, the commission's uninflected bureaucratic style momentarily gave way to a flash of passion in this matter. The senators recorded that "The abbé David shall be informed that the commission has constantly supported his claims to the Minister of Police. The seventh protest by the abbé David shall be transmitted to the Minister, and he shall be told of the sensation which that protest has caused among the members of the commission." In what must have been a *pas de deux* by now, the minister laconically replied that "the latest protest appears to have no foundation, and the commission knows the intention of His Majesty regarding the demand that David be freed." For the moment the commission had no choice but to enter "*ajournée*" on its records. But a few months later it went back to the ramparts when a new petition from David occasioned yet another conference with the minister. Futile as it may have been, this is what the commission had been created to do.[27]

THE ANNUAL REVIEW

In April 1809, Napoleon convoked an ad hoc group of trusted subordinates to review the status of all "prisoners of state" and others being held in preventive detention. For this *conseil secret* (as it was called), the ministry of justice presented the standard five categories of prisoners for review. First came 172 "prisoners of state" or, properly speaking, political prisoners; then 27 "seditious priests"; 152 "vicious men" in custody for crimes but for whom sufficient evidence was lacking to win a conviction; 27 incorrigible vagabonds; and 97 individuals tried for crimes and acquitted, whom the ministry believed to be guilty and too dangerous to release. When this "secret council" held its first meeting, Napoleon sent the last three lists back to a committee for further work. He wanted more information from relevant local officials such as prefects or public prosecutors, and if necessary wanted an *auditeur* of the Council of State sent to interview particular prisoners. Meanwhile, the emperor proceeded to consider the first two, more amply annotated, lists of political prisoners and priests. In two sessions (with the addition of a supplementary list in the second) the council reviewed a total of 253 cases, and recommended the release of 67 prisoners.[28]

The *conseil secret* of 1809 proved to be a trial run for a systematic annual review of all extra-legal incarceration. Under a decree of March 1810 hammered out by the Council of State after discussion with the emperor, the government committed itself to undertake annual inspections of the Empire's seven "state prisons" and to interview all "prisoners of state" in preventive detention. The decree's preamble described the problem (now brought into public view) with disarming candor: "a certain number of our subjects are detained in our State prisons, without it being opportune either to bring them before the courts or to release them." As on the issue of censorship, Napoleon juggled a conviction that the government must be free to do anything necessary to preserve order or repress subversion with a sense that the Empire must be a rational and just polity operating with fixed rules. The emperor initially wished to jettison the term "prisons of state" altogether as reminiscent of a regime "that one is far from wishing to reestablish," although he later let that appellation stand. More fundamentally, he could not bring himself to admit that preventive detention without benefit of trial and conviction was arbitrary. He merely wished to regularize this practice as much as possible, and to assure that such prisoners were not simply forgotten.

The state prisons [*prisons de haute police*] are not arbitrary means of detention (he told the Council of State). They are there to receive men who are guilty towards the State but whose offense cannot be [formally] characterized, and also those whom one wishes to remove from the severity of the courts so as to shed as little blood as possible. It is with such intentions that we incarcerate conspirators, certain seditious priests, brigands escaped from the Vendée who foment trouble and disorder, and agents of England. . . . [But] the minister of police should not have the right to send someone to these prisons simply on his own authority. . . . It is up to the sovereign alone to decide if the circumstances require deviating from ordinary rules. A panel should determine each year whether the detention should continue, and the prisons should be inspected annually by counselors of state. These committees should be invested with the power to free those whom they judge to be inappropriately detained.[29]

An annual review of all such cases—political prisoners, irreconcilable priests, dangerous ex *chouans* and foreigners, alleged British spies, bands of brigands who intimidated juries, hardened criminals who had managed to gain acquittals at trial, incorrigible vagabonds, and social misfits—would assure that these persons were sequestered (as the decree's preamble stated) "only for legitimate causes deriving from the public interest and not out of private considerations or passions." In sum, the government would employ "legal and solemn forms" to review routine extra-legal practices dictated by reasons of state.[30] The irony of this policy was not lost on Lewis Goldsmith when he penned his well-informed and scathing attack on Napoleon and his collaborators in 1810. In his entry on Merlin de Douai (a key revolutionary jurist in the Council of State), Goldsmith printed the newly minted decree of March 1810 alongside the law of suspects of September 1793 drafted by Merlin for the National Convention, which institutionalized the preventive detention of political suspects during the Terror. The parallels are indeed striking, although he could as easily have drawn comparisons with the use of *lettres de cachet* by the Bourbons or with the harsh measures adopted by the Directory against royalist militants.[31]

In any case, as the regime passed from an ad hoc *conseil secret* to routinized annual reviews of preventive detention, the participation of a blue-ribbon group of collaborators in a *conseil privé* helped provide the sense of legitimacy that Napoleon sought. When the first such council convened in December 1810, it comprised besides Cambacérès in the chair and Grand Judge Regnier:

Berthier (the minister of war), Savary (minister of police), Garnier (president of the Senate), Abrial (senator and former minister of justice), Regnaud, Boulay, Jollivet, and Faure (all from the Council of State), and Merlin and Muraire (the president and procurator respectively of the Cour de Cassation, the nation's highest tribunal). In the review of 1812, most of these individuals reappeared along with Lacépède (president of the Senate) and counselors of state Dubois and Pasquier, the former and current prefect of police.[32]

Jollivet (a member of the Legislative Assembly of 1791, financial expert, original member of the Council of State, and key official in the satellite Kingdom of Westphalia, among other posts) had been tapped by Napoleon to supervise the inspection of the prisons and interviews with the prisoners. But Napoleon deemed Jollivet's first efforts inadequate and adjourned the council until he could "establish for each prisoner of state a detailed report containing everything related to the period and the motives for their arrest, and any consideration which can enlighten the opinion of the *conseil privé.*" When deliberations resumed in March 1811, it took five sessions stretching over three months to conclude the review. Jollivet continued to be in charge and formulated the recommendations put before the *conseil privé.* But the *conseil privé* was no rubber stamp. Notwithstanding all the work he had put in, and with as much esteem as he may have enjoyed among his colleagues, Jollivet's conclusions did not automatically win support. Jollivet, for example, recommended that General Malet—"accused of having hatched a conspiracy and of having sought to stir up agitation among the anarchists"—be released after spending three years in detention without trial.

IT IS WORTH pausing over Malet, in retrospect the Empire's most significant "prisoner of state" and the principal organizer of two plots against Napoleon: a bumbling performance in 1808, and a serious and fatal one in 1812. In 1808, Brigade General Claude-François Malet was cooling his heels in Paris awaiting final war ministry action against him for serious charges of corruption. Malet's erratic service record (reflecting clashes with civilian authorities, several suspensions from active duty, and a public vote of no in the plebiscite of 1804, among other problems) did not bode well for his future prospects. Indeed, he faced the distinct possibility of being cashiered from the army with loss of pension. In Paris, Malet fell in with a group of discontented, leftish café habitués such as Eve Demaillot, who eventually began fantasizing or planning a coup. At the same time Malet developed an extremely tenuous connection with an entirely different group of oppositional ex-politicians (including the Montagnard *conventionnel* Florent-Guiot, whom Cambacérès and Berlier had placed as secretary of the Conseil des Prises, and the former war minister Servan, who died suddenly in May of that year). The latter circle was united by its concern over what would happen to France should Napoleon be killed in battle. Malet's plan capitalized on Napoleon's absence on campaign in 1808: a spurious *senatus-consulte*, plastered all over Paris, would proclaim the emperor's death in Spain and the restoration of the republic, while promising, among other popular appeals, to abolish conscription.

In the end, nothing came to pass. Loose talk by Eve Demaillot and others soon reached the wrong ears, prompted a denunciation to the prefect of police, Dubois, and led to the arrest of Malet and his associates, although they managed to destroy any tangible evidence of their plot before the ax fell. Dubois went further and hauled in the "Servan circle" of more prominent individuals, who in fact had nothing at all to do with Malet's cabal. Fouché intervened in behalf of the latter group and with Cambacérès's support finally managed to exculpate them months later, but Malet remained in jail without benefit of a trial, his interrogations having confirmed in the government's eyes "the existence [not of acts] but of proposals, demarches, and hopes." It was a classic use of preventive detention with the virtue of avoiding negative publicity for the regime.[33] When Jollivet concluded his presentation about this enigmatic figure and recommended his release three years later, Cambacérès polled the *conseil privé*. "The majority of the members of the committee believe, contrary to the opinion of commissioner [Jollivet] that it is appropriate to keep ex-general Malet in detention for the next year, with a new determination to be made at the end of that time."[34]

They certainly made the right call, as it turned out, although holding Malet in detention did not suffice to rein him in. In 1810, Malet had been transferred from the Force prison to a supposedly secure private sanitarium because of ostensible health problems. Before long he was plotting with another inmate of the Maison Dubuisson, a hard-core ultramontanist named abbé Lafon. For once, the old canard of collusion between the two extremes came to pass. Malet and Lafon found common cause in the belief that ridding France of Napoleon would fulfill their respective goals: bringing back the republic and winning freedom for the captive pope. In the lax conditions of his detention, Malet planned his second attempt to overthrow the regime, and when the moment came in 1812, he escaped with ease and even managed to free two other cashiered republican generals from the Force prison, using his elegant general's uniform and bogus orders to hoodwink the jailers. This time, Malet used Napoleon's absence in Russia to support the claim that the emperor had died and that the Senate had established an interim government. And this time the plotters passed from words to deed, as they sequestered Police Minister Savary and Prefect of Police Pasquier, and convinced several credulous army officers and high civilian officials, including the Prefect of Paris Frochot, that firm action was needed to fill the vacuum—as if no heir to the imperial throne was waiting in the wings. Finally, a skeptical commander of the Paris garrison called Malet's bluff and after a brief scuffle arrested him. In short order, a military commission tried Malet and several co-conspirators. They were executed before the emperor even learned of these distressing events, which revealed the extraordinary fragility of the imperial regime.[35]

In the review of 1811, incidentally, Jollivet also recommended the release of two alleged co-conspirators in the first, abortive Malet plot of 1808: Eve Demaillot, and Rigomer Bazin (a well-educated *homme de lettres*, as the ministry accurately described him), one of the most impassioned and unregenerate Jacobins in the entire country.[36] But the majority of the *conseil privé* again reversed Jollivet's recommendation and determined that their incarceration should continue—possibly saving their lives by keeping them out of harm's way in prison, thereby precluding their involvement in Malet's failed coup of 1812. On the other side of the spectrum, Jollivet's proposal that the former *chouan* François Pioger should be released after years of preventive detention also met a unanimous rejection by the *conseil privé*, in the belief "that it would be dangerous to return this prisoner to freedom." Altogether, the *conseil privé* of 1811 reviewed 802 cases, which it decided as follows:[37]

	Number	*Remaining in Prison*
Prisonniers d'Etat	156	127
Prêtres	44	40
Repris de justice	340	305
Hommes vicieux	141	83
Vagabonds	121	102
Total	802	657

To his credit, Napoleon raised the issue of preventive detention again in 1812, although the decree of March 1810 had met most of his wishes. While perfectly comfortable with incarcerating violent hotheads and potential plotters, he fretted that the net of preventive detention perhaps reached too widely when used against petty offenders, unfortunates, or felons acquitted by juries. Some veteran collaborators tried to allay his qualms by recalling that old regime "policing" in Paris had utilized the equivalent of preventive detention for disorderly persons, *gens sans aveu*, prostitutes, and reckless coach drivers, but other counselors such as Réal did not wish to demean the Paris prefecture of police with such petty matters. Napoleon finally concluded that "the undomiciled *gens sans aveu*, prostitutes, sharpers, coachmen, and others that have been indicted should be under the hand of the police. They can be sent to prison, but only for one month at most, and they have the right to appear before a tribunal."[38]

The case of hardened criminals who had managed to win acquittals from juries remained a more vexing issue. Over the years the Council of State had debated the jury system exhaustively, stymied in part by a canvass of the judiciary which revealed the presiding judges to be deeply divided over whether to retain the exalted but much criticized institution or abolish it. Eventually, the liberal revolutionary veterans, partisans of this "palladium of liberty," won Napoleon over to an historic compromise despite his personal distaste for the jury system. The new Code of Criminal Procedure of 1808 jettisoned the grand jury (making the indictment stage more professional and less uncertain) but retained the trial jury for felonies. The pool of citizen jurors contracted markedly, however, as the eligibility requirements were raised "to narrow the circle from which the jurors are chosen in order to guarantee good choices." Similarly, the new code streamlined the questions posed to the juries in order to reduce the complexity of their task as well as their latitude. But even in this attenuated form, the survival of a supremely revolutionary innovation could be counted as a victory for the liberals.[39]

Now, in effect, the question was back on the table: if indicted felons acquitted by juries could still be held in prison or placed under close police surveillance after their release, what did this say about the power of the citizen-jurors or the rights of defendants? Liberally oriented counselors argued that continuing to hold acquitted felons could not be justified. Boulay and Berlier maintained that under current law, only convicted criminals could be subjected to incarceration or even to tight police surveillance. "It is impossible to establish this against those who have been acquitted,"

Berlier insisted, "without overthrowing the principle of judgment by juries." Finally, however, Napoleon proved unwilling to abandon this practice, although he wished to delimit it. "The police may provisionally seize acquitted individuals whom it is dangerous to release," he concluded. "A commission of the Cour Impériale . . . should examine, within a short interval, the motives for this detention; it should decide if there is cause to prolong it and if so, shall fix its duration."[40] As far as one can tell, this procedure was never actually implemented before the fall of the Empire, but the annual *conseil privé* at least provided a potential check on the abuse of preventive detention against political offenders, acquitted criminals, or local troublemakers.

WHILE the routines of preventive detention largely occurred beyond their purview, liberal senators and counselors of state were obliged to confront its ramifications directly. Initially, the commission on individual liberty burnished the Senate's self-image as guardians of the public trust, and no doubt bolstered its complacency. But did it have any meaningful impact? Or worse (as historian Jean Thiry suggests), did the commission have a negative impact simply by providing a fig leaf behind which preventive detention continued apace? Overall, the senators certainly failed to display aggressiveness or zeal in filling their mandate. Whenever the government dug in its heels, they usually desisted with deference. Yet the commission could unquestionably be an irritant to the police and justice ministries, and its interventions did yield results from time to time. At the least the commission obliged the ministry to investigate its own actions and verify that a given extra-legal sequestration was not a careless mistake or a casual use of police power. The number of releases recorded in the commission's register was not negligible, although one cannot often tell whether a given release would have occurred as a matter of course anyway. Presumably its intervention speeded up the disposition of certain cases that ended in release. Most important is the simple fact that the senatorial commission, ostensibly independent of the executive branch, offered a ray of hope to individuals plunged into the frustration or despair of prolonged preventive detention. Beyond question, the senatorial commission and (after 1810) the annual review by a *conseil privé* each abetted the regime's extra-legal practices while ostensibly serving as checks or correctives upon them. Yet the final word might as easily go in the other direction. Thanks to the existence of the senatorial commission and later of the annual *conseil privée*—in contrast to the methods of modern totalitarian regimes—

persons imprisoned arbitrarily under the Empire did not simply fall into a black hole and disappear.

THE QUESTION OF CENSORSHIP

With its deep roots in the Enlightenment, freedom of the press seemed to be a consensual liberal ideal by 1789. In pre-revolutionary France, the battle for the free expression of ideas had been waged primarily in the realm of books and pamphlets rather than the tightly restricted periodical press. Authors could circumvent an ostensibly comprehensive system of book censorship either by connivance with the authorities (securing "tacit permission" rather than formal authorization to publish) or by finding publishers and distributors in the lively networks of the illicit book trade. Suddenly in 1789 everything changed. The royal censorship apparatus collapsed and, with few qualms as yet, the National Assembly emblazoned freedom of expression in the Declaration of the Rights of Man and Citizen. Like other natural rights proclaimed in that foundational manifesto, however, the right to publish was limited by the interests of society as formulated in positive law.[41]

Simultaneously in the summer of 1789, newspapers instantly became the print medium par excellence in the Revolution's new political culture. Freed of both royal censorship and corporate privileges and controls, journalism blossomed as an unregulated entrepreneurial endeavor. A few old hands and many newcomers jostled to launch weekly or daily newspapers in Paris and the provinces, and while many folded quickly, others enjoyed durable commercial success and substantial political influence. Suddenly France exceeded England or the United States as the land of unfettered political journalism. But backlash and retreat were not long in coming. Veritable press freedom gave visibility to every point on the political spectrum, from rejectionist royalism to the violent polemics of Marat, but such liberty lasted only three years. Starting with the overthrow of the monarchy, no regime proved willing to tolerate outspoken journalistic opposition. Royalist newspapers were the first to succumb immediately after the insurrection of August 1792, followed the next year by journalists allied with the Girondins, and then by others whose loyalty to Montagnard policy seemed suspect.

The fall of the Robespierrist government in 1794 once again permitted virtually unlimited freedom for journalists of all persuasions, but it was not only repressive Montagnards who could not abide such a free press. By the time of the Directory, moderate revolutionary veterans themselves had backed away from that ideal. Unable to solve the conundrum of when press freedom turns into license or dangerous subversion, they inscribed their ambivalent position in the constitution of 1795. Even while reasserting freedom of the press, the new constitution qualified it by granting the government emergency powers to suppress newspapers "when circumstances make it necessary." The Directory used this authority repeatedly against both the left and the right, notably in a sweeping suppression of royalist newspapers during the Fructidor coup of 1797, and in continuous harassment and closings of Neo-Jacobin journals in 1798–99. True, the legislature attempted intermittently to craft a press law that, by spelling out the ground rules for journalistic freedom, might put an end to such arbitrary practices, Berlier's bill of 1799 (alluded to in chapter I) being the last such instance. But these efforts got nowhere because the will to lift the government's hand from the newspaper press no longer commanded much sympathy among the governing elites. Thus the usually principled liberal Pierre Daunou argued in 1796 that if left to themselves, journalists were too unrestrained, too irresponsible to be compatible with order and stability: "one should not grant impunity for Marat out of respect for Bacon and Montesquieu." Most directorial republicans seemed now to believe that French newspapers oversimplified, exaggerated, and needlessly agitated the public. As one historian has put it, republican moderates "did not feel that newspapers deserved the protection given to serious discourse."[42]

TO NAPOLEON, such views were second nature. The first consul had long considered freedom of the press a dangerous shibboleth, and after the experience of the Directory years he encountered scant resistance to muzzling political newspapers decisively. Without any serious constitutional guarantees standing in its way, the Consulate from its inception ordered the closing of most surviving newspapers, coerced the sale of several others to reliable individuals, and eventually instituted formal censorship over those that remained.

Not that the press was entirely comatose during the Consulate. While the regime indeed suppressed overt political journals, broader intellectual currents could still find expression. Most interestingly, a renascent anti-Enlightenment tradition found new voice in the *Journal des Débats*, purchased by veteran conservative publishers, the *frères* Bertin. For several years the Bertins' journal (along with like-minded newspapers such as the *Mercure*) battled it out with Roederer's *Journal de Paris* and with *Le Décade philosophique*—the high-minded organ of the *idéologues*, intellectual heirs of the *philosophes*. Judging by the striking commercial success of the *Journal des Débats* (its circulation having swelled to around 15,000), and by the complaints of Roederer, Cabanis, and the *idéologues*, the counter-Enlightenment was showing an impressive second wind. Its new organs preached the primacy of duty over rights, extolled patriarchy and other traditional values, depicted religion as not only useful but true, and equated religious tolerance with a culpable indifference. The anti-*philosophes* may have been sapping the intellectual foundations of revolutionary liberalism, but as Roederer warned, they were also, at least implicitly, preparing the ground for a royalist restoration, as they would subsequently boast after 1814.[43]

Eventually the regime's tolerance for this contentious discourse wore out. In 1805 the government forced the *Journal des Débats* into a drastic reorganization. The Bertins swallowed up several other newspapers on generous terms to their publishers, pledged absolute fealty to the emperor, took on a new editor named by the government who would lead it out of "an invincible ignorance of present and future political interests," and found a new name for their newspaper, which reemerged as the impeccably bland *Journal de l'Empire*.[44] The Empire's grip on the press tightened inexorably as it taxed surviving newspapers punitively, limited "political" newspapers in the provinces to one per department under the prefect's supervision, and finally reduced the dozen or so surviving newspapers in Paris by another round of confiscations and forced mergers. Already quasi-official in nature, the remaining journals were now subjected to comprehensive pre-censorship so as to eliminate the unpredictability and idiosyncrasies that still nettled the government. As Police Minister Savary explained, "Since the newspapers are generally taken to be organs of the government, it is necessary that they effectively be so, but with precautions such that the government has nothing to fear from the ignorance or indiscretion of the editors. The only way to accomplish this is to subject the contents of these papers to a severe examination before they actually go to press."[45] By 1811, only four daily newspapers were appearing in Paris, all virtual instruments of the government—by coincidence or not, exactly the same number of general newspapers with legal privilege to publish in the capital before 1789.

BOOK PUBLISHING, meanwhile, ostensibly remained free, since the Consulate did not reinstitute old-regime style pre-censorship. But the police ministry had almost unlimited power to suppress any publications it deemed subversive. By 1806, a formal requirement was in place that every publisher must convey to the ministry a copy of each publication before it was placed on sale. From the beginning of the Consulate Fouché had justified the suppression of "corrupt" newspapers and (with admitted misgivings) of certain plays by the simple proposition that "the government exercises its natural right of repression against all who make war on the peace of the Republic," but he boasted that this did not require formal censorship.[46] This peculiar ethos still prevailed in 1806, as the police ministry described its repressive role in a contorted language of liberty: "The more widespread is freedom of the press," explained the functionaries charged with this task, "the greater is the duty of a sound police regime to scrutinize and promptly remedy the excesses which the tolerance of the law have rendered so common. When Your Excellency [Minister Fouché] desired that all publications of the booksellers be made available [to us] at the moment of their appearance, he conceived a simple, just, and necessary idea, which does no more damage to freedom of the press than a census does to individual liberty"—language truly worthy of Orwell's scrutiny.[47]

In 1808, however, Napoleon ordered Regnaud to draft a comprehensive project for the reorganization of the book trade. The project was to include guidelines for licensing and regulating publishers and printers, and the creation of a system for book censorship. In one of its most important undertakings in those years, the Council of State debated Regnaud's project on and off between August 1808 and January 1810, since Napoleon repeatedly sent the current draft back for revision, the main obstacle to consensus being precisely the details of the censorship system. (We are well informed about this protracted debate because Locré, the Council of State's recording secretary, took unusually copious notes and later published them as a book during a debate on press regulation under the Restoration.)[48]

Napoleon participated actively in the debate, pontificating and steering the deliberations in certain directions but also listening attentively to the clashing views of his counselors. "Every government knows that it has the right to smash the instrument that is wounding it," he declared, setting the baseline for discussion. A free press no longer served the public interest in France, he added (with unabashed cynicism), since under its present constitution the people no longer involve themselves with political affairs. Citizens remained free to express their political thoughts orally or in letters, he allowed, but not in print. Books dealing with religion, natural history, or morals did not much concern the emperor. In those relatively innocuous domains, he believed, censors ought to work with authors and not be quick to suppress questionable works. But books "written against the state" must be quashed before they ever found their way into print or distribution.

While Napoleon's intolerance for public political criticism was axiomatic, he seemed equally concerned that the present system of police surveillance and confiscation of books was too arbitrary: "It should not be the case that a book already in print can be suppressed by a simple decision." (Il ne faut pas qu'on puisse supprimer par une simple décision un livre déjà imprimé.) Printers, in particular, needed some security for their business. They could receive such reassurance, Napoleon thought, if they submitted their manuscripts for preliminary clearance by an official censorship agency. If a printer received authorization to publish a manuscript, and should the book later be suppressed for cause by the government, the printer would be entitled to an indemnity. Moreover, the emperor wanted a collective body with procedural guidelines of some kind to make these decisions. Initially, he called for a *collège de censure*, but later he decided to avoid the word "censorship" and suggested the more innocuous designation of a *tribunal de l'imprimerie*.[49]

Despite the emperor's well-known contempt for freedom of the press, it was still possible to defend that idea in his presence, at least in the abstract. To be sure, all counselors acknowledged the right of the state to suppress subversive writing. Moreover, since most shared Napoleon's view that the present powers of the police ministry were arbitrary in the extreme, a return to some form of book censorship could conceivably appear at this juncture as a lesser evil. On the level of sentiment and the symbolic gesture, at any rate, a clear line divided the active participants in this debate between those wishing to honor the ideal of freedom of the press—and to limit the proposed mechanisms of censorship at the margins—as against counselors who considered freedom of the press a specious notion that should not inhibit a rigorous process of censorship. This difference immediately crystallized into a choice between a so-called voluntary or partial censorship—defended by several revolutionary veterans in the Council—as against obligatory, comprehensive censorship, advocated by certain relative newcomers.

The Council accepted major constraints on book publishing with little or no dissent. In the name of an orderly marketplace, to combat overproduction, cutthroat competition, and book pirating, the government restricted the number of printers in Paris to sixty, in effect according them a kind of privilege, and reestablished a corps of inspectors for the Parisian book trade.[50] The Council also readily agreed that printers must maintain a certified register listing the titles of all manuscripts they intended to publish, which list they must present upon request to authorized government officials. Moreover, all books had to be signed with the real name of the author and publisher, upon pain of confiscation and punishment.

But must printers submit their manuscripts for clearance by a censorship bureau before they could lawfully be printed? As against such "absolute censorship," as it was called, Regnaud proposed a censorship agency to which printers *could* submit their manuscripts for clearance if they wished, without being obliged to do so—with the proviso that if a particular title on the printer's register aroused official concern, the bureau could demand to see the manuscript. If printer and author did not voluntarily avail themselves of precensorship by the bureau, their published book could be subject to confiscation if the government later deemed it subversive, and the printer would not be entitled to an indemnity for his loss. But if a book approved by the censorship was subsequently banned, the printer would be indemnified.

Liberals on the Council rallied around this notion of "voluntary censorship" lest a more draconian rule be adopted. In so doing they could at least honor the ideal of freedom of the press and salve their consciences. For the record, Regnaud himself declared, "absolute censorship will always remain an obstacle to the progress of enlightenment." Treilhard, a former colleague in the National Assembly, member of the Convention, and ex-director, likewise claimed that preliminary censorship was both futile and wrong. Along with Berlier, he argued that truly subversive authors would not be deterred by any system of censorship. Worse yet, censors were notoriously subjective and prone to abuse their power. Treilhard and Berlier both observed that censors were bound to be men of letters themselves and thus rivals of those whose fate they decided; to Regnaud, they would likely be exercising power over "authors more enlightened than themselves." I would prefer "the most complete liberty to publish," Treilhard told the Council, but under the circumstances he would support voluntary as against compulsory censorship.[51]

Berlier paid homage to freedom of the press, though he conceded under debate that it was perhaps less a natural right than a kind of convention. Still, he asked, why must the principle be categorically denied when one had the means "to prevent abuses without wounding the principle." With a somewhat convoluted logic, Berlier professed to be comfortable with Regnaud's proposal for voluntary censorship: "Censorship can be useful as long as one is free not to subject oneself to it." Defermon and Réal joined Berlier, Treilhard, and Regnaud in defending the beleaguered principle of press freedom once espoused (they noted) by such figures as Voltaire and Montesquieu. (The reputations of those towering figures, however, as well as the Enlightenment's core principle of freedom of thought, no longer carried an automatic sacrality after several years of anti-*philosophe* polemics in such organs as the *Journal des Débats*.) Réal, usually unsentimental in discharging his police duties under Fouché, asserted that ideally he would prefer no censorship at all, but that voluntary censorship would at least save the principle of freedom of the press. As a practical matter, liberals conceded, the distinction between a strong system of "voluntary" censorship and a blanket requirement for the pre-censorship of all published works might appear small, but (as Defermon put it) "with absolute censorship, all liberty will disappear."[52]

ALIGNED against these veteran liberals with their modest gesture in behalf of press freedom stood a group of more recent recruits to the Napoleonic regime, less invested in the principles of 1789. These hard-line voices included Portalis *fils*, Ségur, Pasquier, and the emperor's aristocratic golden boy, Molé; they were joined in advocating a more stringent approach by two revolutionary veterans, Archchancellor Cambacérès and Grand Judge Regnier. To these counselors, the logic of the government's interest dictated the need for obligatory censorship: compulsory pre-censorship would "prevent the offense rather than punish it." Molé, Regnier, and Ségur all argued that once a dangerous book was published, the damage might be done, whereas routine government censorship would stop it before it ever appeared. Against the argument that under voluntary censorship the bureau could demand to see suspicious titles that had not been proffered for review, Ségur replied that one cannot necessarily judge a manuscript by its title.

Voluntary censorship, Molé plausibly contended, will either fail or evolve de facto into absolute censorship. To this Regnier added that well-intentioned authors will not mind submitting their works for clearance by the censorship, while turbulent spirits will benefit from that intervention, which could save them from themselves, so to speak: "Why not place all authors under the necessity to be prudent?" Among the advocates of obligatory pre-censorship, Portalis *fils* was least inclined to suffer the liberals' sentimental nostalgia for freedom of the press. Voluntary censorship, he argued, was being espoused merely to keep alive a once voguish idea, which certain people are still reluctant to surrender but which is in fact only a prejudice. Publishing, in his view, should be organized just as teaching is under the new University, to assure that "only sane and not dangerous doctrines" are disseminated publicly.[53]

In the end, perhaps surprisingly, Napoleon sided with the advocates of voluntary censorship. The defenders of the idea of press freedom, the advocates of the symbolic liberal gesture, must have taken satisfaction in this small triumph. No doubt it reinforced an implicit belief that their participation in the Empire's inner councils served a larger purpose than their own self-interest. The subsequent outcome, however, would give them small comfort. The new decree empowered a director-general of publishing and the book trade (with his staff of censors) to demand submission of any manuscript whose title, listed in a printer's official register, aroused his concern. After reviewing such manuscripts, as well as those submitted voluntarily, his censors could order changes or outright suppression. The law stipulated that the author could appeal, but this proved a dead letter. (The Senate's stillborn commission on freedom of the press, created during the transition to Empire in 1804, was invoked in the Council's debates only to be dismissed with good reason by Regnaud and Boulay as "illusory.")[54] In effect, notwithstanding the notion of "voluntary censorship," the decree of 5 February 1810 subjected printers, publishers, and authors "to the non-negotiable will of a legal dictatorship," with the director general the dictator.[55]

For this important post the emperor chose Portalis *fils*, an outspoken advocate of "absolute censorship" during the council's debates, and the son of one of Napoleon's most esteemed servitors. Portalis approached his task with repressive zeal in the belief that publishing was not simply a commercial venture but a public trust, which the state must regulate to its interests. Censorship under his aegis proved wide-ranging and highly intrusive, going beyond Napoleon's concern with anything that questioned the "obedience of subjects toward the sovereign, or the interest of the state." Apart from exercising precensorship over manuscripts submitted voluntarily or on demand, the new agency received a copy of every published book or pamphlet, against which it could initiate prohibition and seizure.

In less than a year, it is true, Portalis lost his post. Unthinkingly, he had allowed the circulation of a papal brief attacking Cardinal Maury, the emperor's nominee for archbishop of Paris. In January 1811, after a furious verbal flagellation by the emperor before his Council of State that lasted over an hour, Portalis was summarily dismissed, literally ejected from the room into exile from Paris.[56] Napoleon replaced him with baron de Pommereul, a former general, prefect, and occasional man of letters, who as an inspector for the royal artillery corps had once examined a young aspirant named Bonaparte. Pommereul continued the rigorous approach of Portalis, although he claimed to be uninterested in "literary squabbles" (*tracasseries littéraires*). "It is no inconvenience," he wrote, "that the public should occupy itself or amuse itself with such matters."[57] Even so censorship grew ever tighter, especially in conjunction with the police ministry under the ham-handed General Savary, whom Napoleon had appointed to replace Fouché in 1810. (Savary's foremost victim was Mme de Staël. Her notable book on Germany had been cleared by the censors after certain modifications, but the minister suppressed it on his own authority in keeping with Napoleon's known animus against the author.)

The new agency quickly grew to include twenty censors, six inspectors of the book trade in Paris, twenty-four in the provinces, and two dozen commissioners stationed at the frontiers. In an effort to induce collective amnesia, the censors suppressed or demanded the bowdlerization of most works dealing in any way with the Revolution or the former monarchy. As one censor put it in rejecting a manuscript on the social life of the former royal house, "it is necessary to keep out of circulation anything that might tend to call up memories or stimulate affections which harm the interests of the State." Even Jomini's now classic work on the Revolution's military campaigns ran into difficulties for putting the republic in too favorable a light.[58] Religious works passed muster if they were bland, but allusions to atheism or to the church's "misfortunes" during the revolutionary era set off alarm bells for the censors. One can only imagine the extent of self-censorship and deferral of publication that went on among serious writers. In sum, Napoleon's liberal collaborators may have done their best to defend the beleaguered principle of press freedom, but in the end they failed completely. In the hands of the director general of the book trade and the police ministry's "bureau of public spirit," Napoleon's program of pacification became a prescription for intellectual sedation and cultural torpor.

VIII

The Limits of Loyalty

*O*N SUCH ISSUES as preventive detention and book censorship, Napoleon's liberal servitors could at least engage the emperor and on occasion score a minimal success at the margins. But in the diplomatic and military arena, their counsel was rarely sought and generally fell on deaf ears when offered. With Talleyrand gone from the inner circle after 1807, and notwithstanding the clear-eyed misgivings of such civilians as Cambacérès, the emperor rushed headlong into a military occupation of Spain in 1808. When unexpected Spanish resistance hardened, he faced a quagmire, an "ulcer" that would not heal (as he later put it) despite the commitment of 300,000 French troops. Still heedless of the problem he had created for himself to the south, Napoleon compounded this blunder in 1812 by invading "the colossus of the North" with his Grand Army of 600,000 men drawn from across the Empire and its satellite kingdoms. Over 85 percent of those troops perished on their way toward Moscow or on their catastrophic winter retreat westward.

Yet with an eerie willfulness, Napoleon rebounded almost completely from the unmitigated disasters of the Russian campaign even before he reached his base camp in Poland. As the emperor traversed the Russian steppes in his enclosed sled, with his aide Caulaincourt listening quietly to his musings day after day, Napoleon put the carnage out of mind, regained his optimism, and primed himself psychologically for the next round.[1] By the time he reentered the Tuileries, Napoleon had planned a return engagement against the allies in Germany to defend his Grand Empire. This ability to rally from adversity had served him well before and for the moment it worked again. Soothing his shaken minions in the capital, he exhorted his prefectorial corps in the provinces for the stepped-up extraction of tax revenue and military recruits.

Napoleon's remarkable conscription machine—fashioned from revolutionary models, routinized through years of fine-tuning, and imposed by effective coercive methods—operated at peak efficiency between 1811 and early 1813. Just as he had imagined during the retreat from Russia, he rapidly replenished his decimated army, and ordered a massive requisition of horses to support the troops.[2] The Empire's finances, on the other hand, accommodated this challenge less easily. Against all his inclinations, the emperor was obliged to solicit the legislature's approval for a quick financial fix.

NAPOLEON AND THE LEGISLATURE IN 1813

Napoleon, as we have seen, had progressively eviscerated his parliament. First he browbeat, purged, and finally abolished the Tribunate, the parliament's more active and public chamber. The Legislative Corps, which never engaged in open debate, rarely drew Napoleon's ire but held little esteem in his eyes. He signified his grudging view, for example, during the drafting of the annual "State of the Empire" report for delivery before the legislature in 1805. His aides had thoroughly revised the address at least three times, down to the smallest detail, when Napoleon insisted on changing the opening salutation. Instead of "Legislators!" (a term presumably freighted with residual echoes of revolutionary history), the final draft used the more cumbersome but less evocative "Messieurs les députés des départements au Corps Législatif."[3]

While the Corps continued to vote laws up or down without debate after hearing the government's spokesmen, Napoleon further coopted it by introducing preliminary consultations between its relevant standing committee (finance, legislation, or interior) and emissaries from the Council of State. Together they reviewed the texts of proposed new laws before they were sent on for formal consideration. Nonetheless, the Corps's workload diminished sharply once it had approved the regime's five great legal codes. For Napoleon had decided that most matters (apart from the annual budget and long lists of routine local expenditures) could be dealt with by executive decrees hammered out in the Council of State or by *senatus-consultes* drafted in a *conseil privé*, rather than by new laws requiring legislative action. (Approval of conscription calls, it will be recalled, had long since been given over to the Senate, on the grounds that the Corps might not be sitting when circumstances dictated the need for accelerated or supplementary troop levies.) Like the departmental advisory councils (*conseils généraux*) created after Brumaire, the Corps Législatif suffered from almost terminal inanition by 1812. For Napoleon it was useful solely as a solemn audience for ceremonial rituals such as the opening and closing addresses by the government's spokesmen at each year's parliamentary session or delivery of the annual "State of the Empire" report touting the regime's achievements.

Notwithstanding such useful passive functions, Napoleon regarded the Corps as a collection of tiresome, obscure mediocrities who added nothing to the luster of his regime. But while the members might be sycophantic in their quest for personal or local favors, Napoleon knew that they were also potentially oppositional. As far as he was concerned, the more the Corps atrophied, the better. After the Russian debacle of 1812, however, the emperor required greater financial resources from the French people. Having delivered a bland, exculpatory summary of the Russian campaign and his hopes for a just peace through victory, Napoleon made his move. Given his aversion for borrowing funds or for printing paper money, he hit on the expedient of nationalizing communal properties (*biens communaux*). The revenue windfall for the state would come from privatizing these properties and selling them off at auction to wealthy citizens. But this policy meant that thousands of towns and villages would lose these precious local assets and the annual revenues they generated, in exchange for a dubious promise of annual compensation from the state at a much inferior level. Genuine deputies for the departments might well have denounced such a shortsighted spoliation. But with adept lobbying the government secured endorsement from the Corps's financial committee, followed by a lopsided approval from the whole body in a vote of 303 to 26.[4]

IN OCTOBER 1813 Napoleon's defeat at the Battle of Leipzig imperiled the very survival of the Empire. Again the emperor would have to appeal to the Corps Législatif for support. Typical of his obsession with detail and of his attitude toward imperial institutions, however, he found the time to effect a symbolic change in the rules of that game. Heretofore Napoleon had designated the president of the Corps from a list of five nominees submitted by that body annually. But Napoleon wanted the freedom to name any distinguished person that he wished for this conspicuous honor, even if the designee was not a member of the body. Cambacérès vigorously objected to this "humiliating" innovation, but the Senate duly approved it, notwithstanding a public objection by Senator Cornet, which must have surprised that craven dignitary himself as much as his startled colleagues.[5] Under this new prerogative, Napoleon promptly designated one of his most loyal servitors, the recently retired Grand Judge Regnier. Many deputies surely resented being shut out of this matter, but for the moment could do nothing about it, as the government convoked the Corps Législatif for a special session in December 1813, where it hoped to win moral support for the emperor's diplomatic maneuvering, and approval for an increase in the levels of direct taxation.

Given the unprecedented and grave threats to the French homeland, Napoleon submitted documentation to the legislature to justify his failed diplomacy. The Corps in turn named a committee to review the materials and draw up a report. This was the first time that the emperor's foreign policy would come under official scrutiny outside the precincts of the pliable Senate. The underlying question was: had Napoleon been making good faith efforts to achieve a settlement or did the allies have reason to rebuff him as they inflicted further military reversals on the Empire? For its five-man committee the Corps chose deputies not closely identified with the emperor, including the chair L'Ainé, a highly regarded lawyer from Bordeaux and relative newcomer to the body destined for a distinguished career in government service during the Restoration. After the committee met with Regnier, Cambacérès, and Regnaud to discuss the material, L'Ainé went off by himself to draft its report and produced an extremely critical assessment. Despite strenuous objections by the three outside notables, who urged L'Ainé to modify the draft, the committee accepted his unrevised report and submitted it to the Corps in executive session, where it apparently made a sensation. Looking back on this event, Thibaudeau described the committee's act as "highly courageous, perhaps, but very impolitic." Boulay de la Meurthe took a sharper view: the committee's report was not only intemperate, but was an ill-timed act of opposition. It would encourage the allies and demoralize the country by making it appear that the emperor did not desire peace and that his government did not respect the laws, although the report cited no concrete instances for these charges.[6]

Napoleon took mortal offense at the committee's criticism. (As he shortly observed, disingenuously but plausibly, the time for the Senate or the legislature to criticize or show its independence was during the glory days of success and not when the Empire had its back to the wall.) Convening a *conseil privé*, he asked his advisers whether he shouldn't prorogue the legislature before it could act on the report and amplify the damage. Among others Boulay, despite his irritation at the Corps, argued forcefully that this would be most imprudent. The government, he felt, must attempt to conciliate the committee, explore the reasons for its complaints, and develop good relations with the Corps. Napoleon finally agreed and delegated Boulay to prepare a message to the legislature that he and Defermon would deliver. But the next morning Boulay learned that the emperor had reversed himself and had issued a decree immediately proroguing the legislature, in reaction to its decision in a vote of 233 to 31 the previous day to publish the inflammatory report. Napoleon followed this arbitrary act with a tongue-lashing delivered at a new year's reception for deputies and senators, where he insisted that "I alone am the representative of the people. . . . Even if you think me at fault you should not reproach me publicly." To Napoleon, dismissing the legislature seemed the best way to avoid further embarrassment and put the matter behind him. But his despotic manner would reverberate in people's thoughts when he later returned from Elba claiming to be a born-again liberal emperor.[7]

THE COLLAPSE OF THE EMPIRE AND THE BOURBON RESTORATION

Napoleon could rebound from the Russian disaster but not from the Battle of Leipzig and the defection of his last imperial satellites. Back in France, conscription had finally reached its limits. The desperate call of November 1813 for 300,000 new recruits for the impending battle of France "presents difficulties that no other levy has ever yet offered," lamented one prefect. Despondency and resignation turned into aggressive hostility by the end of the year. As defeatism took hold not only in frontier departments but deep inside the country, a long-standing yearning for peace created a groundswell of ill-will toward the regime. While the military front gave way sector by sector, the home front was collapsing as well.[8]

Apart from the Senate, the fall of the Empire did not pose a crisis of conscience for Napoleon's civilian servitors. The fate of their regime was largely out of their hands and inexorable, although the intensity of defeatism and *sauve qui peut* naturally varied. ("The most shameless," recalled Thibeaudeau, "threw themselves secretly into the arms of the royalists" well before the end came.)[9] While Napoleon withdrew to Fontainebleau, General Marmont capitulated outside Paris, opening the capital to the allies. Tsar Alexander then invited the Senate—the one public institution with even a shred of credibility—to help effect an orderly transition. The senators thus found themselves in the unaccustomed position of facing real choices.

Lest they succumb to indecision, Talleyrand, senator and prince of Bénévent, stepped in to provide a guiding hand. Despite his elevated status in the imperial hierarchy, Talleyrand had long since despaired of Napoleon's unbridled expansionist policies, and by more or less mutual agreement had stepped down from his post as foreign minister in 1807. After years of intrigue behind the emperor's back to bolster the resolve of the anti-Napoleonic powers, Talleyrand concluded in 1814 that a restoration of the Bourbons under favorable terms held the best hope for the future of France and the peace of Europe.[10]

At first glance, the Senate appears as a most implausible vehicle for Talleyrand's maneuvers. No group had behaved more sycophantically toward Napoleon than the senators, who, as Thibaudeau accurately put it, "were enervated by their servility and corrupted by money and honors." Even as reversals began to multiply in 1813, the Senate's docility had not faltered one whit. While the obscure representatives in the Legislative Corps dared to question Napoleon's leadership in December, the grandees of the Senate reviewed the same material and concluded with a ringing endorsement, expressed in his usual cloying prose by Fontanes. The drama that was about to unfold therefore had the hallmarks of a classic betrayal.[11]

For the handful of marginalized liberals in the Senate, to be sure, this was a long-awaited moment for settling accounts with a despot. But most other senators were driven to their act of repudiation by two different kinds of motivation. Clearly they were scrambling to dissociate themselves from Napoleon in order to preserve the very dignities and emoluments that he had lavished upon them; by now most senators doubtless believed that they deserved their honored place in the political order as a veritable meritocracy with or without Napoleon. But the senators could also claim that in this moment of national crisis they were simply placing the interests of France above Napoleon's strong personal claims on their loyalty.

With Talleyrand's aid, Tsar Alexander drafted a statement that nudged the

Senate into action. He reiterated the allied resolve never to negotiate with Napoleon or any member of his family, thus ruling out the regency that Napoleonic loyalists desired. But he also affirmed the allies' respect for the territorial integrity of France, pre-1792, and added that "the allies will recognize and guarantee the constitution that the French nation shall give itself"—presumably an invitation to the Senate to draft that constitution after it deposed Napoleon and named a provisional government.[12] Senator Charles Lambrechts drafted the resolution dethroning the emperor, and he must have done so with relish. A distinguished jurist from Louvain who had thrown in his lot with the French when they annexed Belgium in 1795, Lambrechts had served the Directory as minister of justice and was named in the first cohort of senators after Brumaire. But his name always figured among the tiny group of senatorial dissidents alongside Lanjuinais and Grégoire, and he was known to have voted against the elevation of Napoleon to emperor. Here was one senator who could not be taxed with hypocrisy or betrayal. Lambrechts's resolution, however, contained a bill of particulars against the emperor for abuses of power that created an awkward situation for most of his colleagues. For as Napoleon quickly responded, the Senate's complicity in most of his alleged offenses (including his abuse of the conscription laws) was a matter of record.

None of this deterred the senators from adopting what Boulay de la Meurthe later called "this illegal and odious act." Former revolutionaries with liberal reputations such as Sieyès, Roger Ducos, Emmery, Garat, Grégoire, Lanjuinais, and Lenoir-Laroche lined up to sign the dethronement resolution. While most of the sixty-odd signators were men of low profile, a few of the senators most closely associated with Napoleon over the years—including Fontanes, François de Neufchâteau, and Fabre de l'Aude—also came forward to sign, although by design or circumstance a few others in that category managed to avoid signing even if their sentiments at the moment differed little from those of their colleagues.[13]

Between the Senate's vote on 2 April to dethrone Napoleon, and the emperor's unconditional abdication on 6 April 1814 (following the desertion of almost all his marshals, and his abortive attempt two days earlier to abdicate in favor of his son), the Senate completed work on a constitution. Designed to restore the Bourbons to the throne on terms that bound them to the basic gains of the Revolution, the senatorial constitution declared that the Bourbons were returning at the invitation of the French people. It not only reaffirmed certain principles of 1789 but restored liberal practices that the Empire had eroded or repudiated altogether, such as a free press and an elected chamber of deputies with legislative initiative. The Senate's proposed constitution embodied a wistful hope for a Bourbon restoration without a counterrevolution. Beyond that, however, it not only protected but enhanced the senators' own interests by transforming their body into an hereditary institution modeled on the British House of Lords. (Some senators had gingerly suggested such a change in 1804, it will be recalled, only to be rebuffed by the newly crowned emperor.) This blatant attempt at self-aggrandizement helped discredit the Senate's initiative, and later made it easier for the Bourbons to jettison the senatorial constitution in favor of a "charter" (as they called it) of their own design.

A RESTORATION of the Bourbons had seemed unlikely even as the Empire tottered at the end of 1813, but by April 1814, under the guns of the allies, their return took on an air of inevitability for want of a viable alternative. But how would the Bourbons behave? Once Napoleon was out of the picture, would they attempt to build a consensus or would they engage in a reactionary politics of revenge? The early omens were ambiguous. The Bourbons realized that they possessed enough leverage to ignore the senatorial constitution and to draft a charter of their own on rather different terms: one they deigned to bestow on the French people from the throne, and which would not be subject to acceptance by the citizens in a referendum. Indeed, the date on the preamble to the Bourbon Charter rendered 1814 as "the nineteenth year of Louis XVIII's reign." On the other hand, the Bourbons pledged a general amnesty and seemed to mean it. Although popular royalist violence exploded in the Midi and elsewhere, the king renounced any persecution or prosecutions for past political opinions or votes. Like a biblical scapegoat, Napoleon alone would bear the official royalist animus against twenty-five years of revolution and usurpation. While the pariah was banished to the toy principality of Elba, his close collaborators would be left in peace to enjoy their pensions, titles, and memories at home.

To be sure, a hard core of ex-revolutionaries and Napoleonic servitors did not wish to swear fealty to the Bourbons under any circumstances. The regicide, counselor of state, and prefect Thibaudeau, for example, resigned from his prefecture when he first learned of Napoleon's dethronement so as to spare himself from officially proclaiming the restoration of the Bourbons in the Bouches-du-Rhône department. This gesture coincided with simple prudence: as a regicide, Thibaudeau saw no place for himself in the new regime and rightly wished to flee the volatile Midi, where political lynching was a tradition. His departure in fact reads like an escape saga, complete with nocturnal exits and disguises.[14]

Back in Paris, regicide Théophile Berlier hoped to avoid any pubic submission to the Bourbons as well. But when the comte d'Artois entered Paris, the Bourbon emissary convoked the "great political bodies" to receive their felicitations. Since all five presidents of sections in Napoleon's Council of State had followed the regency council to Blois a few days earlier, Berlier, as the remaining member with the greatest seniority, was expected to convey the Council's homage to the Bourbons. By the stratagem of tapping the oldest member to act as spokesman instead, Berlier managed to avoid that "*corvée.*" But he could not evade his responsibility as president of the Conseil des Prises (the commission that regulated maritime seizures) when Artois summoned members of second-line institutions for the same purpose. Berlier made the best of it by publicly expressing his hope that France would find tranquility under a government "which desires all public powers to be sagely ordered, and individual rights adequately guaranteed"—something he scarcely expected. At this point Berlier sought nothing more than to take his pension and retire. But the reasoned plea of a former colleague, now the Bourbon's minister of marine, that Berlier wind down the affairs of the Conseil des Prises induced him to remain in that post for several months. He then exited as quickly as he could and returned to private life.[15]

For most former revolutionaries and Napoleonic collaborators, the issue was less how they would react to the Bourbons than how the latter would deal with them. Before long, the Bourbon regime began to snub compliant former revolutionaries despite its pledge not to "disturb" people for their past opinions. When the royalist government reconstituted the Senate into a new House of Peers, it categorically excluded twelve ex-senators as regicides, along with another twenty non-regicides associated with the Revolution and Empire, including Chaptal, Garat, Grégoire, Monge, and Roederer. Naturally the Bourbons made a clean sweep of the Council of State: not only were its four regicides excluded (Berlier, Merlin de Douai, Quinette, and Thibaudeau), but twenty-six others were also shown the door for their service to Napoleon. Moreover, the government slashed their expected pensions in the bargain. The Bourbons also purged the Cour de Cassation, the nation's high court, excluding not only regicides Lamarque and Merlin (the procurator general) but Muraire (the presiding judge), who had been deported by the Directory in Fructidor 1797 for his supposed royalist leanings.[16]

The Bourbon purges violated the spirit of their pledge if not its letter, but even if deprived of their public positions, Napoleon's prominent servitors were left in peace to enjoy the comforts of home and family. Cambacérès, for example, while subjected to merciless caricature and excluded from any role in public life despite his august standing, could maintain at least a semblance of his sumptuous lifestyle. At dinner parties in his Paris town house, former revolutionaries and Napoleonic collaborators reminisced, argued about revolutionary events, and recalled conversations with the emperor.[17] In this sense, Napoleon's exile to Elba occurred in a strange kind of isolation.

It soon became apparent, however, that hope for a restoration without counterrevolution was a fantasy. The reactionary atmospherics and policy discussions in government circles increasingly alarmed those on the wrong side of the divide. To Thibaudeau, it seemed that counterrevolutionary passions were blinding the Bourbons and leading the old nobility to behave like a conquering race full of hauteur and disdain for everyone else. In Boulay's view, the king failed to recognize the rights of the nation. Boulay saw national honor insulted by the appointment as the Bourbons' first war minister of General Dupont, who had disgraced the French uniform in Spain, and by the rise of émigrés who had waged war against France to the highest military ranks. Growing threats against owners of *biens nationaux* threatened to undo years of painstaking adjudication by Boulay as director of the Contentieux des Domaines, while religious fanaticism mocked the liberal defense of Catholicism that he had mounted during the Directory years and after. When the erudite Boulay read the divine-right preamble to the Bourbon Charter, he told his family: "I am going to write a history of the last Stuarts!"[18]

IT IS INSTRUCTIVE at this point to revisit Napoleon's first war minister and renowned public critic, Lazare Carnot. Soon after his remarkable speech opposing the transition to Empire, Carnot's term in the Tribunate expired and he retired to private life. In 1809, however, he was driven to make contact with the emperor. Financial desperation caused by severe investment losses forced Carnot to seek imperial help in claiming full pension rights as an *inspecteur des revues*, the military post he had vacated when the Côte d'Or department elected him to the National Convention in 1792. This minimal favor he managed to gain, although other promises of recognition did not materialize. No matter. When the allied offensive threatened France in 1814, Carnot volunteered for service and accepted assignment as governor general of Antwerp. Carnot organized the defense of this redoubt of French power, now cut off by the allies, with a flurry of resolute actions reminiscent of 1793 and all too rare elsewhere. Like Hamburg under Marshal Davout, Antwerp was one of the last French strongholds to surrender and acknowledge the Bourbons. Stall as he might, however, Carnot finally oversaw the transition to the Bourbon regime.[19]

Carnot made his peace with the Bourbons in light of their promise in the charter to renounce "all scrutiny of opinions and votes cast prior to the Restoration." But by July, his distress at the discord created by ultraroyalist influence prompted him to compose a long letter to the king, which he forwarded via Beugnot, a royal minister who had once served as a Napoleonic prefect. Through a series of misunderstandings probably beyond Carnot's control, a publisher got hold of his letter and printed it in October as a tract entitled *Mémoire Adressé au Roi en Juillet 1814*. The government raced unsuccessfully to suppress the pamphlet, which naturally caused a sensation.

The return of the Bourbons had produced a "universal enthusiasm," Carnot admitted, shared even by former republicans like himself who had found Napoleon's tyranny oppressive. But this goodwill soon vanished. Carnot denounced the regime's purges and its strident hostility to the regicides which, he was certain, would soon escalate into attacks on former revolutionary activists all across France who had shown their support for the regicide Convention. The future was all too apparent: "Who can fail to see that we are being prepared for the debasement of everyone who took part in the Revolution, for the abolition of anything that still clings somewhat to liberal ideas, for the return of the *biens nationaux*, for the resurrection of all the prejudices that make imbeciles out of the people?"[20] The real agents of France's calamities in the 1790s, and in a sense the real regicides, Carnot argued, were the royalists whose misguided opposition had plunged the Revolution into turbulence, especially the émigrés who "took up arms against their fatherland" whilst abandoning their hapless king to his fate. In this light, the members of the Convention were simply defending the *patrie* and doing their duty as duly constituted judges. But now the ultraroyalists were treating the majority of patriotic Frenchmen as despised strangers in their own land.[21]

While Carnot took several swipes at Napoleon, his pamphlet implicitly identified the two features of Napoleon's reign that had won the loyalty of Frenchmen, and which the Bourbons ignored at their peril. First: "only forgetting the past can conciliate all interests and reunite all Frenchmen in love for the King." Repeatedly Carnot exhorted the king to forget past grievances, to "bring together all parties," "extinguish the parties," "extinguish the spirit of party." Second was the contempt shown by ultraroyalists for national honor, for the twenty-year legacy of patriotic and military glory during the Revolution and Empire. "The French Revolution was composed of heroism and cruelty, of sublime traits and monstrous disorders," Carnot recalled. But the heroic defense of the fatherland in 1793 and the ensuing military glory evoked his unalloyed enthusiasm. Projecting his own values onto the French population at large, Carnot waxed nostalgically about the honor of defending the fatherland and the glory of continuous military success across twenty years. In "this glorious defense of the fatherland," he maintained, the vast majority of the French people participated, sacrificed, and furnished their young men. "What is it that made Napoleon's tyranny bearable for so long? It is the fact that he excited national pride. With what devotion did even those who detested him the most serve him! It was despair alone that finally caused one to abandon his eagles."[22]

In his blunt criticism of the Restoration, Carnot did not invoke the republic or a return of Napoleon as alternatives. He simply pleaded with the Bourbons to honor their better instincts: to lead a restoration without a counterrevolution, to unite all Frenchmen in a common loyalty to the fatherland. As Carnot's biographer points out, most contemporaries focused on his assaults against the ultraroyalists and overlooked the pamphlet's weary distancing from the Revolution, with its "vainly pursued chimeras" and its manifest incapacity to institute liberty. By the same token his view of Bonaparte at this juncture remained unforgiving, in the pamphlet and in private. "He is a tyrant whom no one can like and whom the friends of liberty cannot abide," Carnot wrote to the English liberal, Lord Brougham.[23]

Yet the *Mémoire Adressé au Roi* suggests in hindsight why Carnot could rally to Napoleon after his return from Elba, despite his deep-seated contempt for the emperor's tyranny. To be sure, amid the ill-feeling generated by the Restoration during its first year, Napoleon scarcely figured at all. As in Carnot's pamphlet, the conflict pitted former revolutionaries (regicides and non-regicides alike) against ultraroyalists and vengeful émigrés. Yet the emperor's attempted return was a logical response to the growing contempt for the governing royalists and the resultant collapse of any national consensus. The Bourbons had their priorities backward: they scorned huge swaths of their subjects, were insensible to national pride, and craven in their relations with the allies. Napoleon at least had never dishonored the fatherland and had never given the nation's foes an inch. A chastened Napoleon, an emperor shorn of his despot's habits but adept in leading his armies, might just square the circle.

THE CRISIS OF THE HUNDRED DAYS

Fouché once remarked to the comte d'Artois in 1814 that Napoleon on Elba was to Europe as Vesuvius was to Naples.[24] Yet few of the emperor's former stalwarts imagined that he would actually return to France and fewer still planned for such an event. When Napoleon did land on the mainland on 1 March 1815, however, efforts to stop him quickly collapsed. Troops and commanders in Grenoble and Lyon succumbed to his electrifying defiance, and when the hapless Marshal Ney in Auxerre disobeyed royal orders and defected, the path to Paris lay open. By the time Napoleon reached the capital, Louis XVIII had hastily decamped for Belgium and the emperor's return gave the misleading appearance of being an unopposed national redemption. In reality his presence raised as many problems as it might solve, and posed a troubling conundrum for his former collaborators.

True, few of the military or civilian servitors of Napoleon who had rallied to the Bourbons accompanied Louis XVIII into exile or remained resolutely on the sidelines. (Only Berthier and Marmont among the marshals took that first decisive step.) After one year the Restoration had utterly discredited itself in the eyes of many former revolutionaries and anti-Napoleon liberals who had reconciled themselves to the Bourbons in 1814. Such Frenchmen—perhaps even the allied leaders themselves—now had to be wondering what they had ever hoped for in the Bourbons. But along with the workers and artisans who turned out to cheer the emperor en route (whom Napoleon could never bring himself to appreciate, lest he depend on the streets for his power), the real enthusiasts for his return were veteran army officers hungry, unlike the sated marshals, for a reprise of the glory days.[25] Demoralized by its recent losses and decimated by forced retirements and budget cuts in 1814, the army clearly constituted a potential zone of support for "the little corporal."

Two problems, however, dampened the spirits of all but the most zealous Napoleonic loyalists. First came the stark decree from the allies at the Congress of Vienna outlawing Napoleon and pledging never to negotiate with the usurper. With his habitual self-confidence, the emperor himself dismissed this as a mere gesture, convinced that the ignominious flight of the Bourbons, his own arrival in Paris without firing a shot, and the seeming assent of the nation would soon undercut the allies' resolve. But most of those who fatalistically rallied to the emperor were doubtful. As Napoleon headed toward Paris, Thibaudeau arranged a meeting between Fouché (ostensibly representative of former revolutionaries) and Maret (the staunchest "bonapartist"). Fouché argued that a regency for Napoleon's young son was their best hope, which Metternich might be induced to support in the interest of the child's Austrian mother. Maret, however, insisted that Napoleon's abdication at Fontainebleau was now null and void, and that only the emperor himself could energize the army and the French people.[26] Even as they assembled in the Tuileries and took their places in Napoleon's new government, some of the closest collaborators of old (including Cambacérès and Davout) showed a marked lack of enthusiasm. They knew that the resurrected Empire confronted a well-armed and implacably hostile Europe.

Did the national cause, betrayed by the Bourbons, now depend on Napoleon for redemption? Or, on the contrary, did linking the national cause to this European pariah threaten to drag the French people down to new depths of misfortune? Cutting across each individual's calculations on this basic question were his personal interests; or as Thibaudeau unkindly put it (thinking especially of Cambacérès): everyone was trying to balance "personal interest, egoism, fear, and cowardice; their town houses, châteaux, and decorations."[27] A former Napoleonic servitor might sully his honor by staying conspicuously on the sidelines or by opposing the emperor after his daring return, but the risk was even greater that in now rallying to Napoleon he might compromise his future irrevocably should the emperor's resurrection abort.

A few tried to keep a safe distance from Napoleon by accepting innocuous posts, most obviously Molé, the young scion of a notable aristocratic family of émigrés, whose career had skyrocketed under Napoleon's wings, culminating with his appointment as minister of justice in 1813 at the age of thirty-two. The emperor had apparently been mesmerized by Molé's aura, sought out his company at court receptions, and claimed to value his advice. But Molé now turned down Napoleon's offer to head either of two ministries, and would only agree to serve as director of roads and bridges (Ponts et Chaussés), which he had headed for a while during his rapid ascent. Cambacérès's tepid commitment was also apparent to everyone, although the archchancellor's pleas about age and infirmities had more plausibility than Molé's pathetic excuses of ill-health. Indeed, a politically exhausted Cambacérès would have much preferred to lay low, but knew that he could not.[28] He accepted titular appointment as minister of justice, on the understanding that Boulay de la Meurthe would carry the actual responsibilities, and also turned up during the Hundred Days chairing important meetings and advising Napoleon in customary fashion. His discomfort was palpable, but the sway of loyalty and habit prevailed.

A second, persistent problem created friction from the moment Napoleon reached Paris. Almost everyone agreed that the emperor must now become a new man, a less despotic, less ambitious, and more liberal version of himself. Colonel La Bédoyère, whose defection with his regiment at Grenoble first opened Napoleon's way to Paris, set this tone even as he heralded the emperor's return: "No more ambition, no more despotism," he cried in the plainest of language. "We wish to be free and happy. Your Majesty must abjure the system of conquests and of extreme power that brought misfortune upon France and yourself."[29] But how could this to be assured, how could Napoleon's worst instincts be kept at bay? Or was this simply the wrong question to be asking at a moment when circumstances demanded unity of purpose behind Napoleon's leadership?

Even if Napoleon finally renounced any desire to reconstitute the bloated Grand Empire, he was not about to abandon his imperial persona. As Thibaudeau observed, Napoleon's return brought an "imperial restoration," complete with "his old cortège of dignitaries, ministers, counselors of state, marshals, and chamberlains, most of whose friendship was more than doubtful, who were discredited in the eyes of public opinion, and very few of whom were disposed to sacrifice themselves for the fatherland or for him." It all appeared to this former regicide and Napoleonic official as a situation lacking real appeal, "a provisional building constructed with old material." (In contrast, Thibaudeau's personal fantasy called for Napoleon to return not as an emperor but as "the avenging arm of a revolutionized France, exercising a dictatorship until the nation . . . could constitute its own government.")[30]

True, the imperial structure did receive a transfusion of liberalism upon Napoleon's return from Elba. Surprisingly, Benjamin Constant put aside his long-standing animus against Napoleon, and agreed to design a liberal facelift for the Empire. Instead of starting afresh, however, Constant produced a lengthy constitutional addendum known as "The Additional Act to the Constitutions of the Empire." After a committee of the emperor's trusted aides—Cambacérès, Maret, Regnaud, Defermon, and Boulay—vetted the document, Napoleon accepted it and agreed to submit it for a referendum to the people. Constant's "Additional Act" set a liberal tone and firmed up the Empire's parliamentary institutions, but in a rather halfhearted fashion. Why, some complained, leave standing the previous constitutions or *senatus-consultes* of 1802 and 1804 that all but sanctioned one-man rule? Boulay, among others, regretted this impolitic failure to make a genuine fresh start. Moreover, enamored of the British model, Constant (as the Bourbons already had done in 1814) provided for an hereditary Chamber of Peers alongside an elected Chamber of Deputies. Napoleon himself expressed skepticism about an hereditary peerage, doubtless for self-interested reasons, but former revolutionaries like Carnot were also offended by such aristocratic trappings. The Additional Act did promise to restore veritable (indirect) elections and to make the Chamber of Deputies a genuine partner in government. But it left open the ultimate balance of power between the emperor and his parliament.[31]

The referendum on the Additional Act produced mixed results. On the one hand, it garnered about 1,550,000 "yes" votes as opposed to a mere 5,700 nays. But in relation to France's approximately 5,000,000 eligible voters, and in contrast to turnouts in excess of 3 million votes for the plebiscites of 1802 and 1804, abstentions ran high. The historian of this subject concludes that about 60 percent of the votes in 1815 came from republicans of one type or another, who voted yes in an anti-Bourbon reflex. He notes, in passing, that two-thirds of the surviving regicides in the Convention came out and voted yes. Conversely, unlike Benjamin Constant or Lazare Carnot, certain liberals dubious about Napoleon probably abstained. Regionally, abstention was massive in certain royalist-leaning regions like the Midi and the West. And among local notables and bourgeois moderates across France who had supported Napoleon as the harbinger of stability and peace in 1802 and 1804, many now sat on their hands, committed by default to the royalist option.[32]

With the promulgation of the Additional Act, the question arose whether to implement it immediately by calling elections for the Chamber of Deputies or deferring them until the crisis had passed—the emperor's instinctive preference. Several advisers regarded postponement as a fatal error that would ignite the deep-seated distrust of Napoleon, even though they knew that the chamber was likely to badger him once it convened. They tapped Regnaud to convince the emperor, and according to Thibaudeau, Regnaud succeeded only after threatening to resign.[33] The government quickly convoked the electoral colleges and despite a dismayingly low turnout of electors, especially in the royalist South, those assemblies chose their deputies, who quickly assembled in Paris with more of a mandate than their counterparts had possessed when the Senate designated the members of the Legislative Corps between 1800 and 1814. Generally liberal in orientation and anti-Bourbon, the new Chamber of Deputies manifestly distrusted Napoleon.

Meanwhile, Napoleon named a new, hereditary Chamber of Peers, 117 in number, including 60 military officers. Twenty-seven of the new peers had been senators complicit in his dethronement in 1814—a generous concession, no doubt, but perhaps a bad omen for the imperial future. Napoleon kept his three iron men out of the peerage. Boulay, Defermon, and Regnaud could serve more usefully as heads of section in the Council of State, ministers of state without portfolio, and governmental liaisons with the parliament. In a throwback to the old days, Napoleon named Cambacérès and Lacépède as president and vice president of the Peers. (Thibaudeau, who had lobbied unsuccessfully for election to the Chamber of Deputies in the electoral college of his native Vienne department, was surprised to find himself named a peer by Napoleon. He reluctantly accepted, he claimed, in order not to rock the boat, and was chosen by his colleagues as the body's secretary.)

Napoleon's problem with the Chamber of Deputies immediately surfaced when it elected Lanjuinais as its president. Since Lanjuinais had been outspoken during the senatorial dethronement of Napoleon in 1814, this could reasonably be taken not simply as a show of independence but almost as an affront to the emperor. Having little alternative, however, Napoleon swallowed his customary pride and officially welcomed Lanjuinais. Similarly, the emperor had to abide the prominent place in the new chamber occupied by the nettlesome Lafayette and by several figures from the confrontational legislative session of December 1813. In fact, both houses of parliament were fixated on the need to delimit the emperor's powers. The deputies and peers remembered all too well how tyrannically he had treated the Legislative Corps in 1813, and they bridled at any hint of despotism coming from the Tuileries. The parliament saw itself as separate from and above Napoleon, as the ultimate instrument of the national interest. But Napoleon's inner circle, led by Boulay among others, was determined to work with the chambers and to resist any notion of proroguing the parliament under pretext of the national emergency. To the pessimistic Thibaudeau, the ensuing posturing— the prickliness of the chamber over its independence, Napoleon's quibbling over the language of various addresses, "the puerile discussions, the [cascade] of words in the presence of a conspiring Europe"—seemed all but pointless.[34]

TWO INDIVIDUALS stood out in Napoleon's new government: Fouché, the logical if risky choice to head the police ministry; and Carnot, who exuded great moral force even if he was not suited to the grinding detail of the interior ministry. Both had been spurned by Napoleon in the past, held a jaundiced view of the emperor, and had no wish to see him return in 1815. But Carnot now embraced Napoleon as the best hope for redeeming the national cause and saving the revolutionary legacy from oblivion. To the surprise of some, moreover, Carnot renounced any notion of a 1793-style dictatorship of public safety and clung to a liberal, legalistic approach to the exercise of power.[35]

Fouché, on the other hand, played a game of his own design whose motivations remain opaque—even if one grants him a measure of sincerity rather than accounting for his actions by simple opportunism or instinctive deviousness. Fouché could not get past the idea that Napoleon would be an obstacle to any settlement with the allies, despite the salutary effect of his return from Elba in driving out the Bourbons. Initially, Fouché hoped that Napoleon might proclaim a regency for his son, which might placate the allies, prevent a second restoration, and thereby protect the men and ideals of the Revolution. Getting nowhere with this proposal, Fouché promoted it indirectly by intriguing to hamstring Napoleon. Acting through a group of allies in the two parliamentary houses, Fouché encouraged suspicions of Napoleon and defiance of his will. By stoking the deputies' distrust of the emperor, by dissuading them from backing him wholeheartedly, Fouché's followers obliged the emperor to worry about betrayal back in Paris instead of focusing exclusively on leading his army. And instead of fortifying Napoleon's hand as the critical moment approached, Fouché entered into back-channel negotiations with various figures in the allied coalition.[36] The lukewarm to frigid stance of most Napoleonic marshals likewise undercut Napoleon. Even Davout had initially been reluctant to get involved, and when he did throw himself into the fray as Napoleon's war minister, the "iron marshal" rarely exhibited his customary decisiveness.

ENDGAME: AFTER WATERLOO

As long as Napoleon held out hope of leading the French army to a crushing victory over the allies that would induce them to negotiate, his reluctant collaborators could suspend disbelief. Waterloo, of course, removed that comforting possibility completely and produced the ultimate crisis. All easy hopes and most illusions vanished, although France was still unconquered the day after the battle. In the regime's inner circles, various degrees of panic or demoralization took hold, but so in some quarters did the determination to fight on. Regnaud and others now called for Napoleon to abdicate in favor of a regency for Marie-Louise and his son, but Boulay, Carnot, and Lucien still resisted that course. Lucien and Davout talked about proroguing the chambers to secure Napoleon's political flank, but others opposed that dubious move. Before any decision could be reached, Lafayette (seconded by Fouché's minions in the Chamber of Deputies) moved and carried a decree that the two chambers henceforth would meet *en permanence*, thus preempting any action by the executive.[37] Anti-Napoleonic sentiment also erupted in the Chamber of Peers, where Boissy d'Anglas among others chastised apologists for the emperor such as Roederer. Napoleon had feared just such parliamentary agitation in the aftermath of Waterloo, and this concern caused him to rush back to Paris instead of moving immediately to regroup his scattered forces. In that sense parliamentary hostility, nurtured behind the scenes by Fouché, effectively scuttled Napoleon's last stand before it could occur.

Inside and outside the government, Waterloo left one simple question: could national independence be salvaged by unqualified unity behind Napoleon and the remnants of his armies or, on the contrary, by severing Napoleon from France so that negotiations might begin short of complete defeat? In the latter view, France could no longer prevail by military means; only the parliament could lead the nation out of the abyss to a negotiated peace once Napoleon was gone. Sentiment for abdication mounted among the deputies, the peers, the ministers, and even some of Napoleon's brothers, although Cambacérès refused to put such a motion to a vote in the Chamber of Peers, while Lucien, Carnot, and Boulay resisted in the ministerial council.[38] But after several spasms of defiance and indecision, a dispirited emperor decided to abdicate in favor of his son.

That agonized decision in fact settled little. With the head of state gone, Regnaud proposed that a five-man provisional government be named by the two chambers to govern in Napoleon II's name. The chambers gratefully accepted the abdication but avoided proclaiming Napoleon II emperor, nor would they refer to the resultant provisional government as a regency council. The star of bonapartism was sinking out of sight. On 23 June Napoleon sent his three iron men to the Chamber of Deputies to assert his son's succession rights. Boulay's spirited intervention had a particular edge when he warned the deputies: if you now declare the imperial throne vacant, you will doom France to the fate of a Spain or a Poland. But the chamber ducked the question by simply moving to the order of the day.[39] Behind the scenes, Fouché was dispatching additional back-channel emissaries to pursue negotiations with the allied camp.[40]

The Chamber of Deputies duly named three members for the provisional government, choosing Carnot (with 324 votes on the first ballot), Fouché (with 296 votes on the first ballot), and General Grenier on a second ballot.[41] In the Peers, where Sieyès, Cambacérès, and Thibaudeau declined to be considered, Foreign Minister Caulaincourt was chosen (by a vote of 52 out of 70) along with the regicide Quinette (with 48 votes). Carnot assumed that coming in with the most votes from the Chamber of Deputies he would be designated as president of the provisional government, but Fouché managed to gain that post, perhaps by tricking Carnot to vote for him out of courtesy while Fouché in turn voted for himself. The provisional government then named Berlier, a regicide and veteran member of the Council of State, as its secretary.

The provisional government had to decide whether to continue military resistance. Could the army regroup, hold off the allies before the Prussians and English linked up, defend Paris, and by this resistance secure a cease-fire, after which negotiations might start? Fouché made it plain that he opposed continued resistance: capitulation rather than fighting to the bitter end offered the best hope for the future. Behind this obvious predicament lay the specter of a second Bourbon restoration: was it inevitable or could some kind of regency be put in place to keep the Bourbons at bay? In sum, was continuing the military struggle the only way to avert a restoration, or was further resistance sure to make the inevitable capitulation even harsher? As Carnot's biographer puts it: was the approaching endgame a time for heroic defiance in a revolutionary spirit or for maneuvering in the corridors?[42]

As secretary of the provisional government, Berlier's eyewitness account of "ten of the most agonizing and unhappy days of my [public] life" is a terse, suggestive guide to this somber interlude. Fouché took the helm in more than name. When Berlier was asked to draft the provisional government's official proclamation to the French people, Fouché urged him to make it vague and laconic. Berlier prudently refrained from mentioning Napoleon II, but he did state that the government hoped to master the present crisis "without having to subject France to the return of a power [i.e., the Bourbons] that would not be in the national interest." Fouché glanced at Berlier's draft, pocketed it, and told him that he would revise it himself.[43]

Fouché's four colleagues, bitter over the prospect of a second Bourbon restoration, resented their president's machinations but could offer no viable alternative. On 27 June, for example, shortly before Napoleon finally left for the port of Rochefort and exile, he offered to lead the army as a simple general; but Fouché rebuffed him, and his colleagues reluctantly concurred, assuming that the chambers would react furiously to any such resurrection. Then, when the *fédérés* (civilians who volunteered for military service against the invaders) petitioned for arms that they knew to be available in the capital, Fouché opposed the request in disparaging language. Carnot bristled at this gratuitous insult, but did not object to passing the petition on to the war minister, who was likely to bury it. In the most frustrating incident recounted by Berlier, it became known that Fouché had been meeting with a royalist agent named Vitrolles, whom Fouché had previously freed from prison. Carnot lashed out in fury, but Fouché stood his ground. "You understand nothing," Fouché retorted; "your vain resistance will not save the country." As Thibaudeau's private conversations with him reveal, Fouché felt further resistance to be pointless at this juncture. One could only maneuver for small gains by reconciling with the Bourbons, placating the allies, and playing on differences among them.[44]

A final *conseil de guerre* chaired by War Minister Davout, with the defeatist marshals in attendance, recognized that the left bank of the Seine lay open to the allies' advanced units. After inspecting the terrain personally, Carnot reluctantly concluded, for both tactical and humanitarian reasons, that Paris could not be successfully defended, and should therefore be spared a siege and the depredations of an assault. Since that was what Davout wanted to hear, the endgame was over, Fouché prevailed, and the Bourbons returned.[45]

AS DAY follows night, the fate of Napoleon's leading collaborators, "the instigators and authors" of the Hundred Days, could scarcely be in doubt after the second Restoration of the Bourbons. Even if the shaken Louis XVIII was himself prepared to be relatively indulgent, his ultraroyalist supporters were out for blood. Leaving aside the "white terror" in the South, where vigilante justice and massacres again erupted in that unforgiving region, the reckoning came in two waves. Even before a newly elected Chamber of Deputies could convene, the king signed a so-called amnesty decree on 24 July 1815 most notable for the exceptions that it specified. The decree singled out two categories for retribution. Nineteen high-ranking military officers, accused of participating in the overthrow of royal authority, were slated to go before military courts-martial for treason. Thirty-eight men, mainly civilians, who had publicly favored the usurper's return, were to be exiled from France. The second group included Maret, Carnot, Boulay de la Meurthe, Regnaud, Defermon, Thibaudeau, Réal, and Merlin de Douai.[46]

The king himself would have stopped there, but the ultraroyalists of his new Chamber of Deputies clamored for a more comprehensive retribution. After complicated parliamentary maneuvering, a reluctant king agreed to a bill aimed more at former regicides than prominent Napoleonic collaborators. Again, the bill in question was ostensibly an amnesty law, which then excluded a composite category of "relapsed regicides" (as historian Daniel Resnick calls them): deputies to the National Convention who had voted to execute the king in 1793 and who had later signified their approval of Napoleon's return by their "yes" votes in the referendum of 1815 on the Additional Act, votes recorded in special communal voting registers at that time.[47] Under this law of 12 January 1816, about two hundred ex-*conventionnels* were driven into exile, including certain men closely associated in one way or another with Napoleon, such as Berlier, Cambacérès, Chazal, Cochon, Lamarque, and Sieyès. (Ex-regicide Fouché was later forced into exile himself, notwithstanding his performance in 1815.) The deportation of the "relapsed regicides" was only the harsh tip of the iceberg. Purges at every level of government and administration finished the job. To take but one example, ex-*conventionnel* Daunou, neither a regicide nor a notable Napoleonic collaborator (having been purged from the Tribunate in 1802), was later appointed by Napoleon as head of the French imperial archives. The Restoration government ordered its chief archivist to supervise the scrutiny of the 1815 voting registers, which would be used as evidence against his former regicide colleagues. No sooner had Daunou completed that task than he lost his own post.[48]

Certain exiles, including Cambacérès and Regnaud, were permitted back into France after a few years, but most of the survivors had to wait until the fall of the Bourbons in 1830 to regain their native soil. While the exiles scattered across Europe and even to America, the largest contingent ended up in or around Brussels. According to the unregenerate Montagnard exile Marc-Antoine Baudot, the Napoleonic nobles in their ranks like Merlin de Douai and Thibaudeau clung to their titles and were mocked for their pretension by their fellow exiles as the *magnats*, not exactly a term of endearment. The biggest snob was of course Cambacérès, who never ceased playing the prince, and who certainly had the wherewithal to support an opulent lifestyle. Berlier, on the other hand, was one Napoleonic notable exempt from Baudot's scorn, and his son in fact married Berlier's granddaughter.[49] Indeed, if there is a truly sympathetic protagonist in this saga, it is that unpretentious and thoroughly decent individual—that nostalgic republican, dedicated public servant, and family man. Berlier's long exile in Brussels had a particularly bittersweet quality since he had spent time there in 1806 on a mission to investigate hundreds of questionable detentions and appalling conditions in the city's main prison. In the course of his mission Berlier uncovered personal vendettas by certain officials and various illegal practices; he personally questioned many prisoners, and expedited the procedures that in due course led to the release of 90 percent of the detainees. On his return to Brussels as an involuntary exile ten years later, Berlier found a circle of welcoming Belgians who remembered his beneficent actions as Napoleon's emissary.[50]

Finally, there is the case of Sieyès, with whom, in a manner of speaking, it all began back in 1789 and again in Brumaire. Sieyès had decamped for Belgium in 1815 even before the law of January 1816 ordered him out of France. Though ailing and withdrawn, he found in his psyche a residual kinship with his erstwhile revolutionary colleagues. Now a wealthy man, Sieyès made funds available to help the most destitute of these former deputies to the Convention who had never shared in Napoleon's largesse.[51]

REFLECTIONS

To catch our breath after this vertiginous denouement, let us briefly digress to another time and place, namely, Washington, D.C., at the height of the Vietnam War. In retrospect, then Secretary of Defense Robert McNamara, the leading civilian hawk in the Johnson administration, informs us, he had gradually concluded that the war was futile, unwinnable on any but the most extravagant and unacceptable terms. Yet McNamara persisted despite his misgivings. As the body count on both sides soared, the secretary led internal debates on particular tactical options from time to time but never pushed to reverse the tide of escalation.[52] True, such advocacy could be found in the administration's inner circle, which tolerated Undersecretary of State George

Ball as a kind of in-house dissenter or devil's advocate for deescalation and military disengagement. But Ball's ritualistic dissent was essentially discounted by his colleagues for its predictability and thus rendered innocuous; even if his own conscience was assuaged. In the words of an observer: "Ball felt good, I assume (he had fought for righteousness); the others felt good (they had given a full hearing to the dovish position); and there was minimal unpleasantness. The club remained intact."[53]

As Albert Hirschman argues, Ball had renounced in advance his strongest weapon: the threat to resign under public protest. McNamara, who increasingly shared Ball's misgivings, as we now know, entirely foreclosed that option as well. "Many friends, then and since, have told me [McNamara recalled in his memoir] that I was wrong not to have resigned in protest over the president's policy. Let me explain why I did not. The president . . . is the only elected official of the executive branch. He appoints each cabinet officer, who should have no constituency other than him. That is how cabinet officers are kept accountable to the people. A cabinet officer's authority and legitimacy derived from the president." Not content to state this once, McNamara reiterates it on the next page: "Some said I should have used [my power] by resigning, challenging the president's Vietnam policy, and leading those who sought to force a change. I believe that would have been a violation of my responsibility to the president and my oath to uphold the Constitution. . . . I was loyal to the presidency and loyal to him, and I sensed his equally strong feelings toward me. Moreover, until the day I left, I believed I could influence his decisions. I therefore felt I had a responsibility to stay at my post."[54] All of this, needless to say, has an uncanny similitude to the posture of Napoleon's leading subordinates.

McNamara and Ball evidently shared the feeling that however uncomfortable their positions, they were duty-bound to remain in order to exert some kind of positive influence within an administration rife with so many adamant hawks, civilian and military. "Opportunism," Hirschman aptly concludes, "can in this situation be rationalized as public-spirited." To Hirschman, protest resignation or "exit" is the strongest weapon that a dissenting government official possesses, and he laments the extreme rarity of its use, since "exit has an essential role to play in restoring quality performance of government, just as in any organization. . . . The jolt provoked by the clamorous exit of a respected member is in many situations an indispensable complement to voicing dissent [within the government]." McNamara had arguably misplaced his loyalty. As the establishment journalist James Reston wrote in 1969: "Most who stayed on at the critical period of escalation gave to the President the loyalty they owed to the country."[55]

The appearance of McNamara's memoir years later only strengthens this argument. Ronald Steel, for example, makes much the same point in a scathing review of that volume. "McNamara honored what he believed to be his duty to Johnson above what many others would consider his duty to his country. . . . What is useful about this evasive book is the appalling picture it portrays of men caught in the prison of their own assumptions and of their bureaucratic roles." Steel broadens his critique in language that again resonates with the Napoleonic experience, maintaining that McNamara's memoir "inadvertently reveals a great deal about the self-contained bureaucratic machine in which he operated so successfully . . . hermetically sealed as a spaceship. . . . It ignored dissonant views, rationalized unpleasant facts and, when proved wrong, simply redoubled its efforts. . . . [It] reveals a leadership class so in thrall to power, so convinced of its own intellectual superiority, so cut off from, and even contemptuous of the wider society it has been empowered to serve, that it was willing to sacrifice virtually everything to avoid the stigma of failure." [56] Similarly *The New York Times* editorialized: "Mr. McNamara believes that retired Cabinet members should not criticize the Presidents they served no matter how much the American people need to know the truth. . . . Perhaps the only value of 'In Retrospect' is to remind us never to forget that these were men who in the full hubristic glow of their power would not listen to logical warning or ethical appeal. When senior figures talked sense to Mr. Johnson and Mr. McNamara, they were ignored or dismissed from government. . . . [At the end] Mr. McNamara, while tormented by his role in the war, got a sinecure at the World Bank and summers at Martha's Vineyard."[57]

LET US LEAVE Robert S. McNamara to his contorted second thoughts, and return to Napoleon's collaborators, better equipped perhaps to assess their behavior. For if excessive or misplaced loyalty to the chief is not specific to dictatorships but can bedevil democratic polities as well, in a dictatorship the consequences are surely exacerbated by the paucity of countervailing sources of information or dissent, especially the absence of an independent legislature and a free press.

France in 1800–14 was far from resembling an unabashed dictatorship in the style of a *caudillo* in the nineteenth century or a junta of colonels in the twentieth, let alone a Nazi or Soviet regime, where protest or "exit" would earn a bullet in the back of the head, if one were lucky. We are dealing rather with the gradually unfolding, gilded authoritarianism of Napoleon Bonaparte, the dictatorship that dared not speak its name. In this environment, the civilians closest to Bonaparte were known for their loyalty: if they served France (as they believed) it was by way of faithfully serving Napoleon Bonaparte.

After 1814, however, this loyalty began to appear excessive even to certain complacent participants. The emperor's devoted private secretary Fain, for example, whose own functions were entirely clerical, had ample chance to observe Secretary of State Hugues Maret, the official with the most unencumbered access to Napoleon. Fain later testified that once Napoleon decided on a measure, Maret permitted himself no reservation or dissent, whatever his personal opinion. Maret regarded this as the measure of probity in a faithful minister. But even the loyal Fain noted that Maret had since been reproached "for never having disapproved and for having, on the contrary, constantly defended all of Napoleon's political operations."[58] Prefect of Police Pasquier made a similar point about that other prominent official with almost daily access to Napoleon: "There is reason to believe that had he shown a little more courage in expressing his thoughts, and more firmness in defending his opinions, Cambacérès would on many occasions have induced the chief, to whose fortunes he had attached himself, to come to many a valuable determination."[59]

Perhaps so. More likely, had Maret, Cambacérès, or other prominent servitors shown more determination in resisting Napoleon's willfulness, either in his early transgressive acts or in his later imperial adventures, they would have found themselves pastured out to the Senate or to an early retirement without any access or influence at all. A more specific and tantalizing question, equally unanswerable, follows: what if one or several prominent servitors had resorted to "exit" at a key juncture in the developing trajectory of tyranny at home or abroad? What if Cambacérès, or a valued minister, or a president of section in the Council of State, or an important senator had publicly resigned his position in protest at some major crossroad? Napoleon's collaborators could not have been unaware of this option, but none chose to employ it. If there is an exception it is Talleyrand, but his case is highly ambiguous. His exit was neither painful nor public: by a kind of mutual consent in 1807, Talleyrand slipped quietly out of the foreign ministry into a munificent sinecure in the imperial court. Yet his departure was understood abroad as a sign of encouragement to Napoleon's adversaries (with whom Talleyrand remained in secret contact) that they should resist the emperor's grandiose ambitions. Being notorious for his cynicism and opportunism, Talleyrand is hard to hold up as an example of integrity or courage, and in France his behavior has understandably been viewed as equivocal if not traitorous. But his machinations in the interest of France (as he saw it) and as a good European stand in better repute today than in the past.[60]

OBSERVATIONS about lack of courage or the absence of "exit" among Napoleon's servitors are in any case easy enough to make. But the history of Napoleon and his collaborators has a more positive if problematic side as well. The ex-revolutionary collaborators in particular kept aloft the banner of liberal revolutionary principles, however selective, symbolic, or observed in the breach they may have become.[61] They repeatedly managed to inscribe certain "gains of the Revolution" in the regime's acts of self-representation—in the proclamations surrounding Brumaire, the necrologies of senators, the pivotal orchestration for the transition to Empire, even the launching of the imperial nobility, notwithstanding the contortions this last development required. The old hands of the National Assembly and their spiritual heirs—strengthened by their obligatory reunion across the awkward Fructidor divide—kept an attenuated set of revolutionary values on the table. Napoleon always insisted that he was the only guarantee against a return of the Bourbons, but he otherwise found talk of public liberties tiresome at best. The enduring presence of his ex-revolutionary collaborators, however, obliged the emperor to retain a modicum of grudging respect for such sentiments.

Beyond that, Napoleon's servitors lent to his regime the competence they had acquired from the Revolution's decade of administrative and legislative experience. The Cambacérès who stood at Bonaparte's side was not simply the judge of the old regime Cour des Comptes in Montpellier or the self-important collector of honors and emoluments, but the seasoned veteran of political vicissitudes and endless legislative labors in the National Convention. The same was true of other civilian stalwarts, not least Napoleon's "iron men," Boulay, Defermon, and Regnaud.

Even as the dictatorship took shape, battles remained to be fought. Soon after Thermidor, conservatives had started to attack various innovations of the Revolution. The often stalemated legislative debates of the Directory years had fended off some of the most drastic assaults, but a new wave of reaction seemed possible after Brumaire. Former revolutionaries in Napoleon's inner circles, however, managed to defend certain beleaguered liberal institutions. Their small victories included preservation of the Revolution's landmark equal inheritance law of 1793 (retained in the new Civil Code with only modest concessions to a father's testamentary discretion), and trial by jury in felony proceedings, upheld after a grueling debate in the Council of State that ran on and off for years. On a more symbolic level, I have suggested, the "men of the Revolution" like Treilhard, Berlier, and Regnaud doggedly defended the idea of press freedom. Napoleon demanded the reestablishment of book censorship, and nothing could be done to prevent this, but his servitors on the Council of State won the day for a "voluntary" rather than obligatory form of censorship. While the distinction proved illusory in practice, they at least protected the venerable principle from annihilation. Likewise they kept the routine use of preventive detention in the spotlight, with the Senate committee on individual liberty obliging the police ministry to at least review its own actions and justify them in certain cases. Some of Napoleon's collaborators tried to mitigate the regime's repressive practices by making them less blatantly arbitrary and by subjecting them to a degree of oversight.

OBVIOUSLY, if one aspired to public service, to a lawmaking or administrative role, in the newly depoliticized government of France, one could do so only from the inside. The first year of this new order offered considerable satisfactions to the regime's leading participants. The high purpose and rafts of serious business occupying the Council of State profited from the forced reconciliation of the revolutionary elite that had been fractured in the Fructidor coup of 1797. The installation of the prefects seemed to resolve the vexing issue of relations between Paris and the provinces. With a cascade of patronage to be managed, almost every regime notable could exercise some influence, even to the point of assisting certain ex-regicides otherwise outside the pale. Liberal revolutionary legislator and counselor of state Français de Nantes, for example, appointed the stalwart ex-Montagnard Charles Duval as a bureau chief in the agency for the Droits Réunis which he directed, and by one account allowed Duval to occupy that post as a kind of sinecure. Similarly, Berlier employed his former Montagnard colleague, the dissident Florent-Guiot, as secretary general of the Conseil des Prises which he headed.[62] This opportunity to make a difference put collaboration with Bonaparte in an appealing light even to former republicans like Berlier or Boulay, let alone constitutional monarchists like Roederer or Regnaud, and its afterglow lasted for years.

Participation in the Napoleonic regime was hardly a form of selfless behavior. First and foremost it served pure self-interest—political security, financial advantage, social prestige, and one's sense of honor, the desire to be useful to society in some fashion. Such opportunities for generously rewarded public service, however, could easily create a presumption of merit and entitlement, which could in turn erode one's capacity to act independently once the atmosphere began to change. For working within the bosom of this evolving dictatorship eventually meant facing unpleasant realities and demoralizing situations. The first and most jarring moment of truth came quite suddenly and unexpectedly in December 1800, with Bonaparte's ferocious extra-legal assault on alleged former terrorists. Touched off by a genuinely shocking event, the royalist attempt of 3 Nivôse to assassinate the first consul with a powerful bomb, the subsequent deportations ultimately had no direct connection with that pretext. They were in fact exceedingly cruel and utterly arbitrary, notwithstanding their aura of a long-overdue exorcism and settling of accounts for the Terror. Far more than the Brumaire coup itself, and well before the transition to Empire, this episode was a pivotal event in the slide toward dictatorship. As we have seen, it perplexed most of Bonaparte's hand-picked collaborators on the Council of State and made several of them extremely uncomfortable. But like the exclusion of Daunou from the Senate, or the purge of the Tribunate, or the manipulated plebiscite on the life consulship, the deportations provoked scant opposition, let alone any "exit."

After those transgressive acts, the die was cast on the domestic side. Later, when the regime became preoccupied with foreign relations and far-flung military campaigns, it was much too late to interpose any check on Napoleon's will or power, as the Legislative Corps learned with its abortive effort to remonstrate with the emperor in December 1813. During the later years of the Empire, Napoleon sucked the air out of his regime. The latitude for independent opinion within the government vanished, as the emperor began to elevate mediocre sycophants to high positions (including Maret himself as foreign secretary, Molé as minister of justice, and the odious Savary as minister of police). In Paris, the regime's center of gravity shifted from the Council of State to the stuffy and servile atmosphere of the imperial court. Legislation gave way to administration, in whose details Napoleon certainly continued to show a keen interest. Above all, the growing militarization of the Empire reduced Napoleon's civilian collaborators (other than the prefects) to a diminishing role, excluded as most of them had always been from strictly diplomatic and military affairs.[63] But a remnant of their prominence can be found in the *conseils privées*, where their procedural role formed a final, residual barrier to unchecked tyranny.

SCRUTINY OF Napoleon's personal attitude about the Revolution will show, I believe, that his vaunted appropriation of the French revolutionary legacy, his identification with 1789, had largely to do with its clearing operations and had little resonance with its more demanding positive values. To the extent that certain "gains of the Revolution" not only motivated the Brumaire coup (which is self-evident) but remained a component of the Napoleon dictatorship even after the first consul became an emperor, it was the ex-revolutionary collaborators who should receive whatever credit is due. Their presence in turn helps explain the last act of the Napoleonic episode (apart from the creation of the Napoleonic legend), the strange experience of the Hundred Days. That unexpected and unstable amalgam of Revolution and Empire was grounded in the wish (or fantasy) that a non-aggressive France would now be led by a liberal emperor. The public lineaments of Napoleon's resurrection in 1815 reflected the values not of the impatient "usurper" himself but of the cautious ex-revolutionaries who still surrounded him. The evanescent prospect of a liberal empire was their vision, not Napoleon's, vindicating, it might well have seemed, fourteen years of collaboration.

Acknowledgments

OR STIMULATING discussion, particular suggestions, or other kinds of assistance, I wish to thank Ann Adelman, Jean-Paul Bertaud, Steven Clay, Mel Edelstein, Steve Forman, Ray Grew, Don Lamm, Peter Loewenberg, Sergio Luzzatto, Mel Richter, Louise Tilly, Alex Woloch, David Woloch, and Nancy Woloch. I would also like to express my appreciation to Jean Tulard for his many indispensable publications in this field, not least his guide to the memoir literature, his exhaustive *Dictionnaire Napoléon*, his edition of Cambacérès letters, and his monograph on the Napoleonic nobility, all of which facilitated my own work.

I began the research for this project while a fellow at the Center for the History of Freedom at Washington University (St. Louis), for whose congenial environment I thank the director, Richard Davis. Along the way I had the opportunity to present some of my thoughts on Napoleon's collaborators at The New School; the NYU Institute of French Studies; and a conference at Hunter College on Bonapartism, with thanks to my hosts in each of those venues. Finally, I am grateful for the long-standing support of Columbia University and my publisher, W. W. Norton & Company.

A Note on Sources

ARCHIVAL SOURCES

Given the unusual focus of this project, it was difficult to anticipate where the most useful archival documents could be found. I therefore sampled many sources in the Archives Nationales that in the end proved of little or no help, but also found many that yielded substantial material for my quest. (It should be noted that the main repository of papers from the Council of State did not survive the fire of 1871 during the siege of the Paris Commune.)

From Series **AF IV,** the papers of the executive branch, Consulate and Empire, organized by the secretary of state, I have used the following cartons:

1023 (mission of Regnaud); 1025 (mission of Pelet); 1041 (Senate, Tribunate); 1042 (Grand Judge, Council of State); 1043 (police); 1065 (minister of interior); 1227 (*conseils privés*); 1236–37 (prisoners of state); 1238 (administrative council: interior affairs); 1229–30 (council of ministers); 1231 (administrative council); 1232 (*conseils privés: grâces*); 1304-06 (misc.); 1314–15 (police); 1326A (Council of State); 1337 (Council of State); 1424 (Senate candidates); 1429 (electoral colleges); 1432 (plebiscites); 1446–48 (Attentat de Nivôse, An IX: addresses).

Other series that I drew on included:

F¹ᶜ I 13: Exposition de la Situation de l'Empire
F¹ᵈ I 32–34: Préfectures: demandes de places, An VIII
F⁷ 6271: Police: Attentat de Nivôse An IX
BB I 138: Conseil d'Etat: Auditeurs
BB II 850A, 850B, 851A: Adresses militaires, An XII
BB³ 140–45: Justice: délits politiques
AD XIXA 3: Conseil d'Etat
CC 50, 60–62, 64, 69: Sénat

In the Series of Private Papers in the Archives Nationales, I looked at about a dozen collections, but only four proved truly useful for my purposes:

27 AP: François de Neufchâteau Papers: 14, 16
29 AP: Roederer Papers: 75, 78
199 AP: Lamarque Papers: 1, 2, 4, 5, 7
286 AP: Cambacérès Papers: 1, 3

In addition, the Berlier Papers in the departmental archives of the Côte d'Or contained a couple of illuminating documents, but not as much as one would have hoped.

PUBLISHED PRIMARY SOURCES

For guidance to the vast memoir literature on the Napoleonic era, I am, like all scholars, indebted to Jean Tulard's reliable *Bibliographie critique des mémoires sur le Consulat et l'Empire* (1971). It will be evident that I have drawn most heavily on the two sets of memoirs published by Thibaudeau; on Berlier's memoir (written, he said, for the use of his descendants); and on the memoir/ biography of Boulay de la Meurthe compiled by his son but based largely on Boulay's own words, and like Berlier's, intended for the family. The latter two, I believe, have been entirely and unwarrantedly neglected by historians. Other memoirs from this voluminous literature most useful for my purposes included those by or compiled in behalf of Barante, Lucien Bonaparte, Bourrienne, Cambacérès, Caulaincourt, Chaptal, Cornet, de Broglie, Dumas, Fain, Fouché, Gohier, Meneval, Molé, Mollien, Pasquier, and Roederer.

Tulard's two-volume edition of Cambacérès's letters to Napoleon was of course invaluable. Other especially useful material included Lombard de Langres's contemporaneous compilation about the Brumaire coup; Pelet de la Lozère's documents and notes about discussions in the Council of State; Locré's report of debates in the Council of State on censorship and the book trade; Taillender's compilation about Daunou; Oelsner's contemporary celebration of Sieyès; and Baudot's posthumous volume of notes about personalities of the revolutionary and Napoleonic eras. I would also call attention to two precious eyewitness accounts of the Brumaire coup by the deputies to the Council of 500 Bigonnet and Combes-Dounous, used in the first chapter, which have often been overlooked in previous accounts of that event.

Notes*

Preface

1. Readers of French have the outstanding study by J. Tulard, *Napoléon, ou le mythe du sauveur* (2nd edn., 1977), but Anglophones are ill-served by the translation. Works in English include F. Markham, *Napoleon* (1963); A. Schom, *Napoleon* (1997); G. Ellis, *Napoleon* (1998); and my sentimental favorite, J. M. Thompson, *Napoleon Bonaparte* (1952). For two recent and reliable textbook syntheses, see M. Lyons, *Napoleon and the Legacy of the French Revolution* (New York, 1994), and M. Broers, *Europe Under Napoleon* (London, 1996).

2. See P. Geyl, *Napoleon For and Against* (New Haven, CT, 1949), a perceptive and even-handed survey of 19th- and early 20th-century French historiography on Napoleon.

3. See A. Hirschman, *Exit, Voice and Loyalty: Responses to Decline in Firms, Organizations, and States* (Cambridge, MA, 1970),17 and 115–19. (I owe this reference to Louise Tilly.)

Chapter I: Seizing Power: the Joint Venture of Brumaire

1. This notion is invoked in several key articles in F. Furet and M. Ozouf, eds., *A Critical Dictionary of the French Revolution* (Cambridge, MA, 1989 transl.). Their interpretation emphasizes the latent illiberalism of Jacobin ideology, and all but dismisses the role of circumstances in radicalizing the Revolution.

2. For overviews of the Directory years, see G. Lefebvre, *Le Directoire* (1947); D. Woronoff, *La République bourgeoise de Thermidor à Brumaire, 1794–1799* (1972); and M. Lyons, *France Under the Directory* (Cambridge, 1975).

---

*unless otherwise stated, place of publication is Paris.

A.N. = Archives Nationales

B.N. = Bibliothèque Nationale

3. On the Neo-Jacobins, see I. Woloch, *Jacobin Legacy: The Democratic Movement Under the Directory* (Princeton, NJ, 1970), and B. Gainot, "Le Mouvement Neo-Jacobin à la fin du Directoire" (2 vols.), Thèse pour le doctorat, Université de Paris I, 1993.

4. See H. Brown, "From Organic Society to Security State: The War on Brigandage in France, 1797–1802," *Journal of Modern History*, XLIX (1997), 661–95.

5. Biret, curé de Loye (à l'Ile de Rhé), *La Source des malheurs de la République et le moyen d'y remédier* (an VIII), B.N. Lb43 498, pp. 39, 61–62. See I. Woloch, "Republican Institutions, 1797–99," in C. Lucas, ed., *The Political Culture of the French Revolution* (Oxford, 1988), on the revolutionary calendar; and I. Woloch, *The New Regime: Transformations of the French Civic Order, 1789–1820s* (New York, 1994), chap 6, on the school wars.

6. V. Lombard de Langres, *Le Dix-huit Brumaire ou tableau des événements qui ont amené cette journée . . .* (an VIII), 15–16. This is a valuable source that conveys the tendentious views of the brumairians and provides the text of key addresses surrounding the coup.

7. Woloch, *The New Regime*, chap 3; M. Crook, *Elections in the French Revolution: An Apprenticeship in Democracy, 1789–1799* (Cambridge, 1996), chap 6.

8. Lombard de Langres, *Dix-huit Brumaire*, 19.

9. *Ibid.*, 20–21.

10. *Précis de la Vie politique de Théophile Berlier écrit par lui-même et adressé à ses enfans et petits-enfans . . .* (Dijon, 1838), 52–54. (Referred to hereafter as Berlier, *Précis.*)

11. On Sieyès, see C.-D. Oelsner, *Des Opinions politiques du Citoyen Sieyès et de sa vie comme homme public* (an VIII), B.N. Ln27 18957; P. Bastid, *Sieyès et sa pensée* (2nd edn., 1970); and especially J.-D. Brédin, *Sieyès: la clé de la Révolution française* (1988).

12. On this episode, see P. Higonnet, *Class, Ideology, and the Rights of Nobles During the French Revolution* (Oxford, 1981), 234–43.

13. On the Prairial coup, see A. Méynier, *Les Coups d'état du Directoire* (3 vols., 1928), Vol. III, and A. Vandal, *L'Avènement de Bonaparte* (Nelson edn., 1910), Vol. I, chap 1.

14. J.-I. Combes-Dounous, *Notice sur le 18 Brumaire, par un témoin . . .* (1814), 10.

15. Berlier, *Précis de la Vie*, 58–62.

16. *Ibid.*, 54–55, 64–65. On the clubs and press, see Woloch and Gainot.

17. *Boulay de la Meurthe* (1868), 8–9, 18–19, 33–38. This volume, on which I have drawn throughout the book, was compiled by Boulay's son "d'après ses conversations, sa correspondance, ses écrits, ses discours et autres documents authentiques" (note préliminaire). Like Berlier's memoir, it was said to be intended for private rather than public consumption ("Elle n'est point destinée au public").

18. *Ibid.*, 73–81.

19. For perspective on the generals and the regime, see J.-P. Bertaud, *Bonaparte prend le pouvoir: la République meurt-elle assassinée?* (1987), 143–63.

20. *La France Vue de l'Armée d'Italie: journal de politique, d'administration et de littérature française et étrangère* (Milan), nos. 1–3, 6, 14 (continuous pagination). The journal supported a classic anti-Jacobin measure: "La nouvelle de la clôture des clubs promet la cessation de la fermentation qui se manifestait" (p. 31).

21. *Ibid.*, pp. 35, 44.

22. Lucien Bonaparte, *Révolution de Brumaire ou Relation des principaux événements des journées des 18 et 19 brumaire* (1845), 30–33.

23. *Mémoires de M. de Bourrienne sur Napoléon* (10 vols., Brussels, 1829), III: 55, 38, 56.

24. Lucien's relationship with P.-J. Briot, a young democratic deputy purged after Brumaire, endured long after the coup. They would go on to exchange bitter letters about Napoleon's abandonment of republicanism after he took the imperial crown, which Lucien reproduces at the end of his memoir.

25. Lombard de Langres, *Dix-huit Brumaire*, 129; Lucien Bonaparte, *Brumaire*, 42.

26. M.-A. Cornet, *Notice historique sur le 18 Brumaire* (1819), 9; Bourrienne, *Mémoires*, III: 64; Vandal, *L'Avènement de Bonaparte*, I: chap 7.

27. Lucien Bonaparte, *Brumaire*, 43–44.

28. For accounts of the 18th Brumaire, see Vandal, *L'Avènement*, chap 8, and Bertaud, *Bonaparte prend le pouvoir*, 28–40.

29. Lombard de Langres, *Dix-huit Brumaire*, 157; *Boulay de la Meurthe*, 91.

30. Lucien Bonaparte, *Brumaire*, 83.

31. *Ibid.*, 63.

32. Cornet, *Notice historique*, 12.

33. Lucien Bonaparte, *Brumaire*, 19, 69; *Boulay de la Meurthe*, 92.

34. Combes-Dounous, *18 Brumaire*, 19–24, and M. Bigonnet, *Coup d'état du dix-huit Brumaire* (1819), 23. These two precious eyewitness accounts by deputies in the Council of 500 were doubtless written soon after the event but were published only after Napoleon's fall.

35. The phrase is from Lombard de Langres, *Dix-huit Brumaire*, 183.

36. Bigonnet, *Coup d'état*, 24–25.

37. *Ibid.*, 25.

38. Lombard de Langres, *Dix-huit Brumaire*, 200; Bourrienne, *Mémoires*, III:76.

39. Lombard de Langres, *Dix-huit Brumaire*, 220–22.

40. Lucien Bonaparte, *Brumaire*, 110.

41. Combes-Dounous, *18 Brumaire*, 37; Bigonnet, *Coup d'état*, 26–27.

42. Lucien Bonaparte, *Brumaire*, 111–21.

43. Bourrienne, *Mémoires*, III: 83–84.

44. Combes-Dounous, *18 Brumaire*, 36; Bigonnet, *Coup d'état*, 31; *Boulay de la Meurthe*, 98.

45. Lucien Bonaparte, *Brumaire*, 111; Bigonnet, *Coup d'état*, 26–27; *Boulay de la Meurthe*, 98.

46. Overheard by Combes-Dounous, *18 Brumaire*, 38.

47. *Boulay de la Meurthe*, 100.

48. Bigonnet, *Coup d'état*, 28–29, 32; Combes-Dounous, *18 Brumaire*, 40.

49. " . . . ces constitutionnels du poignard et du hors la loi": Lucien Bonaparte, *Brumaire*, 154.

50. *Ibid.*, 180; *Boulay de la Meurthe*, 103.

51. According to Cornet, however, only a minority in the Elders actually endorsed the plan, while "the majority was mournful and silent." Cornet, *Notice historique*, 16.

52. For the official addresses, see Lombard de Langres, *Dix-huit Brumaire*, 230–41, and *Boulay de la Meurthe*, 102–06.

53. I. Woloch, "Réflexions sur les réactions à Brumaire dans les milieux républicains provinciaux," in *Mélanges Michel Vovelle: Sur la Révolution: approches plurielles* (1997), 309–18.

54. Vandal, *L'Avènement*, I: 409. Bastid, *Sieyès*, 247, is skeptical.

55. Vandal, *L'Avènement*, I: 426–30.

56. A. Aulard, ed., *Registre des déliberations du Consulat Provisoire* (1894), 43.

57. Besides the discussion in Bastid and Brédin, see P. Pasquino, *Sieyès et l'invention de la Constitution en France* (1998).

58. *Discours de Boulay de la Meurthe, 21 frimaire VIII, au nom de la section chargée de preparer le projet* . . . (B.N. Lb42 812); Lombard de Langres, *Dix-huit Brumaire*, 395–96.

59. Brédin, *Sieyès*, 474–75; K. Baker, "Representation," in Baker, ed., *The Political Culture of the Old Regime* (Oxford, 1987).

60. Brédin, *Sieyès*, 468–70; M. Gauchet, *La Révolution des pouvoirs: la souveraineté, le peuple et la représentation, 1789–1799* (1995), 214–18.

61. Bastid, *Sieyès*, 254–55.

62. *Boulay de la Meurthe*, 117.

63. Brédin, *Sieyès*, 482.

64. Cited by Gauchet, *La Révolution des pouvoirs*, 223.

65. *Boulay de la Meurthe*, 115.

66. Gauchet, *La Révolution des pouvoirs*, 229–34.

67. "Garat," in J. Tulard, ed., *Dictionnaire Napoléon* (1987), 773–74.

68. *Mémoires de Louis-Jérôme Gohier, président du Directoire au 18 Brumaire*, in the series "Mémoires des Contemporains, pour servir a l'histoire de France . . . " (2 vols., 1824), II: 53–54.

69. "Discours par Garat dans la séance du 23 frimaire, relative à l'acceptation de l'acte constitutionnel," in Lombard de Langres, *Dix-huit Brumaire*, 425–31.

70. Gohier, *Mémoires*, II: 54–55.

Chapter II: Organizing Power

1. For a general overview, see A. Meynier, *Les Coups d'état du Directoire, I: Le Dix-huit Fructidor* (1926).

2. Quoted in T. Tackett, *Becoming a Revolutionary: The Deputies of the French National Assembly and the Emergence of a Revolutionary Culture* (Princeton, NJ, 1996), 227.

3. C. Le Bozec, "Le pas de clerc d'un centriste: Boissy d'Anglas et fructidor," in P. Bourdon and B. Gainot, eds., *La République directoriale* (2 vols., 1998), I: 401–12.

4. The veritable royalists deported in Fructidor included Willot, Imbert-Collomès, and Henry Larivière.

5. See M. Reinhard, *Le Grand Carnot, II: L'Organisateur de la Victoire, 1792–1823* (1952), chap 8.

6. H. Mitchell, *The Underground War Against Revolutionary France* (Oxford, 1965), 214–16.

7. *Dictionnaire des Grands Hommes du Jour, par une Société de très-petits Individus* (Paris, an VIII) in B.N., Lb43 79.

8. *Ibid.*, 27–28.

9. *Ibid.*, passim.

10. A.N. AF IV 1314: Relevé des surveillances accordées par le Citoyen Fouché, 13 thermidor VII–4 pluviôse VIII; Etat des Individus condamnés à la déportation par des actes Législatifs. See also *Mémoires de M. de Bourrienne sur Napoléon* (10 vols., Brussels, 1829), III: 217–19.

11. Chaptal, *Mes Souvenirs sur Napoléon* (1893), 311; O. Connelly, *The Gentle Bonaparte: A Biography of Joseph, Napoleon's Elder Brother* (New York, 1968), 41.

12. F.-N. Mollien, *Mémoires d'un ministre du trésor public, 1780–1815* (1898), I: 231, 234–35.

13. An interesting example of the prevailing mood: When Prefect of Police Dubois suddenly ordered that François de Neufchâteau's play *Pamela* be pulled from the theatrical repertory because it contained several pointed anti-Jacobin verses that might provoke public demonstrations, the veteran man of letters and former minister of interior for the Directory reacted furiously and invoked his freedom of expression. But Minister of Interior Lucien Bonaparte, implicitly apologizing for Dubois's brusque order, appealed instead to François' patriotism. "Quand le Gouvernement donnait l'exemple d'un pardon généreux, les citoyens ne doivent pas reveiller des passions haineuses," Lucien argued. Better to condemn such villains to "*un éternel oubli*" than to continue agitating over their crimes or stupidities. Faced with this kind of sincere request, the newly named senator swallowed his pride and consented to delete the provocative passages, although he warned that the audience might not be so forgiving. François de Neufchâteau Papers: A.N. 27 AP 16, doss. 5: Lucien Bonaparte to F. de N., 19 germinal VIII, and response.

14. Chaptal, *Souvenirs*, 311–12; J. Fouché, *Mémoires*, ed. M. Vovelle (1992), 148–49.

15. A.N. AF IV 1448, fol. Seine: Bremontier to the first consul, 4 nivôse IX.

16. A.-C. Thibaudeau, *Mémoires, 1799–1815* (1913), 41–43.

17. M.-J. Cornet, *Souvenirs Sénatoriaux* (1824), 5.

18. J. Thiry, *Le Sénat de Napoléon* (1949), chap IV; Bourrienne, *Mémoires*, III: chap 10.

19. See J.-L. Halperin, "Sénat," in J. Tulard, ed., *Dictionnaire Napoléon* (1987), 1562–66.

20. A.N. CC 69: Sénat—Nécrologie.

21. *Ibid.*

22. *Ibid.*

23. A.N. CC 69; Garran-Coulon, *Notice sur J.-A. Creuzé-Latouche, membre du Sénat et de l'Institut National* (brumaire IX) in B.N. Ln27 5161.

24. W. Giesselmann, *Die brumairianische Elite*, in the series "Industrielle Welt": Vol. 18 (Stuttgart, 1977), 168–72, 282–84, 426–32.

25. See the informative work of I. Collins, *Napoleon and His Parliaments 1800–1815* (London, 1979).

26. A.N. F1d I 34, fols. Seine-et-Marne, Seine-et-Oise, and Seine Inférieure; A.N. F1d I 32, fol. Loiret for a divided deputation.

27. A.N. F1d I 32, fol. Aveyron. See also F1d I 33, fols. Marne and Puy-de-Dôme.

28. A.N. F1d I 33, fol. Puy-de-Dôme; F1d I 34, fol. Seine. Dulaure was not appointed.

29. Drouet to minister of interior, pluviôse and germinal an VIII in A.N. F1d I 33, fol. Marne.

30. J. Tulard, "Les Préfets de Napoléon," in J. Aubert et al., *Les Préfets en France, 1800–1940* (Geneva, 1978); Fouché, *Mémoires*, 148.

31. E. Lemay, ed., *Dictionnaire des Constituants, 1789–1791*, Vol. II, and J.-L. Thiry, *Le Département de la Meurthe sous le Consulat* (Nancy, 1957), 23–29.

32. See the important article by E. Whitcomb, "Napoleon's Prefects," *American Historical Review*, LXXIX (October 1974), 1089–1118.

33. A.N. F1c III: Seine Inférieure 8, an X.

34. F. Rocquain, ed., *L'Etat de la France au 18 Brumaire* (1874), 285–86.

35. A.N. AF IV 1052.

36. Pelet de la Lozère, ed., *Opinions de Napoléon au Conseil d'Etat* (1833), 268–72.

37. A.N. AF IV 1043: Ministre de police: Rapport aux Consuls, messidor, an VIII. Fouché believed that most returned émigrés "sont loin d'être assez généreux pour oublier les maux."

38. Rocquain, ed., *L'Etat de la France*, 271, 212, 250.

39. A.N. AF IV 1065.

40. A.N. AF IV 1065: Ministre de l'Intérieure: Rapport sur l'Analyse des procès-verbaux des Conseils Généraux des Départements, an XI: Tableau 3.

41. *Ibid.*, and Thiry, *Meurthe*, 23–29.

42. A.N. AF IV 1065.

43. Lamarque figures prominently in I. Woloch, *Jacobin Legacy: The Democratic Movement During the Directory* (Princeton, NJ, 1970).

44. Lamarque Papers: A.N. 199 AP 4: unsigned letter to F.L., 13 frimaire 8; Cambacérès to F.L., 12 pluviôse 8.

45. A.N. 199 AP 2: "Observations sur la situation actuelle de la République," 2 pluviôse VIII.

46. A.N. 199 AP 2: F.L. to Roux, 19 germinal 8; F.L. to Lacombe, nd.

47. A.N. 199 AP 2: F.L. to Lucien Bonaparte, 11 floréal 8; F.L. to Roux, 23 floréal 8.

48. A.N. 199 AP 2: F.L. to Didot jeune; A.N. 199 AP 7: Tableau analytique des grandes époques . . . de la Révolution de 1789, extrait des Mémoires de F. Lamarque (never published), and fol. "Résumé."

49. A.N. 199 AP 4: Lucien Bonaparte to F.L., 4 messidor 8; A.N. 199 AP 2: F.L. to Roux, 27 messidor 8.

50. A.N. 199 AP 2: F.L. to Cambacérès, 24 floréal 10; A.N. 199 AP 4: Bordas to F.L., nd.

51. A.N. 199 AP 6: *Notice pour F. Lamarque, l'un des trois Candidats, présentés par S.M. L'Empereur pour Juge de la Cour de Cassation.*

52. A.N. 199 AP 5: Roux-Fazillac to Cambacérès, 21 floréal 12 (11 May 1804)(copy).

53. A.N. 199 AP 5: Roux to F.L., 21 floréal and 24 prairial XII, enclosing a letter to Berlier; Roux to Réal (copy), 19 germinal XII.

54. A. Kuscinski, ed., *Dictionnaire des Conventionnels* (1916; 1973), 539.

Chapter III: Early Warning Signs

1. A. Soboul, "Religious Sentiment and Popular Cults During the Revolution: Patriot Saints and Martyrs of Liberty," in J. Kaplow, ed., *New Perspectives on the French Revolution* (New York, 1965), 342–50.

2. A.N. BB3 140 [Délits politiques]: *Avis Au Peuple français*, forwarded by the commissioner to the criminal tribunal of the Pyrénées Orientales to minister of justice, 6 and 15 nivôse IX.

3. R. C. Cobb, *The Police and the People: French Popular Protest, 1789–1820* (Oxford, 1970), 172–211.

4. Historian Stephen Clay, who studies revolutionary Marseilles, is working on the downside of the amnesty in the Midi, its stimulus to the endemic violence of succeeding years in that region.

5. For a panoramic consideration of Neo-Jacobinism in 1799, see B. Gainot, "Le Mouvement Neo-Jacobin à la fin du Directoire" (2 vols.), Thèse pour le doctorat, Université de Paris I, 1993.

6. *Journal de Seine-et-Oise*, no.5, 20 brumaire VIII.

7. A.N. BB3 140: Prefect to minister of interior, nivôse IX.

8. A.N. BB3 140: Commissioner at the tribunal to minister of justice, 14 germinal IX.

9. A. Martel, *Etude sur l'affaire de la machine infernale du 3 nivôse an IX* (1870), 168; Fouché, *Mémoires*, 159.

10. H. Gaubert, *Conspirateurs au temps de Napoléon Ier* (1962), 47–70.

11. A. C. Thibaudeau, *Bonaparte and the Consulate*, trans. G. K. Fortescue (London, 1908), 51. The volume was originally published as *Mémoires sur le Consulat, 1801–1804, par un ancien conseiller d'état* (1827).

12. *Souvenirs du Baron de Barante, 1782–1866*, ed. C. de Barante (2 vols., 1890), I: 72.

13. Fouché, *Mémoires*, 162. See also A. Hayward, ed., *Indiscretions of a Prefect of Police: Anecdotes of Napoleon . . . from the Papers of Count Réal* (London, 1929), 1–11; and P.-M. Desmarets, *Quinze Ans de Haute Police sous le Consulat et l'Empire*, ed. L. Grasilier (1900), 45–66.

14. Gaubert, *Conspirateurs*, 92.

15. A.N. AF IV 1446–48: Attentat de Nivôse, An IX.

16. Also Prefects of Lozère, Drôme, Haute-Loire, and Saône-et-Loire: A.N. AF IV 1446–48; and A.N. F7 6271.

17. A.N. AF IV 1446–47.

18. A.N. AF IV 1448.

19. *Boulay de la Meurthe*, 143; Réal, *Indiscretions . . .* , 6.

20. P.-L. Roederer, *Mémoires sur la Révolution, le Consulat et l'Empire*, ed. O. Aubry (1942), 164.

21. *Boulay de la Meurthe*, 140–46; also C. Durand, *Etudes sur le Conseil d'Etat Napoléonien* (1949), 632–35.

22. Fouché, *Mémoires*, 167; A.N. F7 6271: Arrêté du 17 nivôse IX.

23. Thibaudeau, *Bonaparte and the Consulate*, 65–68. See also the account of Roederer, *Mémoires*, 157–71.

24. A.N. F7 6271: Rapport du Ministre de Police Générale, 14 nivôse IX and *senatus-consulte* of 15 nivôse.

25. Martel, *Machine infernale*, 167, 170.

26. F. Rocquain, ed., *L'Etat de la France au 18 Brumaire* (1874), 293–94.

27. *Boulay de la Meurthe*, 145–46.

28. Berlier refers only briefly in his memoirs to his forceful but unsuccessful intervention with Bonaparte, but directs his readers to Thibaudeau's previously published account. See *Précis*, 81.

29. *Ibid.*

30. See J. Destrem, *Les Déportations du Consulat et de l'Empire* (1885). This work was compiled by a descendant of one of the deportees, the Neo-Jacobin deputy Hugues Destrem, who had railed at Bonaparte when he illegally entered the Council of 500 on 19 Brumaire. See also M. Fescourt, *Histoire de la double Conspiration de 1800, contre le gouvernement consulaire, et de la déportation . . .* (1819).

31. A.N. F7 6271: Etat des 70 personnes déportés aux Iles Séchelles, 1808.

32. A.N. F7 6271: Les français soussignés, mis en surveillance spéciale à Mahé, Iles Séchelles, 29 Janvier 1807.

33. Destrem, *Les Déportations*, 253–54, 261–69.

34. Barante, *Mémoires*, I: 73.

35. See J. Thiry, *Le Sénat de Napoléon* (1949), chap VI.

36. Taillender, *Documents biographiques sur Daunou* (1847).

37. Thiry, *Le Sénat*, 72–78.

38. See G. Gusdorf, *La Conscience révolutionnaire: les Idéologues* (1978), 316–29.

39. M. Staum, *Cabanis: Enlightenment and Medical Philosophy in the French Revolution* (Princeton, NJ, 1980), 287–95.

40. M.-A. Cornet, *Souvenirs sénatoriaux* (1824), 63–64.

41. *Ibid.*, 62–63.

42. Oelsner, *Sieyès*, 242, 248, 250–51.

43. Quoted in Thiry, *Le Sénat*, 263–64.

44. See *Observations* (a four-page pamphlet in which Bourrienne had a hand) criticizing the Tribunate for its opposition to a proposed law creating special courts without juries to hear serious cases of brigandage. "Les étrangers qui ignorent l'état veritable de la France pourraient penser, en lisant les séances du Tribunat . . . que l'esprit de faction s'agit encore." Roederer Papers, A.N. 29 AP 75.

45. J. L. Halperin, "Tribunat," in J. Tulard, ed., *Dictionnaire Napoléon* (1987), 1655–57; Collins, *Napoleon and his Parliaments*, 58–62; *Boulay de la Meurthe*, 152–55.

46. See R. R. Palmer, *J.-B. Say: An Economist in Troubled Times* (Princeton, NJ, 1997), 49–55; Gusdorf, *Les Idéologues*, 315–30.

47. Napoléon, *Correspondence*, no. 5927: 1 pluviôse X; *Cambacérès, Lettres inédites à Napoléon, 1802–1814*, ed. J. Tulard (2 vols., 1973) (cited hereafter as *Cambacérès: Lettres inédites*), Vol. I, Nos. 20, 25, 30, 32, 34, 36, 38–39; Collins, *Napoleon and His Parliaments*, 63–67. One exception was the *idéologue* Andrieux, whom Bonaparte agreed to abide. See also *Cambacérès, Memoires inédits*, ed. L. Chatel de Brancion (2 vols, 1999) Vol. I: 602–04.

48. *Cambacérès: Lettres inédites*, Vol. I, Nos. 489–90.

49. M. Staum, "The Class of Moral and Political Sciences, 1795–1803," *French Historical Studies*, XI (1980), 371–97.

Chapter IV: From Consulate to Empire

1. J. A. Chaptal, *Mes Souvenirs sur Napoléon* (1893), 308–09.

2. A. C. Thibaudeau, *Bonaparte and the Consulate*, ed. and trans. G. K. Fortescue (London, 1908), 217, 221.

3. *Ibid.*, 219–21.

4. *Ibid.*, 222–23; J. Thiry, *Le Sénat de Napoléon* (1949), 96–97.

5. Thibaudeau, *Consulate*, 225.

6. *Boulay de la Meurthe* (1868), 158–59.

7. Berlier, *Précis*, 88.

8. Thibaudeau, *Consulate*, 232–33.

9. C. Langlois, "Le Plébiscite de l'an VIII ou le coup d'Etat du 18 pluviôse an VIII," *Annales historiques de la Révolution française* (1972), 43–65, 231–46, 391–415.

10. C. Langlois, "Napoléon Bonaparte Plébiscité?" in *L'Election du Chef de l'Etat en France, de Hugues Capet à Nos Jours* (1988), 81–93.

11. Roederer Papers in A.N. 29 AP 75: circular, 25 floréal an X.

12. A.N. AF IV 1432, doss. 3: Exécution de l'arrêté du 20 floréal an X: lettres des préfets.

13. A.N. AF IV 1432, doss. 3: M. I. Rapport au Consuls, 8 thermidor an X.

14. Fouché, *Mémoires*, 146–48; see also P. Metzger, "Cambacérès, son rôle comme remplaçant de Bonaparte, An VIII–XII," *La Revolution française*, XLIII (July 1902), 546–62.

15. Thibaudeau, *Consulate*, 255.

16. P. L. Roederer, *Mémoires sur la Révolution, le Consulat et l'Empire*, ed. O. Aubry (1942), 203–11.

17. *Ibid.*, 126–29.

18. Thibaudeau, *Consulate*, 255, 257; Roederer, *Mémoires*, 126–27.

19. Roederer, *Mémoires*, 203–11; O. Connelly, *The Gentle Bonaparte: A Biography of Joseph, Napoleon's Elder Brother* (New York, 1968), 50–55.

20. See J.-P. Bertaud, *Bonaparte et le Duc d'Enghien* (1972), part 2.

21. Cambacérès Papers, A.N. 286 AP 3, doss. 32: Ms Carnet.

22. "Projet de déclaration pour l'établissement de l'Empire proposé au Conseil d'Etat par les présidents des sections en 1804," in Pelet de la Lozère, *Opinions de Napoléon au Conseil d'Etat* (1833), 302–05.

23. Thibaudeau, *Consulate*, 311–14.

24. See also Pelet, *Opinions*, 54–60.

25. Berlier, *Précis*, 92–95.

26. *Ibid.*, 95.

27. *Boulay de la Meurthe*, 162–65.

28. A. Aulard, ed., *Paris sous le Consulat: recueil de documents* (1909), IV: 769–70; Cornet, *Souvenirs Sénatoriaux*, 27; but cf. M. Reinhard, *Le Grand Carnot, II: L'Organisateur de la victoire* (1952), 273.

29. Reinhard, *Carnot*, II: 271–72.

30. The debate may be followed in the *Moniteur*, 11–15 floréal XII. There is a clipping of Carnot's speech in Roederer's papers, along with his refutation: "Observations sur le discours du Cit. Carnot contre l'heredité," *Journal de Paris*, 22–24 floréal XII (12–14 Mai 1804). (A.N. 29 AP 78).

31. Pelet, *Opinions*, 302–04.

32. *Moniteur*, 12–15 floréal XII.

33. Still, the debate in the Tribunate suggests that certain recent historians may in turn have overstated the radicalism of the National Assembly. François Furet and Ran Halévi have argued that already in 1789, the sheer radicalism of the Assembly's break with the past made France a republic in everything but name, with the king relegated to inconsequentiality from the start ("L'Année 1789," *Annales E.S.C*, 1989). But the reliance of tribune after tribune on original intent in 1789 as a rationale for a return to monarchy in 1804 ought to give pause. It suggests that in the National Assembly's initial formulation of revolutionary ideology—the only one that mattered by now—hereditary monarchy stood as one cornerstone for stability in the new regime and should not be dismissed as mere window-dressing. An older historiographical view of 1789–90 as a compromise with the old order that fell far short of democracy and republicanism thereby finds support in this unlikely setting, in this revalorization of original intent in 1804.

34. A.N. BB II 851A: Letters from Generals Bourcier, Junot, and Soult to Berthier, 28–30 pluviôse XII.

35. A.N. BB II 850B.

36. A.N. BB II 850A: Adresse présenté au Premier Consul, 22 floréal XII.

37. A.N. BB II 850B.

38. A.N. BB II 851A: especially Le Général Commandant . . . Camp de Montreuil, 9 floréal XII.

39. *Moniteur*, no. 226, 16 floréal XII: "Réponse du Sénat, 14 floréal." For the Senate's role in general, see Thiry, *Le Sénat de Napoléon*, 125–30.

40. Thibaudeau, *Consulate*, 262.

41. *Ibid.*, 235, 264, 251–55.

42. A. M. Roederer, ed., *Oeuvres du Comte P. L. Roederer* (7 vols., 1854), III: 508–10.

43. *Ibid.*, 507–08.

44. Roederer Papers: A.N. 29 AP 78: Ms. Notes.

45. See G. Livesey, "An Agent of Enlightenment in the French Revolution: François de Neufchâteau," Harvard Ph.D. dissertation, 1994.

46. François de Neufchâteau Papers: A.N. 27 AP 14, fol. 1: à Saint-Cloud, 19 May 1806. See also François to Roederer, 5 November 1804, on planning for the Senate session that would approve the transition (Roederer Papers: A.N. 29 AP 78).

47. *Moniteur*, no. 226, 16 floréal XII.

48. Thiry, *Sénat*, 140, citing H. Grégoire, *Mémoires*, 439–41. When it actually came time to vote, the ailing Lanjuinais could not join his dissenting colleagues.

49. Thiry, *Sénat*, 135–36; Pelet, *Opinions*, 61–63.

50. A.N. AF IV 1432, fol. 3.

Chapter V: The Second Most Important Man in Napoleonic France

1. A. Vandal, *L'Avènement de Bonaparte* (Nelson edn., 1910), II: 34–35.

2. See P. Metzger, " Cambacérès, son rôle comme remplaçant de Bonaparte, An VIII–An XII," *La Révolution française*, XLIII (July 1902), 531n.

3. P.-F. Pinaud, *Cambacérès, 1753–1824* (1996), 43–50. This is the only recent full-scale biography and by far the best compared to the older ones. As my own book was going to press, the long-lost manuscript of Cambacérès's memoirs suddenly appeared in print: *Cambacérès, Mémoires inédits*, ed. L. Chatel de Brancion (2 vols., [November] 1999). (For first alerting me to this I thank Annie Jourdan.) The history of this voluminous manuscript is well-known up to a point. Cambacérès had plenty of time to draft these recollections after 1815, but had not brought them to publication when he died in 1824. The royalist government attempted to suppress the manuscript at that time—an effort that deterred his heir, who subsequently lost interest. Eventually the manuscript passed into the hands of a private collector and friend of the family, who placed the manuscript in a trunk and forgot it. The present editor is the grand-daughter of that individual, who has at last recognized its importance and consecrated the considerable labor necessary to bring it to publication.

Over 1200 closely-set pages in this printed version, the document (alas but predictably) eschews most private matters and gossip, and is generally circumspect in its comments on other people. Altogether it is a dry, rather monochromatic chronicle of its times, and above all an apologia (although the author would deny this)—an endless representation of the rectitude, sincerity, common sense, and tribulations of Cambacérès. Over a third of the space is devoted to his volatile experience during Revolution. As for the Napoleonic era, much of the content clearly draws upon and in some instances virtually duplicates Cambacérès's correspondence with Napoleon (which itself disappeared for a long time and was not published until the 1970s). Unfortunately, a notable quality of these volumes is their excessive reticence and the author's consequent silence on important issues and personalities of the time. Worse yet, the memoir's coverage comes to an abrupt end in December 1813 and therefore has nothing to say about the collapse of the Empire, the first Restoration, or the crisis of the Hundred Days. The text deserves careful study, but seems to offer few genuine revelations.

4. Pinaud, *Cambacérès*, 72–73.

5. Cambacérès Papers in A.N. 286 AP 3, doss. 32: untitled Ms Carnet.

6. Bourrienne, *Mémoires sur Napoléon*, III: 182; *Memoirs of Chancellor Pasquier* (trans. C. E. Roche 2 vols., New York, 1893), 254. Cambacérès begins his memoirs with the claim that he was not a regicide. (*Mémoires inédits*, I: 31–35.)

7. A.N. 286 AP 3: doss. 32.

8. A.N. 286 AP 1: Livre de Raison, an VI.

9. See I. Woloch, *Jacobin Legacy: The Democratic Movement Under the Directory* (Princeton NJ, 1970), chap XI on the electoral assembly of the Seine in 1798.

10. Marquis de Noailles, *Le Comte Molé 1781–1855: Sa Vie—Ses Mémoires* (3rd edn., 1922), I: 70. To all intents and purposes this volume is a firsthand account based on Molé's manuscript memoirs and other papers.

11. A.N. 286 AP 3: Ms. Carnet: "qu'il faut savoir marcher avec son siècle . . . Je dus céder au movement général et s'abandonner au torrent des innovations." The best he could do was to try "à en ralentir la marche, au lieu d'en accélerer les progrès."

12. *Memoirs of Chancellor Pasquier*, I: 252–53.

13. *Ibid.*, 254–55.

14. *Ibid.*, 255, 370.

15. J.-A. Chaptal, *Mes Souvenirs sur Napoléon* (1893), 259; for a specific example, see 255–56.

16. *Cambacérès: Lettres inédites* II: 851, 3 June 1809. For a discussion of this capital source, see below.

17. *Le Comte Molé*, 70.

18. For a balanced overview, see also J. Thiry, *Jean-Jacques-Régis de Cambacérès: Archichancelier de l'Empire* (1935), the most reliable study before the appearance of Pinaud's recent biography.

19. For the details, see J. Tulard and L. Garros, *Itinéraire de Napoléon au jour le jour* (1992).

20. See Metzger, "Cambacérès, son role comme remplaçant de Bonaparte, An VIII–An XII," 528–58, but also J. Bourdon, " Le Role de Cambacérès sous le Consulate et l'Empire," *Bulletin de la Société d'histoire moderne*, (November 1928), 71–73.

21. In Cambacérès's view the arrangement was less than ideal: "un plan d'après lequel [Napoleon] ne devait y avoir en son absence qu'un simulacre d'autorité, tandis que tout aboutirait à sa personne." As the arrangement was refined between 1805 and 1806, Cambacérès observed in his memoirs: "Ce moyen était sans doute plus ingénieux que solide. Il était

sorti tout entier de la tête de l'Empereur qui, voulant comme je l'ait dit, exercer une autorité sans partage . . . n'avait trouvé rien de mieux que d'être toujours présent à l'aide d'un mandataire spécial, qui n'ayant entre ses mains aucune autorité d'exécution, ne pourrait jamais donner de l'ombrage. . . . (*Cambacérès, Mémoires inédits*, Vol. II: 45–46, 97–98.)

22. J. Tulard, ed., *Cambacérès: Lettres inédites à Napoléon, 1802–1814* (2 vols., Paris, 1973). Citations to this fundamental source will indicate the number of the letter and the date.

23. Indeed: cf. Vol. I, No. 495: 30 November 1806.

24. No. 623: 25 April 1807.

25. Nos. 625 and 643: 27 April and 15 May 1807.

26. No. 644: 16 May 1807. For Napoleon's admonitory letter, essentially summarized in Cambacérès's response, see Napoléon, *Correspondance*, No. 12546.

27. *Cambacérès, Lettres inédites*, Vol. II, No. 829: 3 May 1809.

28. Vol. I, No. 584: 17 March 1807.

29. No. 592: 25 March 1807.

30. Vol. II, No. 771: 5 October 1808.

31. Nos. 774 and 790: 13 November and 4 December 1808.

32. No. 779: 18 November 1808.

33. Vol. I, No. 632: 4 May 1807.

34. Vol. II, No. 789: 1 December 1808.

35. No. 781: 20 November 1808.

36. No. 785: 26 November 1808. In *Cambacérès, Mémoires inédits*, managing the Corps Législatif in its annual sessions is a recurrent theme. On the session of 1808 see II: 245–46, where he reiterates Napoleon's anger over any kind of dissent in that body.

37. For his pre-revolutionary years, see Pinaud, chap 1.

38. A.N.286 AP 3, doss. 31: Testament de Cambacérès à Bruxelles, 1818.

39. Pinaud, chap 12.

40. *Cambacérès, Lettres inédites*, Vol. I, Nos. 208, 226, 230, 11 April, 2 and 8 May 1805; also Beugnot to Cambacérès, 4 floréal XIII in A.N. 286 AP 3, doss.34. The cardinal's letter made a poor impression on the emperor and "acheva de perdre la cause." Ledré, *Le Cardinal Cambacérès*, 428, cited in Tulard's editorial notes, p.225.

41. *Cambacérès: Lettres inédites*, Vol. I, No. 196: 9 October 1804.

42. R. Marquant, "La Fortune de Cambacérès," in *Bulletin d'histoire économique et sociale de la Révolution française* (1971), 173.

43. A.N. 286 AP 1: Livres de Raison, 1792–an VII.

44. A.N. 286 AP 1: Livres de Raison, 1792–an VII; Etat de la Recette de Dépense du Cit. Cambacérès pendant la première année de son consulat (laquelle n'est que neuf mois); idem . . . Troisième année de son consulat.

45. A.N. 286 AP 1: Livres de Raison, 1810, 1813.

46. A.N. 286 AP 1: Livres de Raison, 1807–13; "Etat de Situation au 1er Janvier 1814"; Pinaud, *Cambacérès*, 194–97 on the *hôtel*; Marquant, "Fortune de Cambacérès," 176–77, 184–86.

47. Marquant, "Fortune de Cambacérès," 194–99, 244, 247–51.

48. A.N. 286 AP 1: "Etat de Situation au 1er Janvier 1814"; Marquant, "Fortune de Cambacérès," 172, 188–90, 243; and Pinaud, *Cambacérès*, 204–08.

49. A.N. 286 AP 3, doss. 32: J. P. H. Cambacérès to Brossard, 7 July 1830.

50. A.N. 286 AP 3, doss. 32: untitled Ms Carnet.

51. Marquant, "Fortune de Cambacérès," 227–28, Tableau VI: "Etat des Dépenses." His household expenditures included salaries for secretaries and wages for domestics amounting to 9.6 percent of his outlays, and funds for horses and stabling totaling 11.3 percent.

52. Cf. A. Carême, *L'Art de la Cuisine Française au 19ème Siècle . . .* (1833; 1847), xii–xviii. I owe this intriguing reference to Priscilla P. Ferguson.

53. L. Goldsmith, *Histoire Secrète du Cabinet de Napoléon Buonaparte et la Cour de St. Cloud* (London, 1810), 2nd Appendix: 33–36. Goldsmith is discussed in J. Tulard, ed., *L'Anti-Napoléon: la légende noire de l'Empereur* (1965).

54. Cf. J. Tulard, *Joseph Fiévée, conseiller secret de Napoléon* (1985).

55. J. L'Homer, *Cambacérès Intime: amoureux et gastronome* (1902), 46–47.

56. E. L. Lamothe-Langon, *Les Après-Dîners de Cambacérès . . . ou Révélations de plusieurs grands personnages . . .* (4 vols., 1837), I: 310–11.

57. *Napoleon I im Spiegel der Karikatur / Napoleon I in the Mirror of Caricature . . . A Collection Catalogue of the Napoleon Museum Arenenberg with 435 Cartoons Dealing with Napoleon I* (Zurich, 1998), 128, 495. For referring me to this splendid volume I thank Pascal Dupuy.

58. This reading follows C. Clerc, *La Caricature contre Napoléon* (1985), 156, which reproduces some of the caricatures in question, and the commentary in the Arenenberg catalogue.

59. For psychological insights on Cambacérès's character, I have profited from discussions with my friend Peter Loewenberg.

60. A.N. 286 AP 3: doss.32: untitled Ms. Carnet.

61. A.N. 286 AP 3: doss.32: "Notice écrite sous la dictée par mon oncle," 1821.

Chapter VI: In the Service of the Emperor

1. A. J. F. Fain, *Mémoires du baron Fain, premier secrétaire du cabinet de l'Empereur* (1908), 297. See also C.-F. Méneval, *Mémoires pour servir à l'histoire de Napoléon Ier depuis 1802 jusqu'à 1815* (3 vols., 1893).

2. Fain, *Mémoires*, 27–31.

3. J. Bourdon, ed., *Napoléon au Conseil d'Etat* (1963), 199, and duc de Broglie, *Souvenirs 1785–1870* (4 vols., 1886), I: 122–24. On Barbé-Marbois see Cambacérès, *Mémoires inédites*, ed. L. Chatel de Brancion (2 vols., 1999) II: 66–69.

4. See the accounts in *Boulay de la Meurthe* (1868), 198–200, and Cambacérès, *Mémoires inédits*, II: 420, 423, 426.

5. See C. Durand, *Etudes sur le Conseil d'Etat napoléonien* (1949).

6. For Bonaparte's extensive reliance on the heads of sections, see Roederer Papers: A.N. 29 AP 75: Conseil d'Etat, Ans VIII–X.

7. See J. Humbert, *J. G. Lacuée, Comte de Cessac . . . Ministre de Napoléon Ier, 1752–1841* (1939). Upon succeeding to Lacuée's seat in the Académie Française, Tocqueville, who had no love for the Napoleonic regime, was obliged to give his eulogy.

8. See T. Lenz, *Roederer, 1754–1835* (Metz, 1989), 126–45. On participation in National Assembly debates, see T. Tackett, *Becoming a Revolutionary: The Deputies of the French National Assembly and the Emergence of a Revolutionary Culture (1789–90)* (Princeton, NJ, 1996), 320–21: Appendix 3 on the top forty deputy speakers.

9. *Boulay de la Meurthe*, 120–21. This valuable (and generally neglected) source, it will be recalled, was compiled by his son "d'après ses conversations, sa correspondance, ses écrits, ses discours et autres documents authentiques. . . . Elle n'est point destinée au public." In effect, it is a sanitized but often quite detailed memoir.

10. *Ibid.*, 148–55.

11. *Ibid.*, 167–70, 172.

12. *Ibid.*, 165–66, 170–74.

13. See the entries in E. LeMay, ed., *Dictionnaire des Constituants*, and J. Tulard, ed., *Dictionnaire Napoléon*. Also J. Defermon, *Motifs du Projet de loi générale sur les finances* for 1808, 1809, and 1810 in A.N. AD XIX A/3: Conseil d'Etat, An XII–1813.

14. Tackett, *Becoming a Revolutionary*, 320.

15. A. Darnis, *Essai sur la vie de S.E. le Comte Regnaud de St. Jean d'Angély* (Poitiers, 1859), 19–24. Unfortunately this hagiographic pamphlet, written perhaps to curry favor with Louis Napoleon, is the only substantial biographical sketch of Regnaud.

16. Darnis, *Essai*, 28–30; Marquis de Noailles, *Le Comte Molé, 1781–1855: Sa Vie, Ses Mémoires* (1922 edn.), 73–74. Like the volume on Boulay, this is a hybrid of memoir and biography written by an admiring descendant, but based largely on Molé's unpublished memoirs and papers. Molé, incidentally, does not repeat the rumor that Mme Regnaud rebuffed Napoleon's amorous advances.

17. A.N. AF IV 1042.

18. L. Goldsmith, *Histoire secrète du cabinet de Napoléon Buonaparte et de la Cour de St. Cloud* (London, 1810), 2nd Appendix: 44.

19. A.N. AF IV 1042: Rapport à S.M. l'Empereur sur les travaux de la Section de l'intérieur de son Conseil d'état pendant l'année 1809; and Regnaud to Napoleon, 18 January 1810.

20. A.N. AF IV 1326A: Récapitulation, Décembre 1810.

21. A.N. AD XIX A/3: Conseil d'Etat, An XII–1813, and especially *Discours de M. le Comte Regnaud . . . au clôture du Corps Législatif, 21 Avril 1810.*

22. Cambacérès to Regnaud, 19 August 1807, in Cambacérès Papers, A.N. 286 AP 1.

23. His emoluments are listed by the well-informed Goldsmith, *Histoire secrète,* 2nd Appendix: 105.

24. A.N. AF IV 1326A: Etat des Conseillers d'Etat en service ordinaire. . . . An XIV.

25. A.N. AF IV 1238: Conseil d'Administration, 15 nivôse VIII.

26. The first of his memoirs, covering the years of the Consulate, was published in 1827 and has been translated by G. K. Fortescue as *Bonaparte and the Consulate* (1908). The second version, very different from the first, is entitled *Mémoires de A.-C. Thibaudeau, 1799–1815* (1913 edn.). In addition, Thibaudeau wrote a valuable multivolume history of the period.

27. See Thibaudeau, *Mémoires*, 79–81, and A.N. AF IV 1042: Thibaudeau to Locré (secretary of the Council of State), 17 brumaire XIII, explaining that he had been unable to collect anything beyond that first year's stipend since then, despite Bonaparte's approval.

28. Thibaudeau, *Mémoires*, 232.

29. *Le Comte Molé*, 41–52.

30. Thibaudeau, *Mémoires*, 263.

31. Quoted in Jean Tulard, *Napoléon et la noblesse d'Empire* (1979), 63–64.

32. *Archives parlementaires* (2ème série), X:12.

33. Tulard, *Napoléon et la noblesse*, 75–78.

34. *Ibid.*, 93–98, 146–54.

35. Berlier, *Précis*, 108–09.

36. Berlier Papers, Archives départementales Côte d'Or (Dijon), 30F 7: Majorat et Dotation; cf. Berlier, *Précis*, 109–10.

37. Berlier's granddaughter had married the son of the Montagnard *conventionnel* and anti-Napoleonic republican Marc-Antoine Baudot. (See M.-A. Baudot, *Notes historiques sur la Convention nationale, le Directoire, l'Empire et l'exil des votants* [1893; 1974].)

38. Berlier Papers, 30F 8: Last will and testament, 1 February 1841.

39. Berlier, *Précis*, 110.

40. *Boulay de la Meurthe*, 172–74.

41. *Ibid.*, 173. Harvard University's copy of Berlier's privately distributed and rare memoir comes from the Boulay de la Meurthe collection, which Harvard purchased in the 1920s.

42. Bourdon, ed., *Napoléon au Conseil d'Etat*, 62–63.

43. Imperial decree of 26 December 1809 in *Bulletin des Lois*, no. 254; A.N. BB I 138: Conseil d'Etat, Nominations: Auditeurs, 1810. On the aspiring attorneys, see Woloch, *The New Regime*, 403.

44. A.N. BB I 138, Nominations, 1810. In general, see C. Durand, *Les Auditeurs au Conseil d'état de 1803 à 1814* (1958).

45. *Boulay de la Meurthe*, 202–03.

46. *Cambacérès: Lettres inédites*, Vol. I, Nos. 527, 545–47: January–February 1807.

47. Mollien, *Mémoires*, II: 155.

48. Fain, *Mémoires*, 205–06.

49. *Ibid.*, 147.

50. *Le Comte Molé*, 74, 80.

51. *Ibid.*, 80; Thibaudeau, *Mémoires*, 41–43. For the debate on *biens nationaux*, see Bourdon, ed., *Napoleon au Conseil d'Etat*, 33–47.

52. Mollien, *Mémoires*, II:141. The firsthand observations of Mollien, Molé, Thibaudeau, and Pelet de la Lozère are valuable standard sources.

53. Thibaudeau, *Mémoires*, 257–58; Mollien, *Mémoires*, II: 151, 142–43.

54. *Le Comte Molé*, 57, 65ff. Cf. *Souvenirs du lieutenant général Mathieu Dumas de 1770 à 1836* (1838), 222–37.

55. *Le Comte Molé*, 53, 57–59, 64, 70–71.

56. C. Durand, "Conseils privés, conseils des ministres, conseils d'administration de 1800 à 1814," *Annales historiques de la Révolution française*, 199 (January 1970), 208–12.

57. These examples come from A.N. AF IV 1229: Conseil des Ministres, 1807.

58. *Ibid.*

59. Mollien, *Mémoires*, II: 138.

60. See Durand, "Conseils," 212–21.

61. A.N. AF IV 1229: Ordre de S.M., 11 Janvier 1808: Conseils d'administration.

62. Mollien, *Mémoires*, I: 378–79.

63. Durand, "Conseils," 219–21.

64. Mollien, *Mémoires*, II: 150, 138–39.

65. Durand, "Conseils," 203–08. On the unusual *conseil privé* convened by Napoleon to dis-

cuss his prospective marriage with a European princess, see Cambacérès, *Mémoires inedits*, II: 325–28. The archchancellor advocated a marriage alliance with Russia.

66. See A.N. AF IV 1227: Conseils privés.

67. *Ibid.*

68. The Grand Judge had warned Napoleon about this small point much earlier: A.N. AF IV 1042: Regnier to Napoleon, 25 December 1808.

69. *Cambacérès, Lettres inédites*, Vol. II, No. 1054, 16 January 1812.

70. Listed in *Boulay de la Meurthe*, 189–90.

71. *Ibid.*, 190–94. For Cambacérès's bland account see *Mémoires inédits*, II: 390–91.

72. See J.-P. Bertaud, *Bonaparte et le Duc d'Enghien* (1972).

Chapter VII: Living with the Erosion of Liberty

1. A.N. BB3 141 [Délits Politiques]: prairial XI.

2. A.N. BB3 141: Commissaire au T.C. [Tribunal Criminel] du Côte d'Or to G.J. [Grand Juge], 4 thermidor XI.

3. A.N. BB3 142: Commissaire au T.C. de l'Isère to G.J., 12 germinal et 30 floréal XII; A.N. BB3 143: P.G. [Procureur Générale] Moselle to G.J., 18 May 1806; also P.G. Allier to G.J., 15 June 1810.

4. BB3 142: Tribunal correctionnel de Besançon, 5 floréal XII; BB3 145: Fouché to G.J., 5 and 10 September 1807. Cf. M. Sibalis, "Prisoners by *Mesure de Haute Police* Under Napoleon I: Reviving the *Lettres de cachet*," *Proceedings of the Western Society for French History*, XVIII (1991), 261–69, for a helpful discussion of the slippery term *"haute police."*

5. BB3 141: Commissaire au T.C. du Nord to G.J., 20 frimaire XII; BB3 143: P.G. T.C.du Nord to G.J., 8 January, 9 February, 17 March 1809.

6. BB3 143: *Proclamation: Le Comité de surveillance extraordinaire à tous les français*; P.G. Loire to G.J., 14 October 1806.

7. *Ibid.:* Fouché to G.J., 21 October.

8. See A.N. AF IV 1232: Conseils Privés de Grâce, Ans XI–XIII.

9. A.N. AF IV 1236, Conseil Privé, 9–10 July 1811: Prisonniers d'Etat.

10. A.N. AF IV 1314: Fouché to Napoleon: Rapport, 5 January 1808, for categories of "individus détenus par mesure de Haute Police." Also A.N. AF IV 1237: Conseil Privé, February 1812. On the propensity of juries to bend the law in reaching lenient verdicts, see I. Woloch, *The New Regime: Transformations of the French Civic Order, 1789–1820s* (New York, 1994), chap 12.

11. C.-E. Oelsner, *Des Opinions politiques du citoyen Sieyès et de sa vie comme homme public* (An VIII), 248, 252–55.

12. Senatus-Consulte Organique of 18 May 1804, Arts. 60–63.

13. The following account draws on two manuscript sources: A.N. CC 60: Registre des délibérations de la Commission sénatoriale de la liberté individuelle—a chronological record of its deliberations; and CC 61–62: registers containing information about specific cases under review.

14. E.g., André, one of the Jacobins named in the deportation decree of 15 nivôse IX, enlisted the aid of the commission from prison while awaiting transfer overseas, but was told that his case was "hors des attributions de la commission." A.N. CC 60: 4th j.c. An XI.

15. J.Thiry, *Le Sénat de Napoléon* (1949), 178–94. Thiry is one of the few historians who has written on this commission at any length. His discussion naturally emphasizes the commission's deference to governmental authority.

16. CC 60: 30 vendémiaire XIII. No similar reports are included in the commission's records, although it may have continued to make such presentations from time to time.

17. Cited in Thiry, *Le Sénat*, 189.

18. CC 60: 14 fructidor XII and CC 61 #104. Badaire was freed only in 1808.

19. CC 60: 28 June 1812. The Canadian historian Michael Sibalis is currently completing an exhaustive study of the commission's case files, and will be able to provide a detailed composite portrait of individuals subjected to preventive detention. Among the cases that the commission pursued, Sibalis has tallied 159 involving brigands or common criminals, 146 concerning political prisoners, 57 cases of vagabonds or beggars, 17 cases of the insane, and 16 cases of persons detained in the interests of their family. (I thank Professor Sibalis for sharing these statistics in a conference at Emory University in November 1999.)

20. A.N. CC 61 #32; CC 60: 28 July 1806; 14 November 1806; 23 November 1808; 28 January 1809.

21. CC 61 #44 and 77; CC 60: 22 thermidor XII; 14 ventôse XIII.

22. CC 60: 28 brumaire et 28 nivôse XIII; CC 61 #138 (d'Atré) and 128 (Couchery).

23. Arnaud was one of the so-called *pauvres de Bicêtre*. CC 60: 18 and 25 messidor XII; CC 61 #4.

24. CC 60: 27 December 1806 and 2 January 1807; CC 61 #232.

25. CC 60: December 1807, June 1809; CC 61 #282.

26. CC 61 #28; Eve Demaillot, *Tableau historique des prisons d'Etat en France, sous le régime de Buonaparte* (1814).

27. CC 60: 1 and 21 February and 14 July 1806; CC 61 #40.

28. A.N. AF IV 1236: P.V. Conseil Secret, 3 and 10 April 1809. On the desolate atmosphere at the state prison in the Château d'If in Marseilles, see the scathing remarks of the prefect A.-C. Thibaudeau—*Mémoires, 1799–1815* (1913), 286–88. He was particularly affronted by the sequestration there of the corpse of General Kléber, who had replaced Bonaparte as commander of the Army of Egypt and was assassinated in Cairo in June 1800. After the French army finally surrendered in September 1801, Kléber's corpse was evidently shunted to the Château d'If, presumably because Napoleon did not wish to reopen the question of his own precipitous flight from Egypt in 1799.

29. J. Bourdon, ed., *Napoléon au Conseil d'Etat* (1963), 104–05.

30. Decree of 3 March 1810 in *ibid.*, 78–79.

31. L. Goldsmith, *Histoire secrète du cabinet de Napoléon Buonaparte* (London, 1810), 2nd Appendix: 127–30.

32. A.N. AF IV 1236: P.V. de la séance du 1er conseil privé concernant les prisonniers d'état, 27 December 1810; AF IV 1237. P.V. du conseil privé tenu à Saint-Cloud, 19 April and 3 May 1812. For his purge of the judiciary of 1808, Napoleon likewise used a blue-ribbon panel, but this time turned exclusively to the Senate for assistance. Interestingly, whereas Grand Judge Regnier proposed a panel of ten veteran collaborators who could be described as the usual suspects, Napoleon named only six of those senators, and added four newer members of his own choosing, passing over Chaptal, Lacépède, Lemercier, and Monge in

the process. See A.N. AF IV 1042, note from Regnier, and AF IV 1231: doss. "Epuration des Tribunaux." In the event, the commission functioned with complete harmony: "Sur 170 juges, dont la commission vous propose la révocation, à l'exception de deux, elle a été unanime sur la totalité."

33. H. Gaubert, *Conspirateurs au temps de Napoléon Ier* (1962), 291–303. Cf. *Cambacérès: Lettres inédites*, II: No. 761 (19 July 1808). Cambacérès. *Mémoires inédits*, II: 220–23 on his mediation between Fouché and Dubois.

34. A.N. AF IV 1236: P.V. Conseil Privé, 18 March 1811.

35. Gaubert, *Conspirateurs*, 303–40. Compare P.-F. Pinaud, *Cambacérès* (1996), 188–90, on the archchancellor's panicky behavior, with Cambacérès's own account of his sangfroid (*Mémoires inédits*, II: 414–22).

36. Cf. C Peyrard, "Rigomer Bazin et Agricol Moreau: deux chefs d'opinion du 'parti républicain' sous le Directoire ou l'impossible oubli de la République démocratique," in P. Bourdon and B. Gainot, eds., *La République directoriale* (2 vols., 1998), I: 379–99.

37. A.N. AF IV 1236: Récapitulation, July 1811.

38. Bourdon, ed., *Napoléon au Conseil d'Etat*, session of 3 April 1812, 105–11.

39. *Motifs du Projet de Loi: Code d'Instruction criminelle (Livre I)*, presented by Treilhard, Réal, and Faure: 5 November 1808; *Exposé de la situation de l'Empire, 1808*; Woloch, *The New Regime*, 375–77; A. Esmein, *Histoire de la Procédure criminelle en France* (1882), "La Question du Jury Devant le Conseil d'Etat," 505–26.

40. Bourdon, ed., *Napoléon au Conseil d'Etat*, 111–12: Session of 3 April 1812.

41. Art. XI: "The unrestrained communication of thoughts and opinions being one of the most precious rights of man, every citizen may speak, write, and publish freely, provided he is responsible for the abuse of this liberty, in cases determined by law."

42. J. Popkin, *Revolutionary News: The Press in France 1789–1799* (Durham, NC, 1990), 168–79; Daunou's *Rapport . . . sur la repression des délits de la presse, 1796*, cited on p. 176.

43. See the illuminating work of Darrin McMahon, *The French Counter-Enlightenment and the Birth of the European Right, 1778–1830* (forthcoming: OUP), chap 4.

44. A.N. AF IV 1314: doss. "Journal de l'Empire."

45. Savary to Napoleon, 1810, reprinted in H. Welschinger, *La Censure sous le premier empire* (1882), 296–97. Cf. A. Cabanis, *La Presse sous le consulat et l'empire* (1975), chap I.

46. A.N. AF IV 1043: Compte Rendu de l'administration de la Police Générale pendant l'an VIII.

47. Rapport du 26 Juin 1806, reprinted in Welschinger, *La Censure*, 272. See also C. Hesse, *Publishing and Cultural Politics in Revolutionary Paris, 1789–1810* (Berkeley, 1991), 225–28.

48. J.-G. Locré, *Discussions sur la liberté de la presse, la censure, la propriété littéraire et la librairie qui ont eu lieu dans le Conseil d'Etat* (Paris, 1819).

49. Napoleon's remarks in Locré, *Discussions*, 9, 12, 16, 57–67, 74, 102–04, 106, 117, 141, 226–27, 231, 241.

50. On this aspect of the new law, see Hesse, *Publishing and Cultural Politics*, 228–39.

51. Locré, *Discussions*, 8–11, 24, 47, 70–71.

52. *Ibid.*, 49–53, 55–56, 65–66, 91–92, 95. On the weakening of freedom of thought as a core value, see McMahon, *The French Counter-Enlightenment*, chap 4.

53. See Locré, *Discussions*, 10, 41–46, 48, 69, 90–93, 105.

54. *Ibid.*, 124–25, 139, 230–31, 258.

55. H. Welschinger, "La Direction générale de l'imprimerie et de la librairie 1810–1815" *Le Livre* (1887), 163.

56. *Souvenirs du feu duc de Broglie* (2nd edn., Paris, 1886), I: 122–24. Broglie notes that only Pasquier and Regnaud had the courage to defend their hapless colleague.

57. Cited in Welschinger, *La Censure*, 313.

58. Cited by Welschinger, "La Direction générale," 167–68.

Chapter VIII: The Limits of Loyalty

1. See the remarkable memoirs of Caulaincourt, *With Napoleon in Russia: The Memoirs of General de Caulaincourt, Duke of Vicenza*, ed. G. Libaire (New York, 1935), parts 4 and 5.

2. Woloch, *The New Regime*, chap.13.

3. A.N. F1cI 13: Compte rendu de la Situation de l'Empire, drafts for 1805.

4. I. Collins, *Napoleon and His Parliaments*, 123–28; Woloch, *The New Regime*, 152–53, on the nationalization of the *biens communaux*.

5. Cambacérès, *Mémoires inédits*, II: 496–97; M.-A. Cornet, *Souvenirs sénatoriaux* (1824), 62–63.

6. Thibaudeau, *Mémoires*, 397; *Boulay de la Meurthe*, 215–16.

7. *Boulay de la Meurthe*, 216–18; see Collins, *Napoleon and His Parliaments*, 134–39 for an account of this episode, including the feeble pretext employed in the suppression decree, namely, that one cohort of the legislature had not been renewed in a timely fashion. Cambacérès objected to the committee's attempt to censure and limit the emperor's authority, but he also opposed Napoleon's arbitrary dismissal of the Corps (*Mémoires inédits*, II: 504–06).

8. Woloch, *The New Regime*, 420–24.

9. Thibaudeau, *Mémoires*, 381.

10. For an assessment of Talleyrand's behavior, see P. Geyl, "The French Historians and Talleyrand," in Geyl, *Debates with Historians* (New York, 1958), 225–37.

11. J. Thiry, *Le Sénat de Napoléon* (1949), 299–300.

12. Cited in *ibid.*, 305–06.

13. *Boulay de la Meurthe*, 233. The non-signers included Chaptal and Boissy d'Anglas, who had earlier accepted missions to the provinces and would probably have signed had they been in Paris, as well as Laplace, Monge, and Napoleon's favorite, Lacépède (who had accompanied Empress Marie-Louise to Blois). For the details of the session, see Thiry, *Le Sénat*, 311–19.

14. Thibaudeau, *Mémoires*, 388–92.

15. Berlier, *Précis*, 118–20.

16. Thibaudeau, *Mémoires*, 411–12; G. Bertier de Sauvigny, *The Bourbon Restoration* (Philadelphia, 1966 trans.), chaps 3–5.

17. E.-L. Lamothe-Langon, *Les Après-Dîners de Cambacérès . . . ou révélations de plusieurs grands personnages . . .* (4 vols., 1837) . The participants included Barras, Roederer, Fabre de l'Aude, and Regnaud.

18. Thibaudeau, *Mémoires*, 414–15; *Boulay de la Meurthe*, 240–41.

19. M. Reinhard, *Le Grand Carnot* (2 vols., Paris, 1952), II: chaps. 11–12.

20. *Mémoire Adressé au Roi en Juillet 1814* (Bruxelles & London [*sic*], 1814), 10 and 14.

21. *Ibid.*, 3–4.

22. *Ibid.*, 15, 17, 18.

23. Reinhard, *Carnot*, II: 304–08.

24. Quoted in Thibaudeau, *Mémoires*, 417. For a lively narrative, which draws extensively on the classic study of Henri Houssaye, see A. Schom, *One Hundred Days: Napoleon's Road to Waterloo* (New York, 1992).

25. These officers included Drouet d'Erlon, Lallemand, Exelmans, and Lefebvre-Desnouettes—not exactly household names. On the issue of popular support, see the shrewd assessment of Tulard, *Napoléon* (2nd edn., 1977), 425–31.

26. Thibaudeau, *Mémoires*, 470, 430–33.

27. Ibid., 472.

28. See the ludicrously self-righteous account in marquis de Noailles, *Le Comte Molé 1781– 1855: sa vie—ses mémoires* (1922), I: chaps 7–8 (drawn from Molé's manuscript "Les Cent-Jours"); P.-F. Pinaud, *Cambacérès* (1996), 227–29.

29. Quoted in J. Tulard, ed., *Dictionnaire Napoléon* (1987), 1010.

30. *Mémoires*, 459–60. For a description of Napoleon's regal installation ceremony at the Champ de Mai on 1 June, see Schom, *One Hundred Days*, 210–19.

31. On the Acte Additionel, see Tulard, *Dictionnaire*, 32–34, and Reinhard, *Carnot*, II:320.

32. F. Bluche, *Le Plébiscite des Cent-Jours* (Geneva, 1974), 120–26 and notes.

33. Thibaudeau, *Mémoires*, 487.

34. *Ibid.*, 499.

35. Reinhard, *Carnot*, II: chap 14; Thibaudeau, *Mémoires*, 463.

36. Boulay, for one, believed that Fouché ultimately did more harm to Napoleon with his maneuvers in the parliament than in his apparent collusion with the foreign enemy— *Boulay de la Meurthe*, 273, 280–82. See also L. Madelin, *Fouché, 1759–1820* (1913), II: chaps 24–26.

37. *Boulay de la Meurthe*, 284–85.

38. *Ibid.*, 293.

39. *Boulay de la Meurthe*, 299–300, 303, 306–08.

40. For a summary of Fouché's diplomatic maneuvers before and after Waterloo, see R. E. Cubberly, *The Role of Fouché During the Hundred Days* (Madison, WI, 1969), chaps 5–7.

41. Fouché managed to box out Lafayette and Lanjuinais, whose prestige might have hampered his own ascendancy: Cubberly, *Fouché*, 89.

42. Reinhard, *Carnot*, II: 326.

43. Berlier, *Précis*, 128–29, 135.

44. *Ibid.*, 130–35; Thibaudeau, *Mémoires*, chap 32. On the *fédérés* see R. Alexander, *Bonapartism and the Revolutionary Tradition in France: The Fédérés of 1815* (Cambridge, 1991).

45. Reinhard, *Carnot*, II: 327–28.

46. D. Resnick, *The White Terror and the Political Reaction After Waterloo* (Cambridge, MA, 1966), 66–70.

47. *Ibid.*, 70–76; Bertier de Sauvigny, *The Bourbon Restoration*, 130–35.

48. A. Kuscinski, *Dictionnaire des Conventionnels* (1916; 1973 repr.), 179.

49. M.-A. Baudot, *Notes historiques sur la Convention Nationale, le Directoire, l'Empire et l'exil des votants* (Geneva, 1893; 1974 repr.), 18–19, 30, 42–43, 76–77, 297, 310–11, 314. On Berlier, see especially 18, 106. For the most part Baudot's fragmentary notes constitute a relentless and vitriolic settling of accounts. For him, the Revolution's brief, egalitarian golden age (embodied by the Mountain and exemplified by his hero Danton) began with the downfall of the Girondins, but was ruined first by the fanatical tyranny of Robespierre, then by the hypocritical bloodlust of the thermidorians. The Directory further eviscerated the republic and Bonaparte consummated its ruin. On Baudot and his fellow exiles, see S. Luzzatto, *Mémoire de la Terreur: vieux Montagnards et jeunes Républicains au XIXe siècle* (Lyon, 1991), chap 1.

50. Berlier, *Précis*, 98–102, 138–40.

51. Kuscinski, *Dictionnaire des Conventionnels*, 568.

52. R. S. McNamara, *In Retrospect: The Tragedy and Lessons of Vietnam* (New York, 1996).

53. James C. Thomson, Jr., writing in *The Atlantic Monthly* (April 1968), quoted in A. Hirschman, *Exit, Voice and Loyalty: Responses to Decline in Firms, Organizations, and States* (Cambridge, MA, 1970), 115.

54. McNamara, *In Retrospect*, 313–14.

55. Cited in Hirschman, *Exit, Voice and Loyalty*, 17, 114–19. Hirschman notes, however, that officials like Ball "ordinarily have no [independent] base in politics or in public opinion."

56. Ronald Steel, "Blind Contrition," *The New Republic*, 5 June, 1995, pp. 34–38.

57. Reprinted in a new appendix to the Vintage paperback edition of *In Retrospect*, 354.

58. A.-J.-F. Fain, *Mémoires du baron Fain, premier secrétaire du cabinet de l'Empereur* (1908), 182–83.

59. E.–D. Pasquier, *Memoirs* (London, 1893 transl.), 256.

60. See Geyl, "The French Historians and Talleyrand."

61. Indeed, the term "liberal" began to have a certain currency only in the Napoleonic years, as far as I can tell, as a relatively unfreighted term of self-description by people like Berlier.

62. On Charles Duval, see Baudot, *Notes historiques*, 34–35; on Florent-Guiot, see Kuscinski, *Dictionnaire des Conventionnels*, 319. Both had barely escaped being swept up in the deportations of December 1800.

63. Until 1813, "depuis la proclamation de l'Empire, jamais Napoléon n'avait mis en délibération les questions relatives à la guerre ou à la paix." Cambacérès, *Mémoires inédits*, II: 429.

Index

Note: Page numbers in *italics* refer to illustrations.